Architecture of Coexistence
Building Pluralism

Architecture
of Coexistence
Building Pluralism

Edited by Azra Akšamija

**AGA KHAN AWARD
FOR ARCHITECTURE**

Table of Contents

6
Foreword: Architecture and Harmony
Farrokh Derakhshani

8
Architecture of Coexistence: Building Pluralism
Azra Akšamija

I. Building Pluralism

26
Beyond Homogeneity: On the Concept of Transculturality
Wolfgang Welsch

36
Immigrant Communities and Their Buildings
Mohammad al-Asad

52
The Architecture of Death in Islam: A Brief Cross-cultural History
Nasser Rabbat

II. Divergence

66
The White Mosque, Visoko, Bosnia and Herzegovina
Interviews and Photo Essay by Velibor Božović

100
Headless, They March On: Cephalophores and Coexistence in Ottoman Bosnia
Amila Buturović

110
Bosnia and the Destruction of Coexistence
Helen Walasek

120
Mosque First: Coming to Terms with the Legacy of Past Abuses in Bosnia Through Heritage Restoration
Amra Hadžimuhamedović

III. Dissonance

136
Superkilen, Copenhagen, Denmark
Interviews by Tina Gudrun Jensen, Photos by Jesper Lambaek

162
Rhetoric of Segregation, Everyday Forms of Coexistence:
Diverging Visions of Diversity and Coexistence in Denmark
Tina Gudrun Jensen

172
A "Border Concept": Scandinavian Public Space in the Twenty-First Century
Jennifer Mack

184
Conflictual Constellations: On Superkilen
Barbara Steiner

IV. Convergence

194
Islamic Cemetery Altach, Austria
Interviews by Robert Fabach, Photos by Nikolaus Walter and Cemal Emden

228
Cultivating Convergence: The Islamic Cemetery Altach, Austria
Azra Akšamija

242
The Islamic Cemetery as an Expression of the Process of Muslim Belonging in Vorarlberg
Simon Burtscher-Mathis

252
An Offer of Leadership
Eva Grabherr in conversation with Azra Akšamija

V. Epilogue

264
Islam, Arts, and Pedagogy
Ali S. Asani

276   Contributor Biographies
282   Image credits
284   Acknowledgements
288   Imprint

Architecture and Harmony
Farrokh Derakhshani

Compared to the lives of our ancestors, the main difference in our societies today is not only the accelerated pace of change, but also our acceptance of it.

Most of us accept rapid change in our societies, whether it is due to the movement of people from rural areas to urban agglomerations, migration between continents, the introduction of new technologies, environmental and natural hazards, or unfortunate wars and conflicts—changes that vastly exceed a country's boundaries. In fact, more and more of these changes are truly global. Nevertheless, whether national or global, we eventually adapt to the transformation of our societies—often resisting it at first, but sometimes embracing it with enthusiasm.

Our most tangible representation of how societies change is reflected in our built environment and the architecture that shapes it. This is especially true of cities. As our cities become more multicultural and multiethnic, stark contrasts in education, wealth, and well-being begin to form. The challenge, therefore, is to both value diversity and mediate its divides.

We surely stand to benefit if we look at the layers of cultures present in our cities as added value and understand the realities of multiple modernities as an asset rather than an obstacle or threat. This is especially true when creating new edifices, urban spaces, and communities: we should be aiming for the creation of shared spaces for societies that are inherently pluralistic. Architects, planners, landscape designers, and other related professionals have an important role to play in creating spaces that represent the aspirations of contemporary societies, but also in facilitating their planning and execution in that same spirit of pluralism.

The Aga Khan Award for Architecture (AKAA) will continue to do its part. Over the last four decades, it has been searching for outstanding projects that have had a positive impact on their users and that could be models for emulation. In this volume, we concentrate on three projects (out of hundreds of winning projects) where people gather: a place of worship, a place for remembrance, and a place of leisure. All of them are situated in multicultural environments. All three evoke important questions that we face today: How do we coexist and live together in a more harmonious fashion?

The three winning projects reflect the mandate and responsibility of the Award—to not only celebrate architectural achievements, but also to analyse, understand, and evaluate a project's historical context, creation process, and life after construction. The Award performs these studies in order to share this information with the world at large and in the hope that it will influence architectural discourse.

We hope, therefore, that this publication becomes a tool, along with other information, reports, films, and events about each of these featured projects, that will instigate further discussions, debates, and events. The ultimate goal, of course, is a better built environment, one that ameliorates the quality of life for future users who must coexist.

Director, Aga Khan Award for Architecture

Architecture of Coexistence: Building Pluralism
Azra Akšamija

I will never forget the opening day of the Islamic Cemetery Altach in Vorarlberg. The morning of the opening, a guided tour was offered to the public. As a designer of the cemetery's prayer space, I met with the small group of project leaders and community members to welcome the first visitors. We were expecting some fifteen, twenty people at the most, which is usually the highest number for such architecture tours.

When the first buses and cars started arriving, those expectations were far exceeded. Hundreds of visitors came from near and far, and surprisingly, most of them were members of the majority, non-Muslim society. Our welcoming team had to split into five groups to be able to show the ablution and prayer space. We were giving rotating tours for hours. The interest in this Islamic cemetery was just beautifully overwhelming.

Later that day, the city of Altach hosted an official celebration, organized together with Islamic communities from Vorarlberg who had prepared a generous meal for all. Thanks to Turkish generosity, the overwhelming number of guests who came to the event enjoyed the food. Of course, our project team was ecstatic to see the tremendous interest in the project, especially the gathering of all these diverse individuals who came to celebrate together.

For the Islamic communities, this celebration was about the inauguration of a shared space for the ninety-five different Muslim communities living in the region. For project initiators and producers, it was about celebrating an inspiring collaboration between individuals who would have never had the possibility of coming together in this way without the project. For many neighbors, local residents, members of the non-Muslim majority society, it was an opportunity to learn about the "other," but also about celebrating cool Vorarlbergian design. Neutral yet celebratory media reports accompanied this opening event, a subtlety that rarely characterizes news about Muslims in Austria today.

The enormous interest that culminated in this beautiful opening made it clear that the Islamic Cemetery Altach had created a bridge between Muslim minority and host majority groups. Moreover, the cemetery represented an important shift in the notion of belonging: for the second and third generation of Muslims in Austria, the definition of homeland was migrating from the family's "country of origin" to the place where one chooses to rest in peace.

What can projects like this teach us about the power of architecture to foster cross-cultural understanding? Can the positive energy, successful collaboration, and the lived experience of pluralism generated by the Islamic Cemetery Altach, and recognized by the Aga Khan Award for Architecture, be transferred to other places? In a time of growing divides, the Islamic Cemetery Altach can offer important lessons for peaceful coexistence.

Architecture of Coexistence: Building Pluralism aims to extend that offer further by demonstrating how built forms can give shape to a more open, pluralistic society. The possibility of pursuing this objective was made possible through an innovation introduced in the 2013 cycle of the Aga Khan Award for the first time in the award's history: instead of distributing the entire prize sum among the winning project's stakeholders, half of the award sum was dedicated to follow-up projects that were meant to advance the mission and social impact of the winning projects.

Hence, this book aims to advance the mission of the Islamic Cemetery Altach in the form of a book with an expanded thematic, geographic, and methodological scope of inquiry about contemporary architecture informed and inhabited by Muslims in Europe. How does architecture express or create a European-Islamic identity? How does it perform as a social medium that positively impacts its communities? What role do aesthetics play in fostering pluralism and a better understanding between different cultures compared to an implementation process? These key questions framing the conceptual scope of the book will be elaborated in conjunction with three internationally celebrated architectural projects that have received the Aga Khan Award for Architecture in the past four decades: the White Mosque in Visoko, Bosnia and Herzegovina (AKAA in 1983), the Islamic Cemetery Altach in Vorarlberg, Austria (AKAA in 2013), and Superkilen in Copenhagen, Denmark (AKAA in 2017). Different positions on the relationship between architecture and coexistence raised by these projects, including issues of migration, identity, visibility, and inclusion, will be elaborated by scholars from disciplines as diverse as architectural history, philosophy, political science, cultural studies, and religious studies. *Architecture of Coexistence* offers a truly multidisciplinary perspective on the subject.

Much has already been written about these award-winning projects, yet this book offers a unique perspective. Instead of viewing a completed architectural project as the endpoint, it examines the social impact of architecture within a longer timeframe. In doing so, this volume examines the social process generated between architectural form and its users. For this reason, the book also includes interviews with both the projects' architects and the everyday users. Together, these essays and interviews provide insights not only into architectural design, but also into architecture's impact on people who inhabit and use these spaces.

Building Pluralism

While projects discussed in this volume are based in Europe, each of them reveals different layers of meaning in relation to the specific sites in which they are located. Moreover, these projects tackle important questions of representation and identity politics—including the rights to presence, rights to visibility, and inclusion in Europe—pointing at societal tensions inherent in the concept of pluralism, and highlighting architecture's capacity to overcome them.

From the Balkan context, we learn about the more than five-centuries-long presence of Islam in this region of Europe, which was inscribed in the architectural landscape of Bosnia and Herzegovina. Mosques, madrassas, housing quartiers, libraries, and cemeteries, many of which were built by the Austro-Hungarian Empire, stand their ground against the claims of some chauvinistic European initiatives, such as Cities against Islamisation, which consider Islamic civilization alien to Europe.[1] These ancient examples of Europe's very own Islamic architecture in Bosnia, together with those in Spain and Turkey, provide material evidence to disprove such false claims.

Considering the more recent European past, this book also offers insights into architecture built by and for Muslim immigrants in regions that have historically been architecturally shaped by non-Muslim majority populations. Architectural historian Mohammad al-Asad provides an overview of the complex social dynamics behind such buildings, which often have to fulfill a number of difficult tasks: to represent different ethnic backgrounds of their very diverse communities within a new cultural context, to express their varied (and at times even contradictory) conceptions of Islam, and at the same time, mediate the community's relationship with the majority society. Taking a closer look at the Danish and Austrian contexts through projects like Superkilen and Islamic Cemetery Altach, the book sheds light on the vital role that architecture can play in the ongoing process of pluralization in Europe. A recurring challenge that these spaces face is how to accommodate the changing concepts of a place that one calls home—a shift from mere presence to permanence.

The theoretical framework of this volume draws from discourses on cultural hybridity in architecture within a globalized context. Recent scholarship on cultural dynamics of globalization has highlighted the need to depart from an understanding of culture as based on clearly distinguished, internally homogeneous spheres, of which the concepts of interculturality and multiculturality are a part. If we are to depart from these two models, as the philosopher Wolfgang Welsch suggests in this book, we need to consider the inherent complexity of modern cultures: our identities are fluid, multilayered, and local. The three key projects featured in this book mediate the dialogue between Muslims and the dominant society, setting new standards for visibility for minority groups in Europe that reveal the paradoxes and capacities of simultaneously belonging to multiple cultural milieus.

In light of the recent rise of populism and white nationalism in Europe and the United States, probing what constitutes the notions of the "local," "homeland," and "tradition" is vital to the political health of democracy in these regions today. Instead of embracing an essentialist idea of culture with clearly defined and internally homogenous boundaries, this book embraces the notion of transcultural aesthetics to talk about identities as multilayered and fluid. In this respect, Nasser Rabbat reminds us of Islam's own history. As we learn from his essay on the architecture of death in Islam, dialogue with, integration of, and building on the preexisting architectural context has always played an important role in Islam. From the funerary practices of early Muslims onward, the long and rich history of cross-cultural pollination and syncretism in the architecture of Islamic societies provides a counter-narrative to Orientalism, nationalism, xenophobia, and religious fundamentalism. In this context, projects such as the White Mosque, Superkilen, and Islamic Cemetery Altach provide tangible media for embracing the fluidity of identity and the changing nature of tradition, demonstrating a respectful reinterpretation of the past in dialogue with the previously existing or the newly imported.

Divergence

The first section of the book, Divergence, focuses on the politics of memory and return in the Balkans and examines how architecture operates as a means to create an identity—ethnic, religious, and/or national—by anchoring cultural memory to a specific territory. It begins with a portrait of the White Mosque in Visoko (built 1980, also known as Šerefudin's White Mosque) through a photo essay and interviews conducted by the artist Velibor Božović (Fig. 1). Personal memories and anecdotes from architects, imams, and people who regularly frequent the mosque or live in the mosque's immediate vicinity speak to the

Figure 1. Šerefudin's White Mosque, Visoko, Bosnia and Herzegovina (1980)

life and perception of this architectural masterpiece forty years after its construction. The White Mosque was designed by the architect Zlatko Ugljen and its modern architectural forms represent a reinterpretation of the vernacular Bosnian mosque.[2] Ugljen's elegant choreography of light tells a transcendental story of Five Pillars of Islamic Worship.

Still celebrated as one of the best examples of religious architecture in Europe, the White Mosque also ties into a longer timescale of the Bosnian architectural palimpsest, as it was built in lieu of a renovation of the previously existing vernacular mosque (dating back to 1477). The project marks a specific time in Yugoslav history, a time in which the Communist regime had become more tolerant to the expression of distinct identities of its multiethnic citizens, and thus more tolerant toward the constructions of new religious buildings. While there has been a continuous tradition of building mosques in Bosnia since the mid-fifteenth century, in the post-WWI period an entire generation of Muslims was allowed to build mosques. The "non-aligned" politics of Yugoslavia since the 1960s increased its contacts with other Islamic countries, which had an influence on the regime's new openness toward religious architecture in this period. At the time when the White Mosque was built, Yugoslavia was a leading member of the non-aligned movement and used its Muslim minority as a means to court Islamic countries for political alliance. Domestically, however, it continued to exert political pressure on the Muslim community and actively suppressed its religious identity.[3] However, in 1968, Bosnian Muslims were finally recognized as a constituent nationality of Yugoslavia and the construction of the White Mosque in Visoko signaled this political shift.[4]

Today, Yugoslav architectural marvels such as the White Mosque, but also the spectacular Communist public monuments, stand alienated in the balkanized territories of former Yugoslavia. The shift from a socialist regime to a multiparty democracy in the late 1980s escalated in the violent conflict of the early 1990s, which tore apart the Yugoslavs living under the motto of "Brotherhood and Unity." Today, more than twenty years after the war, the diverse ethnic groups in Bosnia and Herzegovina still live in a state of mutual alienation, which is fueled by nationalism and religious fanaticism. Essays by Helen Walasek and Amra Hadžimuhamedović explore the relationship between religious architecture, mosques in particular, and the notion of coexistence, and how their meaning has changed throughout this recent history.

Walasek examines how and why cultural heritage, and religious architecture in particular, was targeted in the 1990s war in Bosnia and Herzegovina, arguing that its systematic destruction had been used as an instrument of genocide and ethnic cleansing. Mosques, churches, synagogues, and tombstones that stood side by side for centuries represent evidence of coexistence in the region—their number alone demonstrates that coexistence between the various ethnic groups in the region was not only possible, but also prevalent. As the history of coexistence in Bosnia and Herzegovina stood in the way of creating ethnically homogenous and mutually hostile cultural territories that could be divided into separate nation-states, material traces of this history had to be erased. Religious architecture was thus particularly targeted for its significance as a marker of religious and ethnic identities deemed enemy.

If coexistence can be destroyed through the destruction of architecture, is it possible to rehabilitate coexistence through architectural means? Architectural historian and expert in the preservation of cultural heritage, Amra Hadžimuhamedović investigates this question through the lens of mosques in Bosnia restored after the Dayton Peace Accord formally ended the Bosnian war in 1995. In this story, we learn about the difficulties of trauma recovery, reconciliation, and peace building, which Bosnians face in the process of postwar mosque reconstructions. These processes imply living, working, and building across newly established political borders, coexisting with the "enemy" on a daily basis, and overcoming the corresponding psychological trauma inflicted on people and the build environment through the violence of war and genocide. For an architectural historian, writing about these processes also means finding an approach to reflect on the post-Dayton architectural landscape outside the prevailing dichotomy of the Yugo-nostalgic versus nationalist discourse. Hadžimuhamedović provides a hopeful outlook on the power of architecture to help restore peaceful coexistence after diplomacy had failed.

In light of the systematic destruction of cultural heritage in the Balkans during the 1990s war, during which Islamic heritage was predominantly targeted, as well as the divergent forces of ethno-religious nationalism that intensified in the postwar period, it is important to document and preserve the historical traces of interethnic exchanges in the region. Examples range from minarets in Herzegovina, which look like church towers, to the hybrid cultural practices related to funerary architecture. The latter is elaborated upon by Islamic literary scholar Amila Buturović through case studies of martyr shrines and grave markers of early Ottoman Bosnia. While the notion of coexistence in architecture implies an active form of communication and interaction among the living people, Buturović questions how this concept could be applied to architecture for the dead. Can the violence of the ancient past and the shared practices of mourning Muslim and Christian martyrs help overcome the violence and division of the recent past in pursuit of a peaceful coexistence in the present?

Dissonance

The second section of the book explores architecture's capacity to support democracy and facilitate the inclusion of minority groups in public space. Reflecting on xenophobia and cultural biases toward immigrants and Muslims in Scandinavia, this section is centered on Superkilen in Copenhagen, Denmark (Fig. 2). This kilometer-long urban park is located in the very heart of Nørrebro, one of the most ethnically diverse and socially challenged neighborhoods of Copenhagen. The project was designed as a multidisciplinary collaboration between the architects of the Bjarke Ingels Group, the artist group Superflex, and the landscape architecture firm Topotek 1, achieving remarkable social impact through a unique method of architectural branding and participatory design. Superkilen's design promotes inclusion and peaceful coexistence across lines of ethnicity, religion, and culture through a wide variety of objects representing the numerous nationalities living in the area. Deployed as urban furniture, these objects were gathered and fabricated through an extensive resident-engagement process. The park offers its visitors an encounter with both alien and familiar cultural "samples."

Figure 2. The Moroccan fountain in the Black Market, Superkilen, Copenhagen, Denmark (2012)

How people perceive these forms frames the beginning of this book section in a photo-essay about the park, featuring a series of interviews with local residents conducted by Danish anthropologist Tina Gudrun Jensen and photographs by Jesper Lambaek. Jensen has also written an essay for this section, in which she discusses mechanisms of exclusion and inclusion in Denmark through public spaces and housing projects. Despite strong nationalistic sentiments in Denmark, which are aimed at creating cultural homogeneity through restrictive immigration policies constraining diversity, everyday forms of interethnic coexistence are enabled though architectural projects in Copenhagen that allow for informal encounters among individuals of diverse backgrounds.

In light of the intensification of xenophobic sentiments unleashed as a response to the recent Syrian refugee crisis in Europe, architectural historian Jennifer Mack analyzes the emergence of new public spaces in Scandinavia. These new public spaces are evolving through the inclusion of immigrants as their integral architectural component, whether through an inversion of private and public realms, or through participatory design processes of parks, such as Superkilen. In the case of the latter, as art historian Barbara Steiner argues, participation as curation of conflictual potential is a central feature. The stereotypes of participation go back to an old modernist trope of the passive spectator/consumer. The participatory design process for Superkilen reflected the observation by art critic Claire Bishop that participation does not automatically imply collectivism.[5] Instead, Superkilen deployed participation as a tactic for creating a park collectively rather than for creating a collective or supplementing the work of social agencies. Both Mack and Steiner relate architecture of coexistence to processes of inclusion and exclusion in public space.

The design of the Superkilen park builds on the legacy of participatory art, interventionist art, interrogative design, and relational aesthetics to delineate its own method for a critical design intervention in public space. Its designers called this approach "participation extreme." Fostering intense user involvement and transdisciplinary collaboration, Superkilen designers introduced a new aesthetic for the design of urban furniture for public spaces that function as friendly provocations, mirroring the viewers' perspectives on their own cultural background, while simultaneously alienating them with "foreign" perspectives. This approach creates a sustained difference within the socio-optical space, gesturing toward Chantal Mouffe's notion of public space as an arena of confrontational hegemonies without the possibility of a rational consensus.[6] That is to say, Superkilen's urban furniture is not aimed at mediating the residents' multiple cultural perspectives toward a consensus in the form of a shared perspective. The aim of Superkilen's participatory design is for everyone to come to terms with the limits introduced by irreducibly composite "otherness" in the social sphere.

Ultimately, all three authors of this section tackle the broader questions of who has the right to visibility in public space, showcasing how architecture and art offer means for the creation of inclusive public spaces in Denmark, spaces in which one can encounter something new or something that one has to adapt to. *Architecture of Coexistence* casts the reader toward attempts to create a more heterogeneous society in contrast to ideas of a national homogeneity.

Convergence

The third section concentrates on the creation of the Islamic Cemetery Altach through the theme of convergence, exploring the creation of its transcultural aesthetics in terms of its cultural signification and building process (Fig. 3). This section opens, as the previous sections do, with a personal portrait of the project. Architectural historian Robert Fabach, who lives in Vorarlberg, visited the cemetery together with the architect, the mayor of Altach, and members of the local Muslim community to discuss their perspectives on the impact of the cemetery. Selected segments from Fabach's interviews are accompanied by a photo essay by Nikolaus Walter.

This cemetery, the first of its kind in the westernmost region of Austria, has provided Muslims in Austria with the possibility to be buried according to Islamic tradition. Tracing the history of immigration to Vorarlberg, sociologist Simon Burtscher-Matis argues that the Islamic Cemetery Altach marks an important milestone in the process of establishing Muslim communities in Vorarlberg. His sociological portrait of the region deals with the guest worker migration linked to the industrialization of Vorarlberg in the 1960s. Burtscher-Matis highlights the characteristics of the Muslim migration in Vorarlberg to that of other European regions. From this broader perspective we learn about the cemetery's vital role in the identity formation of the second and third generation Muslims in Vorarlberg: the Islamic Cemetery Altach reflects a major shift in the immigrants' perception of home and belonging and, as such, it represents a significant step toward the establishment of Vorarlbergian Islam.

The cemetery has made a significant impact in the realms of art and architecture, but also in the context of integration politics in Austria. In fact, the project has achieved international recognition as a catalyst for successful integration, and it has been recognized with numerous awards in both Islamic and non-Islamic contexts.[7] My own essay in this section discusses this social and disciplinary impact of the project in regard to its design and the building process. The success of the project would not have been possible without specific design sensibilities. The minimalist design of the cemetery created by Bernardo Bader, with the prayer space designed by myself, gives visual form to pluralism, and establishes a visual bridge between migrants and the host community. The transcultural aesthetics of the cemetery combine local traditions with Islamic dimensions in a new formal language that speaks to both local populations and represents the different Muslim communities in the region though their cultural symbols, materials, and craft.

Beyond the context-sensitive design, to cultivate cultural convergence through architecture means to design and implement an inclusive building process, and to do this in the absence of established organizational structures for the many scattered and diverse Muslim groups in the region. This project was made possible through a special type of non-hierarchical leadership and subtle social and political mediation. The process brought about a new law that would allow for Islamic burial rites to be conducted at a cemetery administered by the local municipality. In an expansive interview, the cemetery initiator and mediator Eva Grabherr elaborates what it means to lead the implementation of such

Figure 3: The Islamic Cemetery Altach, Austria (2011)

a process apart from the construction site itself—the site in her case was the social fabric of Vorarlberg, involving Catholic, Jewish, and ninety-five different Muslim groups. In the end, the many stakeholders' openness to risks of an unfamiliar process—that is, openness to collaborating with one another across disciplinary and cultural borders—fostered cross-cultural dialogue and crystalized organizational structures for Muslim minorities in Vorarlberg.

Conclusion

The three projects discussed throughout this book expand the scope of representational forms for Muslims living within non-Islamic majority societies. Instead of relying on the predominant inspirations drawn from the historical repertoire of Islamic dynasties' imperial styles, the three projects offer creative innovations through a new iconography for contemporary Islam in Europe—an iconography that reflects the diversity, hybridity, and dynamic nature of its interpretations and practices, which are also constantly evolving in dialogue with the local context. The broader political, social, and cultural layers related to the three projects demonstrate how Islamic civilization has been productively shaping the ongoing process of building pluralism in Europe.

Beside their demonstrated sociopolitical impact on the ground, these projects can inform the way we write about and learn about Islamic societies, their architecture and art. Over the past two decades, the field of architecture has seen a dynamic development of topics and exhibitions related to Islamic cultural productions. While this broadening scope of themes and ethnicities in the discipline can be seen as a positive development in terms of the expansion of the canon, labels such as "Contemporary Islamic Architecture" and "the Middle Eastern architect" perpetuate some of the persistent power structures in the field, overlooking the multidimensional identities and methods of global architectural practitioners in favor of exoticism that caters to funding opportunities or current political sentiments. In this respect, this volume aims to provide a critical perspective on these evolving trends through a geographic focus on architecture in Europe, as well as the inclusion of both religious and secular programs into the thematic scope of the book.

The volume concludes with an epilogue that turns the political discussion about architecture to pedagogy, showcasing the innovative approaches to teaching about Islam by Ali Asani. While his courses at Harvard University equally attract Muslim and non-Muslim students, Asani seeks to foster literacy about Islam through a multisensory engagement with the arts and architecture. Instead of presenting Islam primarily as a sociopolitical ideology of identity and hegemony, a lens that dominates most textbooks on Islamic societies and their history, Asani considers the arts as the central pedagogical lens. Creating calligraphy, architecture, and poetry in a history class about Islam allows Asani's students to learn about the arts' seminal role in Islamic history, but also situate its traditions within broader historical and sociopolitical contexts. Simultaneously, students also learn to collaborate and co-create across borders defined by gender, religion, ethnicity, or discipline.

Beyond the dimension of Islam, *Architecture of Coexistence* is really about the capacity of architecture to connect people on the human scale, to bridge ostensibly opposing worldviews in the service of co-creation. Building pluralism means designing and curating social processes that allow for acceptance of difference through a better understanding of each other's qualities. And finally, it is about the capacity of good architecture to transcend petty identity politics. It is about overcoming social alienation through playful, sensory experiences of space, symbols, materials, color, and light that appeal to us as humans.

1 "Conference 'Cities against Islamization,'"
   Cities Against Islamisation, accessed 28 May 2015,
   http://www.stedentegenislamisering.be/En/3/2.

2 Sherban Cantacuzino, "Sherefudin's White Mosque," in
   Architecture in Continuity, ed. Sherban Cantacuzino
   (New York: Aperture, 1985), 105–109.

3 K.F. Cviic, "Yugoslavia's Moslem Problem," *The World Today* 35(9)
   (Sept. 1979): 108.

4 In the first decades of the postwar era, Bosnian Muslims
   continued to be denied the status of a national group and were
   recognized only as members of the Serb, Croat, or Yugoslav
   nation. In 1968, Bosnian Museums were recognized as one of the
   constituent ethnic groups by a decision of the Central Committee
   of the League of Communists of Bosnia and Herzegovina, despite
   the fact that a religion-based nationality appeared to contradict
   the very principles of the anti-religious, communist regime.
   Historian Noel Malcolm argues that their drive for the national
   recognition of Bosnian Muslims in the socialist federation was
   not based exclusively on an Islamic religious movement. Rather,
   it evolved through two simultaneous religious and political
   trends: first, the movement of secular "Muslim nationalism"
   led by Communists and secularized Muslims, and second, a
   "separate revival of Islamic religious belief." Noel Malcolm,
   Bosnia: A Short History (New York: New York University Press,
   1994), 198–200.

5 Claire Bishop, *Artificial Hells: Participatory Art and the Politics of
   Spectatorship* (London and New York: Verso, 2012).

6 Chantal Mouffe, "Art as an agonistic intervention in public
   space." (2007), downloadable from onlineopen.org.

7 Beside the Aga Khan Award for Architecture (AKAA) in 2013, the
   Islamic Cemetery Altach received the International Piranesi
   Award for 2012, Österreichischer Bauherrenpreis der Zentral-
   vereinigung der Architekten 2013, best architect 14 Award 2013,
   and the 7. BTV Bauherrenpreis für Tirol und Vorarlberg 2013.
   It was a finalist for the European Public Space Award 2014, and
   was nominated for the European Union Prize for Contemporary
   Architecture – Mies van der Rohe Award 2013, the DETAIL Prize
   2012, and the Philippe Rotthier Prize 2014.

I. Building Pluralism

Beyond Homogeneity:
On the Concept
of Transculturality
Wolfgang Welsch

The concept of transculturality which I developed in the early 1990s is opposed to the traditional conception of single, national cultures. It corresponds to the current condition of cultures.

The traditional concept of single, national cultures

"Culture" first developed into a general concept, spanning not only a single but all the reifications of human life, in the late seventeenth century. Culture was used in this sense for the first time in 1684 by the natural rights scholar Samuel von Pufendorf (1632–94).[1] He denoted as "culture" the sum of those activities through which humans shape their lives as being specifically human, as opposed to merely animal.[2] Despite the immense increase of different usages of "culture" in modern times, this elementary definition still holds water to the present day.

Prior to this, the noun "culture" had no absolute usage. It had been a relative expression, bearing only on specific realms of activities. Accordingly, in antiquity, Cicero had spoken of the *cultura animi* ("care of the spirit"),[3] patristics propagandized the *cultura Christianae religionis,*[4] and in the Renaissance, Erasmus of Rotterdam and Thomas More pleaded for the *cultura ingeni,* "the culture of the inventive spirit."[5] For centuries, the expression "culture" appeared only in such compounds.

With Pufendorf, the term became a collective singular and an autonomous concept which claimed to encompass the whole of a people's, a society's, or a nation's activities. A hundred years later, this global concept of culture obtained through Herder, especially in his *Outlines of a Philosophy of the History of Man* (1784–91), a form that would remain exemplary for the time to follow.[6]

This traditional concept of single cultures was characterized by three determinants: ethnic foundation, social homogenization, and intercultural delimitation. Firstly, culture was to be the specific culture of a certain people—with French culture, say, being intrinsically different from German culture, or Slavic, or Japanese culture. Secondly, every culture was supposed to mold the whole life of the people concerned, making every act and every object an unmistakable instance of precisely *this* culture. Thirdly, delimitation toward the outside ensued: every culture was, as the culture of one folk, to be distinguished and to remain separated from other folks' cultures.

All three traits have become untenable today, in both descriptive and normative respects. Firstly, the ethnic consolidation is dubious. The idea that cultures are closed spheres, each corresponding to a folk's territorial area and linguistic extent is highly imaginary and fictional and must be laboriously brought to prevail against historical evidence of intermingling.

Secondly, modern societies are differentiated within themselves to such a degree that homogeneity is no longer constitutive or achievable for them. T.S. Eliot's statement, that culture is "the *whole way of life* of a people, from birth to the grave, from morning to night and even in sleep,"[7] is an obviously ideological decree. Modern societies are multicultural in themselves, encompassing a multitude of varying ways of life and lifestyles.

Thirdly, the sphere thesis and the command of ethnically based inner homogenization go hand in hand with outer delimitation. Having noted that "every nation has its *centre* of happiness *within itself* just as each sphere its centre of gravity!" Herder typically enough continues: "Everything which is still the *same* as my nature, which can be *assimilated* therein, I envy, strive towards, make my own; *beyond this,* kind nature has armed me with *insensibility, coldness* and *blindness;* it can even become *contempt* and *disgust*."[8] As the traditional concept advocates the double feature of emphasis on the integrity of the domestic and the exclusion of the foreign, it is a concept of inner homogenization and outer separation at the same time. It tends, as a consequence of its very conception, toward cultural racism. The sphere premise and the purity precept not only render impossible a mutual understanding between cultures, but the appeal to cultural identity of this kind finally also produces separatism and paves the way for political conflicts and wars. The conception's basic failing is thus to envisage cultures as closed spheres. Exclusion and conflict logically follow from this. For different spheres, each closed on itself, cannot communicate or mingle with each other but, as Herder stated, can only *"clash with one another."*[9] (This, by the way, is the original version of the "clash of civilizations.")

To sum this up: The classical model of culture is not only descriptively unserviceable, but also normatively dangerous and untenable. What is called for today is a departure from this concept and to think of cultures beyond the contraposition of ownness and foreignness, "beyond both the heterogeneous and the own," as Adorno once put it.[10]

Multiculturality and interculturality

Are the concepts of multiculturality and interculturality, then, capable of providing an appropriate concept of today's cultural dynamics? They apparently try to overcome some flaws of the traditional concept by advocating a mutual understanding between different cultures. Yet they are almost as inappropriate as the traditional concept itself, because they still remain conceptually bound to its core, to the sphere premise.

The concept of multiculturality takes up the problems that different cultures have living together *within one society.* But the concept remains in the duct of the traditional understanding of culture, for it still takes the various cultures within society as homogenous entities, as separate spheres. From this basis, a mutual understanding or a transgression of separating barriers cannot be achieved. On the contrary, the concept of multiculturality even furthers such barriers, as daily experience has shown for a long time. The concept threatens to engender regressive tendencies which, by appealing to a particularistic cultural identity, lead to ghettoization. The still-prevalent cultural notions of inner homogeneity and outer delimitation engender chauvinism and cultural fundamentalism.

A similar reservation applies to the concept of interculturality. For all its good intentions, it too continues conceptually to drag along the premise of the traditional concept of culture: the insinuation of an island- or sphere-like constitution of cultures. It does recognize that this constitution necessarily leads to intercultural conflicts, and it attempts to counter these by intercultural dialogue, but these conflicts *spring* from this sphere thesis. The classical concept of culture with its first trait—the separatist character of cultures—creates the secondary problem of the difficult coexistence and structural inability to communicate between these cultures. Hence the resulting problems cannot be solved on the basis of this concept.

So, neither the multiculturality nor the interculturality thesis get to the actual root of the problem, but operate on a surface level, cosmetically, so to speak. Both the multicultural and intercultural issues ought to be addressed in a different manner from the outset: in view of today's permeability of cultures.

This brings us to the concept of transculturality. The flaws of the traditional conception of single cultures, as well as of the more recent concepts of multiculturality and interculturality, can be summarized as follows: If cultures were in fact still constituted in the form of closed spheres, then one could neither rid oneself of, nor solve the problem of their coexistence and cooperation. However, cultures today de facto no longer have the insinuated form of homogeneity and separateness, but are characterized through to the core by mixing and permeations. I have called this new form of cultures "transcultural," since it goes beyond the traditional concept of culture and passes through traditional cultural boundaries as a matter of course.[11]

Transculturality

1. Macro level—the altered cut of contemporary cultures
The old homogenizing and separatist idea of cultures has long been surpassed through cultures' external networking. Cultures today are extremely interconnected and entangled with each other. Lifestyles no longer end at the borders of national cultures, but go beyond these and are found in other countries. The way of life for an economist, an academic, or a journalist is no longer German or French, but rather European or global in tone. The new forms of entanglement are a consequence of migratory processes, as well as of worldwide material and immaterial communications systems and economic interdependencies and dependencies. It is here, of course, that questions of power play a role.

A consequence and sign of such permeations is the fact that the same basic problems and states of consciousness today appear in cultures once considered to be fundamentally different—think, for example, of human rights debates, feminist movements, or ecological awareness. They are powerful active factors across the board culturally. According to the old model of culture and its fiction of difference, transnational and transcultural concerns such as these would have been quite impossible, which in turn is evidence of the obsolescence of this model.

Cultures today are in general characterized by hybridization. For every culture, all other cultures tend to become inner-content or satellites. This applies on the levels of population, merchandise, and information. In most countries worldwide, there are members of all other countries living there; more and more the same articles—as exotic as they may once have been—are becoming available the world over; and the global networking of communications technology makes all kinds of information identically available from every point in space.

Cultural mixing occurs not only—as is often too one-sidedly stated—in the consumer industry (think of Coke, McDonalds, MTV, or CNN), but in high culture as well, and this has been the case for a long time—think, for example, of Puccini and Chinese music; of Gauguin and Tahiti; of Picasso and African sculpture; or of Messiaen and India. Western medicine has in the meantime become popular in East Asia, and acupuncture, Yoga, and Ayurveda have, vice versa, become widespread health practices in the West. Forms of life are becoming more and more cross-cultural everywhere. Germans, for example, today have implemented more elements of French and Italian lifestyle than ever before—even Germans today know how to enjoy life!

Strictly speaking, there is no longer anything absolutely foreign. Everything is within reach. Accordingly, there is no longer anything exclusively "own" either. Authenticity has become folklore; it is ownness simulated for others to whom the indigene himself belongs. Today, in a society's internal relations among its different ways of life, there exists as much foreignness as in its external relations with other societies.[12]

2. Micro level

Transculturality advances not only on the social macro level, but also on the individual micro level. This is generally underexposed, but is particularly important. Most of us are determined in our cultural formation by several cultural origins and connections. We are all cultural hybrids. This is not only true, as one often thinks, for immigrants, but increasingly for all people today.

The explanation is simple: since today's adolescents are already familiar with a far greater number of cultural patterns on a daily basis than their parents' and grandparents' generation ever was (they simply meet more people with different cultural and ethnic backgrounds on the streets, at work, in the media than before), they can take up and connect a variety of elements of different origins in their cultural identity formation. The alternatives to the standards of the past are no longer out of reach, but have become part of everyday life. By connecting such different cultural elements to their identity, today's individuals are increasingly becoming transcultural in themselves.

The internal transculturality of individuals is the decisive point. One should not only speak of the fact that today's societies contain different cultural models ("cultural diversity"), but also of the fact that individuals today are shaped by several cultural patterns, combining different cultural elements in themselves. The cultural formation of subsequent generations will presumably be even more strongly transculturally shaped.[13]

In today's conditions, the discovery of this inner transculturality is particularly important and helpful. One of the great advantages of transculturality is that it increases the connectivity, the ability to communicate. Inner transculturality helps in dealing with external transculturality. The more elements an individual's cultural identity is composed of, the greater the chance their identity will overlap with that of others. Spherical identities have nothing in common. Transcultural identities, on the other hand, have intersections. In this way, such individuals can enter into exchange and communication to a much greater extent than before, despite all other differences; they can discover existing similarities and develop new ones.

A cultural identity of this type is, of course, not to be equated with national identity. The distinction between cultural and national identity is of elementary importance. It belongs among the mustiest assumptions that an individual's cultural formation must be determined by his nationality or national status. The insinuation that someone who possesses a Japanese, an Indian, or a German passport must also culturally unequivocally be Japanese, Indian, or German and that otherwise he is without a fatherland, or a traitor to his fatherland, is as foolish as it is dangerous. The detachment of civic from personal or cultural identity is to be insisted upon—all the more so in states, such as ours, in which freedom in cultural formation belongs among one's basic rights.[14]

To sum this up: cultural determinants today—from society's macro level through to individuals' micro level—have become transcultural. The old concept of culture has become inappropriate. It misrepresents cultures' actual form, the type of their relations and the structure of individuals' identities and lifestyles. Every concept of culture intended to pertain to today's reality must face up to this transcultural constitution.

Historically, by the way, transculturality is not a new phenomenon. It has been present to a larger extent than the adherents of the traditional concept of culture want to admit. They blindly deny the factual historic transculturality of long periods in order to establish the nineteenth century's imaginary notion of homogeneous national cultures. For anyone who knows their European history—and art history in particular—this historical transculturality is evident. Styles developed across countries and nations, and many artists created their best works far from home. Albrecht Dürer, for example, who was often considered an exemplary German artist, first found himself in Italy, and he had to seek out Venice a second time in order to become himself completely. In general, Edward Said's observation holds: "All cultures are hybrid; none of them is pure; none of them is identical to a 'pure' folk; none of them consists of a homogenous fabric."[15] Although transculturality rather than purity has long been the rule, the extent of transculturality has indeed risen considerably in the last decades.

3. Counter movements

To be sure, there are also counter-movements to transculturalization. They have been around for a long time: new nationalisms, ethnic and religious tribal incantations in Europe, in the Arab world, worldwide. How are they to be explained and evaluated?

The sociological answer is: they are reactions to real or supposed fears, because one is a loser of globalization, or feels like one. One sees oneself threatened by foreign powers. In such situations we humans (this is our archaic heritage) tend to gang up, to conjure up old and often meanwhile fictitious identities. The artificiality of the proclaimed identity then once again increases the pressure to reinforce it, and thus one approaches the old cultural spheres again with demands of purity and resistance to foreignness.

The psychological answer is: hatred toward strangers is projected self-hatred. In the foreign, one rejects something that one carries in oneself, but which one may not allow in oneself. The internally repressed is combated externally.[16] Conversely, what would be the psychological conditions for coming to terms with external transculturality, which certainly also has its stressful sides? Julia Kristeva pointed out that only those who once have lost the ground beneath their feet will have an open ear for others.[17]

What does the transcultural concept advise? According to it, what is problematic are closed spheres, especially the national ones. What is so implausible about permeable anchoring? That is, what speaks against maintaining open spheres that correspond to regional peculiarities or linguistic communalities, which on the one hand can provide something like comfort, security, and homeland, and on the other hand do so neither at the expense of other homelands nor by forcibly dictating a certain identity? Why shouldn't we have several anchorages that allow us to feel at home in different atmospheres? Why shouldn't someone be a Bavarian who loves the local mountains and is at the same time a fan of Italian cuisine, a friend of meditative practices, and a lover of baseball?

To put it another way: it is good to have a foothold, and for many people the local, regional, or national identity forms this foothold. But the mainstay should not become a clubfoot. Rather, it should allow additional and more extensive movements of the free leg, it should allow openness for others and not exclude them.

Probably we are all looking for anchorages, but they don't have to be in our native country; they can be found elsewhere. In Latin this reads *ubi bene, ibi patria* (where it is well with me, there is my homeland). This does not mean that one can only find home far away from one's first home, the initial roots. But that's a possibility. And in a certain sense, the first home is only ever a real home as a second home, that is, only when one (in view of other possibilities as well) has consciously decided on it, has subsequently chosen and affirmed it for oneself. Only then is *Heimat* (homeland) not a natural, but a cultural and human category.

Transculturality in architecture

Postmodern architecture (and postmodernism in general) was essentially about making the cultural pluralism of modern societies explicit.[18] Charles Jencks, the main propagator of postmodern architecture, stated: "Post-Modernism is [...] extending the language of architecture in many different ways—into the vernacular, towards tradition and the commercial slang of the street. Hence the double-coding, the architecture which speaks to the elite and the man on the street."[19] "It is the discontinuity in taste cultures which creates both the theoretical base and the 'dual-coding' of Post-Modernism."[20]

But how are different cultural patterns to be combined in one and the same work? One possibility is to place the different patterns side by side in a patchwork-like manner; another is to really connect them with each other, so that they can penetrate and fertilize each other.

James Stirlings's famous *Neue Staatsgalerie* in Stuttgart (1984) represents the first type (Fig. 1). The different architectural elements—for example, the massive stone walls and the rotunda in Schinkel's manner, or the curtain wall, which is reminiscent of classical modernism, but put in motion,

Figure 1. James Stirling, *Neue Staatgalerie,* Stuttgart, Germany (1984)

or the handrails in pop colors—stand in separation next to each other. The design is intercultural rather than transcultural.

An excellent example of the second type is Jean Nouvel's *Institut du Monde Arabe* in Paris (1987).[21] Nouvel has achieved a perfect interpenetration of cultural patterns. The squares of the facade are diaphragms, which, similar to photographic apertures, modify their degree of contraction and thus the light supply to the interior according to the varying daylight conditions. They can be perceived as elements of high-tech and as Arabic ornaments at the same time (Fig. 2).

On the inside, this connection of technical installation and Arabic filigree achieves an almost incredible perfection and peculiarity. All in all, the high-tech building which is mainly made of aluminum is so masterfully fine-tuned in gray tones that one can imagine being in a seraglio (Fig. 3). Nouvel has not combined European and Arabic elements in the way of patchwork, but has invented forms that can be read both ways. He has created a truly transcultural architecture.

Transcultural design and architecture can enhance our understanding of the present transcultural condition, and they can make us experience the potential richness and beauty of this condition. The three architectural examples presented in this volume certainly do so.

1   In the second edition of his script *De jure naturae et gentium libri octo* (Frankfurt, 2nd ed. 1684), Pufendorf effected, in several places, the transition from the traditional concept of a specific *cultura animi* to the new talk of a general "cultura" (Book II, Ch. 4, § 1).

2   Ibid., II, 4.

3   Marcus Tullius Cicero, *Tusculanae disputationes*, II, 13.

4   Cf. Wilhelm Perpeet, "Zur Wortbedeutung von 'Kultur,'" in *Naturplan und Verfallskritik. Zu Begriff und Geschichte der Kultur*, eds. Helmut Brackert and Fritz Wefelmeyer (Frankfurt/Main: Suhrkamp, 1984), 21–28, here 22.

5   Ibid.

6   Johann Gottfried Herder, *Outlines of a Philosophy of the History of Man* (New York: Bergman Publishers, 1966). The work first appeared in four separate parts, each of five books, in the years 1784, 1785, 1787, and 1791, published by the Hartknoch press in Riga and Leipzig. The first English edition was published in 1800 in London.

7   T.S. Eliot, *Notes Towards the Definition of Culture* (London: Faber and Faber, 1948), 31.

8   Johann Gottfried Herder, *Auch eine Philosophie der Geschichte zur Bildung der Menschheit* (Another Philosophy of History) [1774] (Frankfurt/Main: Suhrkamp, 1967), 44 f.

1   Ibid., 39.

10 Theodor W. Adorno, *Negative Dialektik*, in: Adorno, *Gesammelte Schriften*, vol. 6 (Frankfurt/Main: Suhrkamp 3rd ed. 1984), 192.

11 See Wolfgang Welsch, "Transkulturalität: Lebensformen nach der Auflösung der Kulturen," in *Information Philosophie* 2 (1992): 5–20; many further elaborations followed, for example "Transculturality: The Puzzling Form of Cultures Today," in Spaces of Culture: City, Nation, World, eds. Mike Featherstone and Scott Lash (London: Sage, 1999), 194–213; most recently: *Transkulturalität: Realität, Geschichte, Aufgabe* (Vienna: new academic press, 2017). When I coined the term "transculturality," I was not aware that the similar notion *transculturación* had been used by Fernando Ortiz already in 1940 when he analyzed the cultural constitution of Cuba determined by the mutual influence of Spanish conquistadors, African slaves, and Asian contract laborers. But it is always good not to be the first person who suggests an idea. Originality is a dubious ideal; companionship is a better one.

12 "[…] cultural diversity tends now to be as great within nations as it is between them." Ulf Hannerz, *Cultural Complexity: Studies in the Social Organization of Meaning* (New York: Columbia University Press, 1992), 231.

13 Amy Gutmann states that today "most people's identities, not just Western intellectuals or elites, are shaped by more than a single culture. Not only societies, but people are multicultural." "The Challenge of Multiculturalism in Political Ethics," in *Philosophy & Public Affairs* 22(3) (1993): 171–206, here 183.

14 Of course, civic and cultural identity can overlap. In many cases they will. The point is that they are not to be *equated*.

15 Edward W. Said, "Kultur und Identität: Europas Selbstfindung aus der Einverleibung der Welt," *Lettre International* 34 (1996): 21–25, here 24. Similarly, J.N. Mohanty states "that talk of a culture which evokes the idea of a homogeneous form is completely misleading. Indian culture, or Hindu culture, consists of completely different cultures. […] A completely homogeneous subculture is not to be found." "Den anderen verstehen," in *Philosophische Grundlagen der Interkulturalität* (Amsterdam: Rodopi, 1993), 115–122, here 118. Jacques Derrida notes: "It is peculiar to a culture, that it is never identical with itself. There is no culture and no cultural identity without this difference *towards itself*" "Das andere Kap," in *Das andere Kap: Die vertagte Demokratie – Zwei Essays zu Europa* (Frankfurt/Main: Suhrkamp, 1992), 9–80, here 12 f.

16 Robert Musil wrote about this: "[…] ethnic prejudice is usually nothing more than self-hatred, dredged up from the murky depths of one's own conflicts and projected onto some convenient victim, a traditional practice from time immemorial." *The Man without Qualities*, trans. Sophie Wilkins (New York: Knopf, 1995, vol. I), 461.

17 "[…] one must have experienced a sort of imbalance, a tottering upon an abyss." *Étrangers à nous-mêmes* (Paris: Fayard, 1988), 30.

18 On the history and the varieties of postmodernism in general, see Wolfgang Welsch, *Unsere postmoderne Moderne* [1987] (7th edition Berlin: Akademie Verlag, 2008).

19 Charles Jencks, *The Language of Post-Modern Architecture* (London: Academy Editions, 1977), 8.

20 Ibid., 6. Already Leslie Fiedler had, with respect to literature, called for a combination of high and low, extravagance and triviality, myth and reality, dream world and machine world, and had defined the postmodern writer as a "double agent," being "equally at home in the world of technology and the realm of wonder." "Cross the Border – Close the Gap," *Playboy* Dec. 1969, reprinted in *A Fiedler Reader* (New York: Stein and Day, 1977), 270–94, here 288 and 294.

21 The institute is jointly supported by the French government and nineteen Arab states and is intended to promote the knowledge of Arab culture and civilization in France.

Figure 2. Facade detail from the *Arab World Institute,* Paris, France (1987)

Figure 3. Interior view of the *Arab World Institute,* Paris, France (1987)

Immigrant Communities and Their Buildings
Mohammad al-Asad

The immigration of communities from places they consider home to a new location is as old as human history. In fact, every one of us has immigrant ancestors. Various communities have immigrated for different reasons. These reasons have included persecution by more powerful groups, which may reach the level of genocide. The persecution may be based on religious, racial, ethnic, tribal, social, or even economic considerations. Although some communities have been targeted because of this sense of "otherness," there also are communities that have found themselves caught in the middle of ongoing conflicts and the violence and disruptions that come with them. Some communities are displaced as a result of natural calamities (famine, earthquakes, droughts). Still, some communities voluntarily move in search of a better life. There also are those who are moved to a different geographic location through coercion, as is the case with slavery. In all cases, however, there is a factor (or factors) that pushes communities out of what was their home. In some instances, certain communities end up going through more than one migration as they search for a new place that accepts—or at least tolerates—them, and that they may be able to consider as a new home. The traumas associated with leaving their homes is often only the beginning of a long process of displacement and adjustment for such communities. This process not only includes the challenges of being accepted by the host society, but also of establishing roots where they end up settling.

Some communities immigrate temporarily, as is the case with guest workers, and some immigrate permanently. Their members may live in host countries legally or illegally. In all cases, the phenomenon of the presence of immigrant communities is often permanent, even if the stay of its individual members in host societies is temporary. It is estimated that about three percent of the world's population are migrants (over 230 million people), although it should be specified that migrants are defined here as those who have lived a year or more outside their country of birth. These numbers of course do not take into consideration internal migrants, that is, those who move within the borders of their country, voluntarily or because they were forced. It is even harder to keep track of their numbers. Conservative estimates place them at over 740 million people.[1]

The issue of immigration, and particularly the acceptance of immigrant communities by host societies, has very recently become highly charged. This not only applies to countries of the Global North, but also the Global South. One constantly comes across media reports highlighting the fear and hatred that members of host societies often express toward immigrants. Although these immigrant communities are by far the weaker of the two, host societies often use them as scapegoats for all sorts of national, communal, and personal disappointments, unrealized expectations, and failures. Not surprisingly, and by extension, there is no shortage of politicians who opportunistically fan such sentiments and emphasize the demonization of immigrants as an integral component of their political platforms. Interestingly enough, however, the hardening of national borders to limit the influx of outsiders coming from the Global South has been taking place in a quieter and less flamboyant, but no less effective manner in the countries of the Global North for decades. These dynamics have been taking place between the wealthier and poorer countries of the Global South as well, but this usually receives less attention in the international media, which gives priority to covering the Global North. This is not surprising considering that this is where much of its audience and advertisers are located.

In spite of such agitated reactions to immigration, it does not seem that it will stop anytime soon, not only because of the presence of large numbers of people who strive to immigrate for various reasons, but also because of the need for people in the Global North—as well as in the relatively more affluent countries of the Global South—who would carry out menial work that locals are not willing to take on. Also important is the Global North's need to address its diminishing natural population growth, which in numerous cases has entered negative territory. Such a drop in population may only be addressed through bringing in immigrants.

Human beings, of course, are social animals and need to organize themselves in groups. Such groups are defined through a wide variety of preexisting and constructed bonds including race, ethnicity, religion, tribal affiliation, social values, ideologies, and economic conditions. We naturally also simultaneously belong to various groups of differing sizes. These various groupings allow us to form our differing identities and be parts of support networks. These groups and identities, however, may also take on the role of forces of oppression and coercion toward their members. Belonging to these groups consequently might require excessive levels of loyalty and conformity, as well as serious sacrifices, which often are for the benefit of the dominant figures and power structures in the group.

We not only define ourselves by our sense of belonging and by our conceived similarities to others with whom we choose to affiliate, or by groups we are born into, but also tend to emphasize our differences from groups with whom we do not affiliate. Such differentiation can easily lead to xenophobia, which very often translates into hostility and violence. It also should be noted that we tend to exaggerate and magnify difference in relation to those who do not belong to our various identity groups. If someone dresses differently than the rest of us, we usually notice this immediately. If a number of people dress differently than the rest of us, we very often unconsciously magnify their numbers. In this context, it is interesting to note that people regularly exaggerate the number of immigrants in their communities.[2]

Such emphasis on similarities and differences within and between groups leads to complex dynamics. Members of an immigrant community usually feel a strong need to band together, partly as a result of the victimization they went through in what was their homeland, and partly to help them survive within the host society, where, as newcomers, they do not have any meaningful contacts and very often may not be welcomed. The host society may even accentuate its differences in relation to a given immigrant community through processes that often take on the form of social, economic, and legal discrimination and segregation. It should also be noted, however, that certain immigrant communities may not wish—or even actively refuse—to integrate or assimilate with the host society, and to emphasize their differences in relation to it, whether such differences are religious, cultural, or racial. In other words, they may engage in a form of reverse discrimination. Here, it should be noted that although immigrant communities are almost always the weaker side in the relation with host societies, hostility is not always necessarily exclusively fanned by the host communities, but may very well also come from members within an immigrant community. An example of this is found in the pronunciations and actions of radical Islamists living in the West, an issue that will be touched upon below.

Immigrant communities may be differentiated in relation to their host societies by inherent physical features, such as skin color. They are also differentiated, however, by various forms of material and non-material cultural expression. These include language, social and religious practices, vocation, dress, literature, performing arts, handicrafts, and food. Some of these may be forced on the immigrant communities, or at least become strongly connected to them, as with dress or vocation.[3] Some of their practices and forms of cultural expression may remain confined within their community, and other forms may spill over to the host society and even be embraced by it. Food and music are very common examples of the latter case.

Immigrant communities, of course, need physical spaces where their members can come together, experience a sense of solidarity, and offer mutual support to each other. They may congregate informally in parks and other open spaces (as with the foreign domestic workers congregating in the public spaces of Hong Kong on Sundays). They also need interior spaces where they can congregate for social events, and, importantly, for religious services. Religion, after all, provides them a sense of identity and also a degree of solace that helps them cope with the various difficulties and challenges they experience and to which they are subjected. Considering the meager financial resources usually available to immigrant groups, such places often are no more than rented or donated spaces that can accommodate a sizable number of people. These may consist of basements and available areas in restaurants and shops. Schools and community centers also may be used in a temporary capacity for prayers for worshippers. In this context, it is interesting to note that of the about 1,000 registered mosques found in the United States during the mid-1990s, less than ten percent were originally designed as such.[4]

The issue, however, extends beyond that of limited financial resources. Such unmarked and informal spaces also allow for a level of anonymity. Immigrant communities may be tolerated, but not necessarily welcomed. Moreover, any form of marked exposure, particularly by immigrant communities that still have not established a multi-generational presence or have not noticeably assimilated in a host community, may even be resented outright by the latter.

It is within this context that buildings differ in relation to other forms of material or non-material cultural expression used by immigrant communities. Buildings, particularly of a public nature, have a marked presence in their surrounding physical environment. They also suggest a level of permanence. Moreover, when these buildings express the use of sizable resources, their symbolic presence is highly magnified, and, in numerous cases, so is the reaction to them. Accordingly, a building dedicated to the service of an immigrant community, particularly a building that emphasizes architectural difference in relation to its physical context, as with a mosque in a non-Muslim setting, may be perceived by the host society as an unwelcomed act of assertion by the immigrant community. A recent example of such a rejection of the architectural presence of the other is the 2009 successful vote in Switzerland to ban the construction of minarets on mosques. Such a reaction is even more noteworthy considering that the country only has four mosques with minarets. It is an example of the exaggerated perception of the presence of the other.[5]

Suffice it say, such buildings can carry considerable—intended and unintended—symbolic charges for both the immigrant community and the host society. Their realization therefore often needs to involve a great deal of negotiation between representatives of the two groups.

I would like to devote the second part of this essay to a discussion of a specific group of such buildings. There is a practically unlimited diversity of buildings relating to the communal use of immigrant communities that one can choose from based on categories such as geographic location, building type, and the communities they serve. We should keep in mind that whatever selection one makes will consequently only address the subject of such buildings from a specific and narrow angle. I will be discussing five mosques located in major Western cities. These are the main mosques of Paris, Washington, D.C., London, Rome, and New York. The five buildings form a coherent group. All are buildings that are intended to serve Muslim communities primarily consisting of immigrants. All are intended to represent Islam. They all belong to the twentieth century, with the earliest being the Paris mosque, which dates to the 1920s, and the latest being the Rome mosque, which dates to the 1990s. They all belong to a period that predates the current horrifying anti-immigrant sentiments that have become increasingly vocal in the Global North, and that have a particularly strong anti-Muslim component to them. They are also buildings for which considerable resources have been dedicated in terms of design and construction. Further, they provide insight into the complex and messy relations that exist between immigrant communities and host societies, as well as other outside players who may be involved in their making. Finally, an adequate amount of information has been published on them, which is not the case for the vast majority of buildings connected to immigrant communities.[6]

Admittedly, using these mosques as a case study presents its share of limitations to understanding this topic. To begin with, one needs to be extremely careful so as not to make any sweeping generalizations based on an examination of a handful of buildings. They do not represent a specific ethnic, racial, or national community, but rather lump different immigrant communities of various sects, ethnicities, and nationalities under a wider identity, that of a religion: Islam. Of course, this is an identity with which a number of immigrants and immigrant groups in the West strongly identify, but definitely is not the only, and not always the most important, one. An emphasis on this general identity in fact may ignore other identities that may be tighter and more closely knit in nature. In some cases, this religious identity even may be a constructed rather than preexisting identity for a number of the various groups placed under it.

In addition to representing a more widely encompassing immigrant identity, these buildings function and communicate at the scale of the city—and even the country—in which they are located, rather than merely at the scale of a neighbourhood or city district. The cities in which these mosques are located are all of national and even global importance: London, Paris, Washington, D.C., and Rome are capital cities of G8 countries, and New York is the largest city in the United States, and a global economic and cultural center.

Figure 1. The Great Mosque of Paris, France (1926)

As I shall explore in further detail below, it should be noticed that immigrant communities generally took on a minor role in the conception and realization of the mosques, even though these buildings were intended to represent and serve them: these immigrant communities were their major users and they take on an important role in the management of the buildings. Instead, when these mosques were conceived, the influence and participation of local communities were very much overshadowed by the involvement of the diplomats of Muslim countries stationed in these cities. Egypt played a major role in the case of the early buildings, and Saudi Arabia played a major role in the case of the later ones. In addition, most of them were also conceived through the involvement of official representatives of the host society, ranging from municipal authorities to national governments. And, of course, none of these buildings have the informal or spontaneous character found in most buildings serving immigrant communities. In that sense, they do stand out, and are in strong contrast with the simpler, modest buildings usually affiliated with immigrant communities.

In discussing those mosques, I of course will address their architecture. My main focus, however, is not their formal compositions, but the messages that the conception and realization of these buildings have conveyed.

The earliest of these buildings is the Mosque and Muslim Institute in Paris (also referred to as the Great Mosque of Paris). The project was conceived between 1922 and 1926. It was built to recognize the North African Muslims who fought alongside the French in World War I. It was sponsored by the

French Government, but since France is a secular state, it was commissioned by the Association of the Awqaf of the Holy Places, which was set up by the French authorities to manage Muslim religious sites in Morocco, Algeria, and Tunisia. An administrative commission of French dignitaries was put together to oversee the project. The Paris Municipal Council donated a prominent 7,500-square-meter site for the project that is located in the center of the city, and the French Government made the sum of half a million French Francs available to the Association to start the project. This amount covered about ten percent of the overall construction costs. The remaining funds came from the governments of French territories in Africa and Indo-China, as well as from individuals in North Africa. The Egyptian government donated the minbar for the mosque as well as Qurans, and continues to contribute to its running costs. The Bey of Tunisia donated the mosaic tiles in its hammam. A group of French architects, all of whom also had worked in North Africa, designed the complex. The design is essentially Andalusian—North African revival, which is not surprising considering France's long colonial connection to North Africa.

The second mosque is the Islamic Center in Washington, D.C., which was completed in 1957. Ambassadors of Muslim countries to the United States played a major role in realizing the project. The idea of constructing the mosque dates back to 1944. More specifically, the conception of the building is linked to the efforts of the Egyptian ambassador in the United States and a Palestinian–American contractor, A.J. Howar, who had immigrated to the United States during the first decade of the twentieth century. Together, they formed the Washington Mosque Foundation.

Figure 2. The Islamic Center in Washington, D.C., United States of America (1957)

Donations for its realization came from governments and individuals in the lands of Islam, as well as from Muslim and also Christian Arab communities in the United States. A 2,800-square-meter plot for the construction of the mosque located in the city's embassy quarter, along the prestigious Massachusetts Avenue, was purchased in 1948 for $95,000. Construction was initiated in 1950, and continued intermittently until the mosque was completed in 1957. The United States Government does not seem to have been involved in the realization of this structure, but President Dwight D. Eisenhower dedicated the building.[7]

The Egyptian Ministry of Awqaf provided the design for the structure, which was carried out by Mario Rossi (d. 1961), an Italian architect residing in Egypt who was responsible for designing a number of important mosques there. The design is an eclectic architectural revival building that includes Fatimid, Andalusian, and Mamluk features. The design was further developed and modified by a Washington-based architectural firm Irving S. Porter & Sons. Among the modifications made to the design was relocating the mosque's minaret from along the street facade further inward within the site. The mosque's minbar was donated by the Egyptian Government, and the tiles used in it were donated by the Turkish Government. The building is currently protected by the Historic American Buildings Survey.[8]

Regarding its later history, it is interesting to note that it has been subjected to inter-sectarian Muslim conflicts, particularly during the early 1980s. For example, a number of opposing Iranian groups attempted to control it during that period and disrupted its daily activities. Moreover, there were disputes between Sunni and Shi'i Muslims regarding who would take on the role of imam of the mosque. A number of visiting imams were appointed as a response.

The third mosque is the London Central Mosque (Regent's Park Mosque), which was completed in 1977. By then, the United Kingdom had over 400 places of worship for Muslims, of which only thirty-five were originally built as mosques. The idea behind the construction of this mosque dates back to 1920, but no action was taken until 1940, when, at the instigation of the Egyptian ambassador in the United Kingdom, the British Government purchased a 0.93-hectare site for the mosque in Regent's Park. This was a reciprocal gesture to the Egyptian Government, which not too long before had donated a plot of land in Cairo for the construction of an Anglican Cathedral. The central location of the site in London was considered an acknowledgement of the importance of the Muslim community in Britain. Up to that time, all mosques in the United Kingdom were located at the outskirts of cities. The site was formally handed to a committee established to oversee the creation of the mosque, which consisted of ambassadors to the United Kingdom from twelve Muslim countries. An existing structure on the site was selected to house an Islamic cultural center until the construction of the mosque.

An initial design for the mosque was developed by an Egyptian architect in the late 1940s. It was not until 1959, however, that plans for initiating construction were set in motion, but the London County Council and the Fine Arts Commission objected to the design for not fitting within its surroundings. The mosque committee accordingly rejected the design. The project then went into sleep mode again for another decade, until 1969, when it was revived by the ambassadors of Saudi Arabia,

Figure 3. The London Central Mosque, United Kingdom (1977)

Figure 4. The New York Islamic Center, New York City, United States of America (1991)

Pakistan, Lebanon, and Kuwait to the United Kingdom. An international competition was held for the design of the mosque. Fifty-two entries from seventeen countries were submitted. A three-person jury consisting of the head of the Royal Institute of British Architects, a member from Pakistan, and a member from Spain selected the submission by British architect Sir Frederick Gibberd as the winning design. The architect was asked to make a few modifications to the design, which was finalized by 1973, and construction began in 1974. Construction costs, which amounted to about ten million USD, were covered by a fund set up by a number of Muslim governments.

The complex includes the mosque in addition to a cultural center (consisting of a library, conference rooms, and a cafeteria), and living accommodations for its staff. It also includes an underground car park. The mosque's prayer hall has a capacity for almost 1,000 worshippers, and can accommodate 4,500 worshippers for special religious events through the use of other spaces including its exterior court.

The structure is dominated by a steel-framed dome with gold-painted copper sheathing that rises to a height of 25 meters, and by a minaret that rises to 43 meters. The rest of the complex is much lower so as not to dominate its surroundings. The dome is inspired by the Safavid domes of the early seventeenth-century Royal Mosque and the Shaykh Lutfallah Mosque in Isfahan. Although it incorporates historically inspired elements including the dome, minaret, arches, and courtyard, the relative simplicity of its overall formal composition and details, its minimal use of surface decoration, as well as its use of modern materials (steel and concrete) and construction techniques provide an attempt to create a mosque that at least makes a nod to a mid-twentieth-century Modernist architectural aesthetic. The mosque also seems to be a source of inspiration for the design of the Great Mosque of Kuwait by the late Iraqi architect Mohamed Makiya, which was completed in 1984. The building recently received protected heritage status.[9]

The fourth project is the New York Islamic Center, which was completed in 1991. The project was sponsored by representatives of the Muslim countries at the United Nations. It was the first to be specifically built for the city's Muslim community.[10] A site for the project in Manhattan's Upper East Side was purchased by the governments of Saudi Arabia, Kuwait, and Libya in 1966, and a non-profit entity was set up to oversee the realization of the project.

The American architectural firm Skidmore, Owings, and Merrill (SOM) was commissioned to design the mosque in 1987. The project's free-standing 40-meter-high minaret was designed separately by another American firm, Haiden Connel Associates, with a Turkish architect working for the firm, Altun Gürsel, taking on the role of lead designer. The Kuwaitis were major supporters of the mosque. The Emir of Kuwait in fact laid the foundation stone for the project. The project provides an abstract interpretation of an Ottoman mosque with a central dome. It can accommodate about 1,100 worshipers.

The fifth mosque is the Islamic Center and Mosque in Rome. It was first used in 1992, but its official opening took place in 1994. The idea of constructing a mosque in Rome, the center of Catholicism, was not welcomed for some time. Mussolini famously commented that he would allow the construction of a mosque in Rome if Muslims would allow the construction of a church in Mecca. The Vatican, however, declared in 1963 that it would not oppose the project as long as it was out of sight of the Basilica of St. Peter and that its minaret would be no taller than the Basilica's dome.

The Rome Islamic Center organization was founded in 1959, and the Islamic Cultural Center Organization was founded in 1966 by presidential decree. The initiative to build the mosque dates back to 1972, when the ambassadors of Muslim countries assigned to Italy and the Vatican, together with representatives of the Muslim community in Rome, approached the President of Italy to set up the Center. Although the intention was to essentially serve the Muslim community, the foundation charter of the Center also declared that it would be a forum to encourage dialogue between Islam and Christianity. A competition was held for the design of the mosque in 1975. Forty-seven entries were submitted. The jury members included professors from universities in the lands of Islam, Italian historians, and ambassadors of Muslim countries to Italy. The jury decided that the designers of two of the entries would collaborate on developing a joint design. These were the office of Italian architect Paolo Portoghesi and Italian civil engineer Mittorio Gigliotti, and Iraqi architect Sami Moussawi.

A committee of thirteen ambassadors from Muslim countries oversaw the project, and contributions for its realization came in from twenty-four countries. The Rome City Council had donated a 2.5-hectare plot for the project in 1974. The city did not provide its approval for the design of the mosque until 1984, with the delay being partly the result of resistance to the project from residents of the area in which it is located. Construction proceeded with numerous interruptions as a result of the lack of funds, but a donation in the amount of ten million USD from Saudi Arabia helped complete the fifty-million-USD project in the 1990s.

The complex includes a mosque and a cultural center that are separated by a court. It can accommodate 2,000 worshippers in its 2,500-square-meter prayer hall.[11]

Architecturally, it may be described as a postmodern structure. Portoghesi in fact is a primary figure in the development of the postmodern movement in architecture, and curated the first Venice Biennale exhibition, *The Presence of the Past,* which is an important event in the promotion of postmodernism. Inspiration for the design of the mosque is found in historical models including the ribbing of the domes and the forest of columns of the Great Mosque of Cordoba (eight to tenth centuries).

A number of observations emerge from examining these five projects. The first relates to the involvement of official local bodies in the realization of the three European examples. This is particularly evident in the case of the Paris mosque. The project was essentially carried out by the French authorities. They took on a major role in terms of conceiving it, financing it, designing it, and constructing it. A good part of the funds for its construction, however, also came from Muslims in the French colonies, either directly through personal contributions, or indirectly through the taxes they paid to the French colonial administrative governments in various Muslim colonies. The land for each of the three European mosques was donated by the local authorities. The fact that the authorities remained uninvolved in the Washington, D.C. and New York mosques is not surprising considering the emphasis on a separation between church and state in the United States, and also its lack of a direct colonial connection to any

Figure 5. The Islamic Center and Mosque, Rome, Italy (1994)

Muslim territories. Still, having President Eisenhower dedicate the opening of the Washington, D.C. mosque with the First Lady attending is of significance in that it indicates official approval of the project, and even a welcoming of it.

Again worth noting is the limited role that the local Muslim communities of these cities took in the realization of these mosques. Their role in fact seems to be nonexistent in the realization of the Paris and London mosques. It is also worth noting that, in both cases, although the mosques were centrally located, the Muslim communities that it was to benefit primarily lived at the outskirts of the two cities. We see an increasing role of local Muslim communities in the realization of the Washington, D.C., New York, and Rome mosques, but their engagement was overshadowed by the role of the diplomatic representatives of Muslim countries in those cities.

It should be added that although France was in total control of North Africa, the French Government nonetheless worked through a North African institution it had set up, the Association of the Awqaf. In addition, the Egyptian Government as well as the Bey of Tunis made in-kind contributions to the mosque. Muslim diplomats played a major role in the realization of the other four mosques, with the Egyptian government taking on an important role in the realization of the London and Washington, D.C. mosques, the Saudi Government taking on a major role in the realization of Rome mosque, and the Kuwaiti Government in the realization of the New York mosque.

The fact that representatives from the relevant local communities ended up taking an active role in managing these mosques is not surprising considering their growing numbers and the long-term presence of many of their members in those cities, in contrast to the relatively short-term tenures and small numbers of members of the diplomatic corps, not to mention the fact that these buildings should be open to all Muslims. This issue of course has had a strong impact on the relation of these mosques to the host society. When under the control of guest diplomats, all sorts of efforts are made to ensure that the institutions that those buildings house maintain a cordial relationship with the host countries. In fact, all of them were conceived not only as places of Muslim prayer, but also places of positive engagement between Muslims and the host society. Once local groups took control over them, they succumbed to the complex and messy relationships that often exist within the communities lumped together under the wider umbrella of Islam. In addition, the no-less-complex and messy sectarian, ethnic, racial, and national compositions of these groups affect the manner in which these institutions are managed. The differences—if not infighting—between them consequently often come to the surface. Moreover, these institutions can, and did, fall under the influence of radical Islamists with anti-Western sentiments, thus negatively impacting the relationship between the communities these buildings are intended to represent and the societies hosting them (see, for example, the section below that refers to remarks made by the imam of the New York Mosque at that time, and to the sermons of preachers at the Regent's Park Mosque).

Also interesting is the noticeable role that local Western architects took on in the realization of these mosques. Local architects essentially fully designed all of the mosques, except for the Washington, D.C. mosque, and, even there, the final design was modified by a local firm. Although the Rome mosque was to be a joint design between Portoghesi and Gigliotti on the one hand, and Moussawi on the other, Portoghesi's dominating stamp on it is indisputable.

The designs of the mosques, however, are very much in sync with the evolution of mosque design globally. The Paris and Washington, D.C. mosques follow the then-familiar model of eclecticism/architectural revivals according to which specific forms and motifs are copied from past prototypes. The London mosque provides for a stripped-down version of an eclectic mix of historical prototypes. It maintains a clear visual connection with them, but tries to take a middle road by making nods to the applied-decoration-free aesthetic of mid-century modernism that was still in force when the mosque was designed and constructed.

In the case of the Rome mosque, the postmodern label applies. We see here clear references to historical prototypes, but these also are reconfigured in a rather exaggerated and playful manner. In the case of the New York mosque, there is an attempt to abstract historical prototypes in a slightly bolder manner than in the London mosque, particularly in the interior. The architecture of all five mosques still subscribes to the domination of the dome and minaret as formal architectural elements, and that has become a sort of shorthand defining mosque design during the twentieth century, even though they do not apply to all historical traditions of mosque architecture around the world.

In none of these mosques do we find examples of the daring approaches of breaking with the past that are evident in the designs of numerous mosques from the lands of Islam dating to the 1970s, such as the Ayshah Bakkar Mosque in Beirut, the Carpet Museum prayer pavilion in Tehran, and Šerefudin's White Mosque in Visoko.[12] The design approaches found in these experimental mosques have been gaining strong momentum since then. In that sense, and in spite of the variety that their designs express, the five mosques in Western cities presented here all remain rather conservative in how they conform to an architectural prototype dominated by the dome and minaret. More importantly, in their emphasis on linking with historical prototypes, none of them established a serious dialogue with ongoing architectural developments taking place in the cities they were located. This is in strong contrast with the more recent 2011 Islamic Cemetery in Altach, Austria, for example, which although a Muslim religious complex, is heavily engaged with local architectural approaches as evident in its crisp unadorned lines and forms, its emphasis on horizontality, its strong connection to the surrounding landscape, and use of exposed concrete surfaces.

Of greater importance is how these mosques connect to the evolution of the relationship between Western host societies and immigrant Muslim communities in their midst over the past century or so. When the Paris mosque was constructed, Islam was viewed very differently in Europe than it is now. It was viewed as more of an exotic—even quaint, though not necessarily fully understood—curiosity rather than the existential threat that numerous xenophobic politicians from the Global North present it as today. Moreover, various European powers during the interwar period viewed Muslims as possible allies in ongoing geopolitical inter-European struggles. After all, the mosque was built to commemorate the Muslims who fought along the French in World War I. The rather modest presence of Muslims in their midst was not only tolerated then, but even welcome, even though in a paternalistic manner. There is also, of course, a darker side to the prior relationship between the West and Islam/Muslims. One should keep in mind that the mosque also was built at a time when France colonized Muslim territories in Africa and Asia, a phenomenon that was characterized by violence, repression, and discrimination. Still, it should be said that a degree of goodwill toward Islam seems to have existed in Europe at that time.[13]

Interestingly enough, the Paris mosque has played a positive inter-religious role in the life of the city. The mosque complex, with the exception of its prayer area, is open to the public, and it even has a restaurant and a hammam that are popular among Parisians. Also worth noting is that during World War II, its administration took a role in saving Jews from detection by the Nazis through giving them Muslim birth certificates.[14]

This spirit of openness is evident in the inauguration of Washington, D.C. mosque noted above. As for the Regent's Park Mosque, its site was provided by the British government. Both it and the Washington, D.C. mosque may even be viewed as post-colonial, postwar updates of the colonial-era Paris mosque, since a process of decolonization was now taking place.

Some reservations, however, were made by local bodies regarding the design of three of these buildings. In the case of the London mosque, the relevant authorities made objections to both the original design and the second design for not fitting well within its surroundings. Although this may be viewed as a case of mild cultural opposition to the presence of the mosque, it may be equally viewed as a case of architectural opposition. In the case of the Washington, D.C. mosque, although the full details are not available, we do know that the design modifications that the local architect carried out for the mosque included moving the minaret from its original location along the street facade further inward, which would give this primary architectural symbol of the presence of Islam a less prominent visual position. This again, however, may be viewed as a form of architectural, and not merely cultural, criticism of the design—that is, to remove an architectural element with a vertical emphasis from the street facade.

As one reaches the 1990s, the situation changes, as is evident in the case of the Rome mosque. Although the Italian Government and the Vatican were receptive to the mosque, and although it is located in an area situated away from the Vatican, there was resistance to it from the local residents of that area. In other words, the opposition presented now was no longer regarding issues relating to the design of the mosque, as was the case in the Washington, D.C. and London mosques, but about the very existence of a mosque. In addition, a darker side of the institutions that those buildings housed appeared with time. The imam of the New York Mosque, for example, made media statements blaming the Jews for the 9/11 attacks. Admittedly, his remarks were immediately disowned by the Center itself, and the imam resigned from his position immediately thereafter.[15] Also, a Muslim female journalist working for *The Daily Telegraph* wrote an article regarding the fanatical and intolerant nature of a number of sermons given by preachers at the Regent's Park Mosque, which also applied to publications sold at its bookstore.[16] With time, these institutions, which started out as showpieces for amiable relationships between Islam and the West, became settings that expressed the often messy and difficult relationships that have come to exist within immigrant communities on the one hand, and between these communities and their host societies on the other hand.

I would like to end by stating that each of the five mosques discussed above are located in cities that have become increasingly diverse and multicultural over the years, and even have become an integral part of the architectural makeup of those cities. This definitely has enriched urban life in those cities for all their residents, regardless of their origins. Many in those cities definitely welcome this increasing diversity. In fact, residents of multicultural cities are generally more embracing of this phenomenon than those living in smaller, less diverse cities and towns or in rural areas, and much of the anti-immigrant sentiment we come across in the Global North is more concentrated in those smaller, less-diverse cities and towns, and in rural areas. Even the 9/11 attacks have not succeeded in making New York a city less willing to embrace the "other."[17] Moreover, London recently elected its first Muslim mayor. As usual, however, there always are exceptions, as with the election of a member of the anti-immigration Five Star Movement as Mayor of Rome in 2016. In any case, although sharing the city with the "other" does enrich life in it, it also includes addressing the friction that arises when a sizable population that also consists of diverse groups of people needs to share the finite facilities and spaces that the city offers. As a result, and under all circumstances, a continuous process of negotiation will need to take place between the groups that make up the city. These not only represent diverse backgrounds and points of views, but also varying population sizes and varying levels of economic and political power. It is a messy process that is characteristic of city life (and of life in general). The conception, realization, and evolution of the five mosques discussed above and the institutions housing them provide insightful examples of such a process of negotiation.

1   Paul Adams, "Migration: Are more people on the move than ever before?" BBC News, 28 May 2015, http://www.bbc.com/news/world-32912867.

2   Jack Citrin and John Sides, "Immigration and the Imagined Community in Europe and the United States," *Political Studies* 56 (2008): 33–56, https://johnsides.org/published-articles; and Alexander Stille, "How Matteo Salvini pulled Italy to the far right," The Guardian, 9 August 2018, https://www.theguardian.com/news/2018/aug/09/ how-matteo-salvini-pulled-italy-to-the-far-right?CMP=fb_gu.

3   Rohingya Muslim men, for example, have been restricted by Burmese authorities to wearing traditional sarongs, or longyis, in their native Myanmar. See Vidhi Doshi, "For Rohingya Refugees, Pants Are a Status Symbol," The Seattle Times, 17 June 2018, https://www.seattletimes.com/nation-world/world/for-rohingya-refugees-pants-are-a-status-symbol/. It is also not surprising that many low-paid jobs in countries of the Global North are dominated by immigrants. See Octavio Blanco, "Immigrant Workers Are Most Likely to Have These Jobs," CNN Money, 15 March 2017, https://money.cnn.com/2017/03/16/news/ economy/ immigrant-workers-jobs/index.html.

4   See Omar Khalidi, "Import, Adapt, Innovate: Mosque Design in the United States," *Aramco World* 52(6) (November/December 2001): 24–33, http://archive.aramcoworld.com/issue/200106/import. adapt.innovate-mosque.design.in.the.united.states.htm; and Arijit Sent, "Evaluating Lived Landscapes and Quotidian Architecture of Muslim Devon," in *Homogenisation of Represen-tations*, ed. Modjtaba Sadria (Geneva: Aga Khan Award for Architecture, 2012), 185–206, https://archnet.org/system/publications/contents/7192/original/DPC4299.pdf.

5   Ian Traynor, "Swiss Vote to Ban Construction of Minarets on Mosques," *The Guardian*, 29 November 2009, https://www.theguardian.com/world/2009/nov/29/switzerland-bans-mosque-minarets.

6   A good deal of the information presented about those buildings in this essay is found in Renata Holod and Hasan-Uddin Khan, *The Mosque and the Modern World: Architects, Patrons and Designs* since the 1950s (London: Thames and Hudson, 1997), 227–53.

7   Andrew Glass, "Eisenhower Dedicates D.C. Islamic Center, June 28, 1957," *Politico*, 28 June 2018, https://www.politico.com/story/2018/06/28/eisenhower-dedicates-dc-islamic-center-june-28-1957-667325.

8   "Islamic Center of Washington," *Archnet*, https://archnet.org/sites/358.

9   "London Mosques given Protected Heritage Status," *BBC News*, 13 March 2018, https://www.bbc.co.uk/news/uk-england-43385587.

10   "Islamic Cultural Center of New York," SOM, https://www.som.com/projects/islamic_cultural_center_of_ new_york.

11   For additional information on the Mosque and Islamic Cultural Center in Rome, see Ashraf Salama, *On-site Technical Review Report - Mosque and Islamic Cultural Center*, Rome, Italy (Geneva: Aga Khan Award for Architecture, 2001), https://strathprints.strath.ac.uk/51602/.

12   Regarding this break with tradition in mosque architecture, see Mohammad al-Asad, "The Mosque of the Turkish Grand National Assembly in Ankara: Breaking with Tradition," *Muqarnas* 16 (1999): 155–68, http://www.archnet.org/library/documents/one-document.jsp?document_id=9709).

13   Marya Hannun and Sophie Spaan, "When Europe Loved Islam," *Foreign Policy*, 5 May 2016. https://foreignpolicy.com/2016/05/05/when-europe-loved-islam-interwar-weimar-republic-wilmersdorf-mosque/. Also, judging from my personal experience as someone of an Arab-Muslim background who has spent most of his life living between an Arab / Muslim country (Jordan) and North America, and also from the experiences of friends and colleagues with similar backgrounds, I can say that the view of Arab and Middle Eastern Muslims in the West as manifestations of the "exotic" other continued until the late 1970s. This view began to erode as a result of a number of factors. These include the acts of violence by individuals, organizations, and governments from the lands of Islam directed against Americans and American interests that started taking place then such as the Iran Hostage Crisis, when fifty-two American diplomats at the United States Embassy in Iran where held hostage in Iran from late 1979 to early 1981; the suicide attack in Beirut that killed 241 United States and 58 French peacekeepers, in addition to six civilians; and the 1988 explosion that destroyed the Pan American aircraft operating a transatlantic flight while flying over the Scottish town of Lockerbie. With the 1990–91 First Gulf War, this exotic view of Islam definitely had come to an end. Following the 9/11 Twin Towers attack in New York City, the Arab and Middle Eastern Muslim had not only ceased to be the exotic other, but had become the ominous adversarial other. Of course, the increased numbers and growing visibility of Muslim populations in North America also contributed to this change in perception.

14   Kait Bolongaro, "The Great Mosque of Paris: A Symbol of Islam in France," *Middle East Eye*, 4 January 2017, https://www.middleeasteye.net/in-depth/features/-behind-doors-great-mosque-paris-islam1623132582.

15   Laurie Goodstein, "A Nation Challenged: The Imam; New York Cleric's Departure from Mosque Leaves Mystery," *The New York Times*, 23 October 2001, https://www.nytimes.com/2001/10/23/nyregion/nation-challenged-imam-new-york-cleric-s-departure-mosque-leaves-mystery.html.

16   Sarah Hassan, "Preachers of Separatism at Work inside Britain's Mosques," *The Telegraph*, 31 August 2008, https://www.telegraph.co.uk/news/uknews/2653266/Preachers-of-sepa-ratism-at-work-inside-Britains-mosques.html.

17   In this context, it is worth noting that New York City has a long history with mosques. See, Rozina Ali, "New York City's Forgotten Muslim Past: A Ph.D. Student Offers a Free Muslim-history Walking Tour in Donald Trump's Home Town." *The New Yorker*, 6 August 2018, https://www.newyorker.com/magazine/2018/08/06/ new-york-citys-forgotten-muslim-past?mbid=social_facebook.

The Architecture of
Death in Islam:
A Brief Cross-cultural
History
Nasser Rabbat

It is remarkable how similar the commemoration of death is around most of the world.[1] We speak, dress, eat, socialize, and inhabit spaces differently. But, to judge from our rituals of burial and remembrance, or even our tombs and cemeteries, we memorialize death in like fashion (exceptions being religions or cultures that do not bury their dead or modern practices that relate to no religion).[2] The same could be said about the atmosphere of our places of burial: they all strive to achieve solemnity and reflect a memorial aura through form, space, and symbols. Their architecture has thus developed common shapes that invoke gravitas and reflection without forgetting the actual functional requirements of disposing of deceased bodies while marking their death. Most societies build crypts or dig holes in the ground, wrap their dead in a shroud or lay them in coffins, mark their burial with calligraphed cenotaphs and tombstones, sometimes build domes over the tombs of notables and heroes, plant certain kind of flowers to embellish them and evergreen plants, evoking eternity, around them.[3] Most of these elements evolved across cultures and over time as manifestations of people's collective anxiety or resignation toward death's absolute power of oblivion and their attempts to assuage it, or at least to circumvent its suddenness, finality, and inevitable force of erasure by keeping the memory of the dead alive.[4]

This is evident in the evolution of Islamic funerary architecture, especially during the formative period from the seventh through the eleventh century.[5] The cross-cultural effects in its forms and symbols are not only a function of shared reactions to death experienced by people of all cultures. It is also the outcome of a historical process through which this rather new religion that quickly spread its dominion learned from, interacted with, and sometimes absorbed the cultures with which it came into contact.[6]

In the first days of Islam as a nascent religion in Western Arabia, the deceased were still hastily buried in minimally marked graves. In that way, early Muslims were adhering to the pragmatic and environmentally sensitive customs of the pre-Islamic Arabs of the Hijaz who adapted their customs and beliefs to their desert milieu with its high temperature swings, vast vistas with few fixed landmarks, and constantly shifting landscapes.[7] But with the spread of Islam over the territories of most of the major empires in the Mediterranean and Western Asia in the next few centuries, new funerary rituals and architecture began to appear that were borrowed from the customs and forms of the absorbed cultures, filtered through the evolving exegesis of the nascent religion, its original cultural milieu, and its forming practices.[8] Then even Medina, the capital of Prophet Muhammad, acquired its built-up cemetery with domed tombs for the Prophet, his wives, companions, and companions of the companions, as well as generations of notable Muslims who piously wanted to be buried in the city of their Prophet.[9] The Saudi Wahhabis, however, the heirs of a modern puritanical religious movement, removed them all in the last few decades, on the pretext that they have become places of un-Islamic practices such as visitation and supplication, except for the Tomb of the Prophet and his two companions, Abu Bakr and Omar, which they left grudgingly under its rather modest green dome lest non-Wahhabi believers riot in their millions.[10] In their own burial practices, the Saudis, true to their fundamentalism, have observed a strict rejection of all commemoration of death. Their kings and common people alike are usually buried in unmarked tombs save for some stone or a modest memorial with the name of the deceased only written on them.

Not so in the rest of the Islamic world. With the successive encounters with sophisticated foreign cultures, the attitudes of the Muslims toward the commemoration of death became undecided at best, before they went all the way toward devising a monumental vocabulary for funerary architecture all their own. On the one hand, Muslim *ulama* (exegesists) wanted to preserve the stoicism inherited from the Prophet and from old customs in Arabia and tried their best to prohibit funerary architecture.[11] On the other, new converts from the old cultures brought with them elaborate funerary ceremonials and architectural memorials that were soon adopted by the rich and powerful patrons, first those new to Islam or diverting from its orthodoxy, but ultimately even the caliphs succumbed to the new practices.[12]

First were the two Abrahamic religions, Judaism and Christianity, which coexisted in the land seized by the Islamic victors for a long time and to which Islam claimed kinship. Islam respected them as divinely revealed religions and allowed their adherents to keep their faith and rituals, which they maintained with relatively minimal hindrance for centuries. Consequently, different Jewish and Christian bereavement habits, like processions, and funerary forms, like tombstones, found their way to the

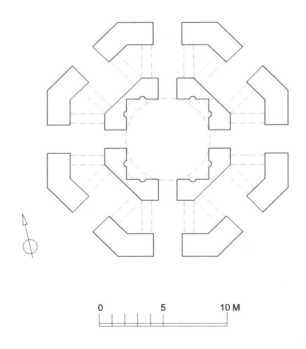

0   5   10 M

Figure 1. Plan of the Qubbat al-Sulaibiyya in Samarra

various Islamic traditions developing in the diverse countries of the Islamic empire, often with slight changes and some sort of Islamization that expressed itself primarily through the avoidance of human figures or crosses, and the use of Quranic verses instead of Scriptural ones on tombstones.[13]

Other cultures and religions, especially the Persian, Turkic, and later on Hindu Indian cultures, which were gradually absorbed by Islamic dominance over a few centuries, did not enjoy the same kind of acceptance as Judaism and Christianity. Yet they influenced the developing Islamic cultural practices all the same, including the funeral ones, even if indirectly and with some resistance among the *ulama* communities. This was especially clear in the monumental funerary architecture, which developed slowly, first in the East (Iran and Central Asia) and then in the central Arab lands and further West in North Africa and finally in India.[14] With the exception of the possible green dome erected over the tomb of Imam 'Ali in Najaf at the doubtful early date of 786, most early Islamic funerary monuments were built for recently Islamized rulers from Iran or Central Asia whose ancestors belonged to the vanquished cultures or religions.[15]

However, one of the earliest instances of a possible caliphal monumental burial known to us is the Qubbat al-Sulaibiyya, ostensibly built for caliph al-Muntasir in Samarra in 862 (Fig. 1).[16] It is an unprecedented octagonal structure with an arcaded ambulatory around a domed square burial chamber, which was later discovered to have been raised on a platform with four ramps. Exhibiting similarities to the classical type used for funerary and religious structures in the Roman and Byzantine empires, the Qubba was initially attributed to al-Muntasir's mother, who was in fact Greek and may have wanted to bury her son according to her tradition as suggested by Ernst Herzfeld, its first excavator.[17] But the poor handling of its excavated remains and the dearth of direct references to it in the historical sources, made it impossible to ascertain its date, occupants, real function or, significance. One thing is for sure, however, it was a funerary dome, since three undated tombs were discovered under it. Its organizational similarity to commemorative domes of both Eastern and Western traditions suggest that Abbasid funerary traditions were changing from the earlier practice of burying caliphs in modest tombs in their own palaces or places of death to what will become the most magnificent aspect of Islamic architecture: the funerary domed mausoleum.[18]

Indeed, despite the scattered admonitions of the celebration of death in exegetical texts produced by several well-known *ulama,* Islamic funerary architecture continued to thrive at the hand of ever more proud rulers and ever more saintly religious figures. The evolving Shi'a doctrines of the sanctity of Imams may have contributed to the development of the funerary dome type as a symbol of veneration, although the evidence from Fatimid Egypt suggests that it was at best one of the factors, bolstered by appropriated commemorative practices from other cultures.[19] Formally and stylistically, the pre-Islamic Persian architecture in Iran and Central Asia played a major role in shaping Islamic funerary architecture. Slowly converted between the tenth and twelfth century, Iranians and Central Asians had the time to translate many of their old rituals into Islamic forms.[20] Thus the ancient Iranian fire temple and Turkic funerary mounds of yore became the ornate domed mausolea of powerful princes, beloved members of Al al-Bayt (family of the Prophet), Shi'a imams, and Sufi masters. The earliest examples appeared in the vast prairies and ancient trade cities along the Silk Road, the same territory in which the pre-Islamic funerary forms have developed. These included the famous Samanid Mausoleum, one of the earliest integrated domed mausolea, built for Isma'il the Samanid in Bukhara (ca. 914), and the less well-known but no less sublime Gunbad-i Qabus, built by Qabus bin Vashmigir outside of his capital Gurgan in northern Iran around 1006–07.[21] Both of these structures illustrate the transition from pre-Islamic forms and practices to Islamic funerary one. Qabus's tower in fact is said to have contained his body hanging by a silver chain from the ceiling in a crystal coffin, a middle stage for this recently converted prince between the old Zoroastrian practices of exposing the body of the dead on the top of a tower to birds of prey and the Islamic requirement of burial underground.[22]

Single-domed mausolea where soon followed by entire necropolises with multiple domes for the members of a ruling family or a dynasty. Examples from the middle period abound. From the East we have the Shah-i Zanda, the necropolis developed by and for the women of the Timurid House outside Samarqand in the fourteenth century during over more than seventy years of building along a central pathway that led to the burial chamber of a semi-mythical hero of early Islam, Qassam ibn al-'Abbas, a cousin of the Prophet who was supposed to have survived after his head was severed by the enemy, hence the title Shah-i Zanda, the Living King.[23] From the West we have the Qarafa of Cairo, the burial area east of the city where numerous Mamluk sultans, princes, and princesses were interred in elegant stone domes from the fourteenth through the early sixteenth century.[24]

A particularly Islamic invention in the development of funerary domes is the muqarnas dome, a visually extravagant concoction that combines the structural properties of the muqarnas with its capacity to form intricate domical crystal series that have been likened to honeycombs and stalactites.[25] The muqarnas, which made its first appearance in Central Asia around the middle of the tenth century before spreading across the rest of the Islamic world, introduced a totally novel and quite enigmatic visual effect. An early experiment is the dome of Imam Dur in Samarra, Iraq, dated to 1085, where five concentric rings of muqarnased squinches end with a small cupola, resulting in a pointed conical profile on the outside and a stunning cascade of gradually lit cusped stars on the inside. This was successively followed by more daring muqarnas domes in Iraq and Syria throughout the twelfth and thirteenth century, such as the Mausoleum of Nur al-Din in Damascus (1167–68), with its five tiers of muqarnas, and the Zumurrud Khatun's tomb in Baghdad with seven tiers, built by this powerful wife of a caliph and mother of a caliph around 1200.[26] These domes used the muqarnas both as an integral structural element of a tiered conical vault and a constituent of a new decorative pattern with infinite geometric variations. And although we do not know for sure what these intricate structures signified, Yasser Tabbaa has imaginatively read them as spatial renderings of the atomistic theory of the Ash'arite theological school that became dominant in the same period.[27] The Ash'aris see the world as a constellation of an infinite variety of shapes constantly changing and kept in place only by the will of God. Using muqarnas domes for mausolea, like the Shrine of 'Abd al-Samad in Natanz, Iran, may indeed have been meant as a visual reminder of the miracle of being: an ascending composition with all of its sophisticated elements suspended as if floating above ground.[28]

Figure 2. Taj Mahal, Agra (1653): General view from the south

The Mamluks of Egypt and Syria took the construction of funerary domes to new heights, literally and aesthetically.[29] Over almost two centuries of steady experimentation, Mamluk stone domes developed a unique attenuated profile and geometric patterns carved on their surfaces that started with simple ribbing or chevron, such as in the domes of Tankiz Bugha and Farag Ibn Barquq and culminated with very sophisticated alternating star and floral motifs, as in the funerary dome of Sultan Qaytbay, before totally disappearing with the onset of the Ottoman period. We still don't know exactly how Mamluk builders produced this complicated geometry.[30] But there is no doubt that they were highly significant for their patrons as they vied with one another to extend their height and elaborate ornamentation in the crowded space of Cairo.

The encounter with the much-developed architectural traditions in India resulted in the refinement of the atmospheric quality of Indian Islamic funerary buildings, especially in the tombs of Sufi shaikhs and great princes.[31] Filtering the light through intricately carved stone screens called Jali in India bestows a mood of both melancholy and mystery on the interior of the tombs, two qualities that very much enhance the enigma of death and the mercy of God for which all believers yearn. The Great Mughal sultans of India further elevated funerary architecture, which reached an unprecedented monumental level under their watch.[32] The first in the line of a spectacular series is the tomb of Humayun, the second Great Mughal, in Delhi built by his wife Bega Begum in 1569–70.[33] Designed by a Persian architect, Mirak Mirza Ghiyath and his son Sayyid Muhammad, and following in the line of great Ilkhanid and especially Timurid mausolea, the tomb of Humayun has a Hasht-Behisht (Eight-Paradise) plan, with the cenotaph of the emperor standing on a low dais in the middle of the central domed hall.[34] Light filters through geometrically simple stone jalis on three levels imbuing the circumambulatory space with a soft, calm, and cool feel.

The Taj Mahal, built by Shah Jahan in memory of his wife Mumtaz Mahal (1632–53) represents the zenith of the Mughal architectural tradition (Fig. 2).[35] Poised and harmoniously proportioned, the monument dazzles with its scintillating white profile infused with a plethora of colored semi-precious stones incised into its marble surfaces in a technic called by its expressive Italian name *pietra dura*. Its interior displays a paler shade of white adorned with the same *pietra dura* but takes the filtering of light a step further by adding an octagonal screened parapet around the two cenotaphs of the sultan and his consort, which is a true tour de force of marble carving.[36] The new naturalism that informs the decoration of the Taj inside and outside manifests itself in the screened panels in the form of interlacing realistic leaves and flowers, some blossoming and some still budding, arranged on a geometric grid of lined-up circles. This intentionally delicate rendering of flowery screens enclosing the cenotaphs is so befitting the image of the beautiful Mumtaz Mahal who died quite young during delivery and whose bereaved husband decided to immortalize her memory in this sublime monument.[37] The addition of the cenotaph of Shah Jahan, who died fourteen years after the completion of the monument, off-center is most probably an afterthought, even though it is infinitely more romantic to imagine these two lovers reunited under this sumptuous dome for eternity awaiting the mercy of God, which he affords his select servants.

Domes continued to be built in India as monumental funerary markers after the Taj Mahal, but no other memorial structure reached its magnificence or poise. Later Moghul and post-Moghul domes in India, including the Bibi Ka Maqbara of Aurangzeb's wife Rabia-ud-Daurani in Aurangabad built in 1660–61 after the Taj Mahal, lacked the striving toward sublimity that characterized the earlier Moghul mausolea.[38]

With the onset of the modern age, new forms derived from other historical styles or more modernistic shapes made their way to the repertory of memorial architecture in the new nation-states of the Islamic world.[39] Examples vary. Many of them, however, are streamlined throwbacks to an imagined pre-Islamic funerary architecture that the particular modern Islamic nation has claimed as ancestral in an attempt to construct a presumed historical continuity of a quintessential national identity. A notable example of this tendency is the Anıtkabir (the Memorial Tomb) of Mustafa Kemal Ataturk, the founder of modern Turkey in Ankara. Built between 1944 and 1953, this huge rectangular hall with a massive marble sarcophagus in the middle is raised on a plinth and surrounded by colonnaded porticoes on all four sides in an arrangement reminiscent of Greek Classical temples. But the columns are quite simple, even austere. Heavy rectangular parallelepipeds in shape, they recall pre-classical architectural traditions, possibly Hittite as the dominant pre-Hellenistic culture in Anatolia, rationalized by a modernistic taste.[40] The image, however, is loudly pre-Islamic and modern at the same time, and this

Figure 3. Sa'd Zaghlul Mausoleum, Cairo (1929): View from the east

historically collapsed message is clearly intentional: Turkey had been for a while undergoing a nationalistic secularization initiated by Atatürk himself. His mausoleum, thus, reflects both a historical rootedness in the land of modern Turkey as opposed to the ecumenical Islamic architectural language and a modernistic geometric clarity symbolizing not only the modernization of the nation but also its new Western orientation.[41]

Another noteworthy example comes from Cairo. Celebrated for its grand architecture of death, Pharaonic Egypt had little direct influence on the development of funerary architecture in the Islamic period. But with the emergence of the modern nation-state in the nineteenth century some attempts were made to reinterpret Pharoanic architecture as a national style, especially at the time of Egypt's revolt against British colonialism when the two branches of the nation, Muslims and Christians, came together in their resistance.[42] Thus the mausoleum of Sa'd Zaghlul, the leader of the 1919 revolution against the British and the "father of the Egyptian Nation," was built in a politically charged neo-Pharoanic style complete with its pylons and lotus columns in 1929 (Fig. 3). The gesture, however, did not take and Egyptian grandees reverted back to building domed mausolea in a neo-Mamluk style, a practice that lasted until the revolution of 1952 and the abolishing of the monarchy in Egypt.[43]

Today, some tombs of important religious and political figures do adopt domes for the same reasons for which medieval rulers used them over their tombs, namely monumentality and symbolism. Otherwise, these mausolea are modern structures emphasizing both the new forms and techniques of construction that proclaim their modernity and the propagandist spirit of the modern nation-state. Thus while the domed tomb of Imam Khomeini in Tehran for instance purposefully draws on the embodied symbolism of the tombs of the major Shi'ite figures such as the Mausoleum of Imam Husayn in Karbala, Iraq, and the Shrine of Fatima al-Ma'suma in Qom, Iran, it also exhibits modern influences in its material, construction techniques, and conception of space of rituals and visitation.[44] Similarly for the burial (cremation is forbidden) of the majority of Muslims: their tombs combine traditional, stripped down forms of tombstones with their names, dates of birth and death, and an appropriate Quranic quotation, with some new invention in display or material. In some countries of the ex-Soviet block in Central Asia and the Balkans, for instance, modernity has seeped into the commemoration practice in the form of stenciled photos of the deceased or attached reliefs of their bust or profile.[45] Multiculturalism clearly lives on in the contemporary Islamic architecture of death.

1   Avril Maddrell and James D. Sidaway, "Introduction: Bringing a Spatial Lens to Death, Dying, Mourning and Remembrance," in *Deathscapes: Spaces for Death, Dying, Mourning and Remembrance*, Avril Maddrell and James D. Sidaway, eds. (London: Ashgate, 2010), 1–8; Antonius C.G.M. Robben, "Death and Anthropology: An Introduction," in *Death, Mourning, and Burial: A Cross-cultural Reader*, Antonius C.G.M. Robben, ed. (Malden, MA, Oxford: Blackwell, 2004), 1–15.

2   See for instance the discussion on natural burial by Andy Clayden, Trish Green, Jenny Hockey, and Mark Powel, "From Cabbages to Cadavers: Natural Burial Down on the Farm," in *Deathscapes: Spaces for Death, Dying, Mourning and Remembrance*, 119–38; expanded in Andy Clayden, Trish Green, Jenny Hockey and Mark Powel, *Natural Burial: Landscape, Practice and Experience* (London: Routledge, 2014), esp. 1–15, 193–202.

3   For an introduction to the development of funerary architecture in the "Western" tradition, see James Stevens Curl, *Death and Architecture: Introduction to Funerary and Commemorative Buildings with Some Consideration of their Settings* (Thrupp, Stroud: Sutton Publishing, 2002); Ken Worpole, *Last Landscape: The Architecture of the Cemetery in the West* (London: Reaktion Books, 2003).

4   The classical reference here is Philippe Ariès, *The Hour of our Death: The Classic History of Western Attitudes toward Death over the last One Thousand Years*, Helen Weaver, trans. (New York: Vintage Books, 1981).

5   A general introduction to the topic is Spahic Omer, *The Origins and Significance of Funerary Architecture in Islamic Civilization* (Kuala Lumpur, Malaysia: International Islamic University Malaysia, 2006); reprinted under a different title but same content, *Death, Graveyards, and Funerary Architecture in Islam* (Kuala Lumpur, Malaysia: A.S. Noordeen Islamic Books, 2008); a concise introduction to Islamic funerary traditions from an archeological perspective is Andrew Petersen, "The Archaeology of Death and Burial in the Islamic World," in *The Oxford Handbook of the Archaeology of Death and Burial*, Liv Nilsson Stutz and Sarah Tarlow, eds. (Oxford: Oxford University Press, 2013), 241–58, http://www.oxfordhandbooks.com/view/10.1093/ofordhb/9780199569069.001.0001/oxfordhb-9780199569069-e-14?print, accessed 19 August 2018.

6   A concise introduction to the topic is Nasser Rabbat "The Dialogic Dimension in Umayyad Art," *RES* 43 (Spring 2003): 78–94; Finbarr Barry Flood, *The Great Mosque of Damascus: Studies on the Makings of an Umayyad Visual Culture* (Leiden: Brill, 2001), 1–14, 184–246, is one of the most elaborate articulations of this process in the art of the Umayyad period. For a broader interpretation of the process that looks into its political and cultural underpinnings, see Garth Fowden, *Empire to Commonwealth: Consequences of Monotheism in Late Antiquity* (Princeton: Princeton University Press, 1993), 3–11, 138–75; idem, *Qusayr 'Amra: Art and the Umayyad Elite in Late Antique Syria*. Berkeley, 2004), 197–226, 248–326; idem, *Before and After Muhammad: The First Millennium Refocused* (Princeton: Princeton University Press: 2014), 1–48.

7   Ignaz Goldziher, *Muslim Studies*, S.M. Stern ed., 2 vols. (London: George Allen & Unwin, 1967–71), 1: 209–38; Th. Emil Homerin,

"Echoes of a Thirsty Owl: Death and the Afterlife in Pre-Islamic Poetry," *Journal of Near Eastern Studies* 44(3) (1985): 165–84; James E. Taylor, "Attitudes, Themes and Images: An Introduction to Death and Burial as Mirrored in early Arabic Poetry," in *Death and Burial in Arabia and Beyond Multidisciplinary Perspectives*, Lloyd Weeks, ed. (Oxford: Archeopress, 2010), 347–52.

8   See the interesting discussion in Leor Halevi, *Muhammad's Grave: Death Rites and the Making of Islamic Society* (New York: Columbia University Press, 2007), 1–13, 234–40, where the divergence from the traditions of other religions and cultures is emphasized.

9   Goldziher, "Venerations of Saints in Islam," in *Muslim Studies*, 2: 255–341; Harry Munt, *The Holy City of Medina: Sacred Space in Early Islamic Arabia* (Cambridge, UK: Cambridge University Press, 2014), 94–182.

10 Understandably, this is a poorly covered subject in both journalism and scholarship. A rare eyewitness to the initial destruction of the Cemetery of al-Baqi', where many famous personages of early Islam were buried with domes over their tombs, in April 1925, is Eldon Rutter, *The Holy Cities of Arabia*, 2 vols. (London and New York: G.P. Putnam's Sons, Ltd., 1928), 2: 255–57, online https://archive.org/details/in.ernet.dli.2015.70025, accessed 27 August 2018. Another eyewitness, but of a later period, is Ziauddin Sardar, "The Destruction of Mecca," *The New York Times* (1 October 2014): A27, online https://www.nytimes.com/2014/10/01/opinion/the-destruction-of-mecca.html?_r=0, accessed 27 August 2018. Among the rare analyses available, see Irfan al-Alawi, "The Destruction of the Holy Sites in Mecca and Medina," https://www.theislamicmonthly.com/the-destruction-of-the-holy-sites-in-mecca-and-medina, accessed 21 August 2018; also, Wikipedia art. "Destruction of early Islamic heritage sites in Saudi Arabia," https://en.wikipedia.org/wiki/Destruction_of_early_Islamic_heritage_sites_in_Saudi_Arabia, accessed 22 August 2018.

11 Thomas Leisten, "Between Orthodoxy and Exegesis: Some Aspects of Attitudes in the Shari'a toward Funerary Architecture," *Muqarnas* 7 (1990): 12–22; Yussef Raghib, "Structure de la tombe d'après le droit Musulman," *Arabica* 39 (1992): 393–403; J. Sadan, "On Tombs and Holy Writ: Some Methodological and Lexicographical Notes on Burial Concepts in Islamic Fiqh (Religious Law), Literature and Practices," in *Milestones in the Art and Culture of Egypt*, Asher Ovadiah, ed. (Tel Aviv: Tel Aviv University, 2000), 171–95.

12 A discussion from an Islamic perspective is Spahic Omer, *The Origins and Significance of Funerary Architecture in Islamic Civilization*, 189–259.

13 Josef W. Meri, *The Cult of Saints among Muslims and Jews in Medieval Syria* (Oxford: Oxford University Press, 2002), 1–5, 12–57; Lawrence Nees, *Perspectives on Early Islamic Art in Jerusalem* (Leiden: Brill, 2016), 144–61; Mattia Guidetti, "Sacred Spaces in Early Islam," in *A Companion to Islamic Art and Architecture*, Finbarr Barry Flood and Gülru Necipoglu, eds. 2 vols. (Hoboken, NJ: Wiley & Sons, 2017), 1: 130–50; Leor Halevi, "The Paradox of Islamization: Tombstone Inscriptions, Qur'anic Recitations, and the Problem of Religious Change," *History of Religions* 44(2) (2004): 120–52, for a revisionist study of early Islamization practices.

14 Oleg Grabar, "The earliest Islamic commemorative structures, notes and documents," *Ars Orientalis* 6 (1966): 7–46, grappled with the same issue; Yussef Raghib, "Les premiers monuments funéraires de l'Islam," *Annales Islamologiques* 9 (1970): 21–36, presents a corrective to Grabar's narrow definition of commemorative structures and broadens the scope of early monuments that fit under this category by including reference to structures over tombs built on tombs of Companions of the Prophet during the lifetime of the Prophet that he found in textual sources.

15 The green dome is credited to the Abbasid Caliph Harun al-Rashid, which is illogical to say the least since this same caliph has restricted visitations to the shrines of both imams 'Ali and his son Husayn in Najaf and Karbala respectively, see Yasser Tabbaa and Sabrina Mervin, *Najaf: The Gate of Wisdom. History, Heritage, and Significance of the Holy City of the Shi'a* (Paris: UNESCO, 2014), 72–76.

16 On the Qubba see, *Thomas Leisten, Excavation of Samarra, Volume I, Architecture: Final Report of the First Campaign, 1910–1912* (Mainz am Rhein: Von Zabern, 2003), 72–78; Oleg Grabar, "The earliest Islamic commemorative structures, notes and documents," 14–15, raises the issues of attribution and terminology.

17 See the discussion of the excavation and the uncertainty of attribution in Alastair Northedge, "Creswell, Herzfeld, and Samarra," *Muqarnas*, 8 (1991): 74–93, esp. 89; also, idem, *The Historical Topography of Samarra: Samarra Studies I* (London: The British School of Archeology in Iraq, 2008), 230–33.

18 Terry Allen, "The Tombs of the Abbāsid Caliphs in Baghdād," *Bulletin of the School of Oriental and African Studies*, 46(3) (1983): 421–31, offers a list of the burial of the Abbasid caliphs from the beginning to the end of the caliphate in Baghdad.

19 Leisten, "Between Orthodoxy and Exegesis"; Christopher S. Taylor, "Reevaluating the Shi'i Role in the Development of Monumental Islamic Funerary Architecture: The Case of Egypt," *Muqarnas* 9 (1992): 1–10, presents careful argument against the ascription of monumental funerary architecture to Shi'a practices in Egypt.

20 A comprehensive study of the adoption of Iranian funerary practices in Islamic architecture is Melanie Michailidis, "Landmarks of the Persian Renaissance: Monumental Funerary Architecture in Iran and Central Asia in the Tenth and Eleventh Centuries," PhD Dissertation, Massachusetts Institute of Technology, 2007, retrievable at https://dspace.mit.edu/handle/1721.1/41720, accessed 27 August 2018. A concise review of the development of mausolea in medieval Islamic architecture is Robert Hillenbrand, *Islamic Architecture: Form, Function, and Meaning* (Edinburgh: Edinburgh University Press, 1994), 253–330.

21 L.I. Rempel, "The Mausoleum of Isma'il the Samanid," *Bulletin of the American Institute for Persian Art and Architecture* 4 (1935): 199–209; Melanie Michailidis, "Dynastic Politics and the Samanid Mausoleum," *Ars Orientalis* 44 (2014): 20–39.

22 André Godard, "The Architecture of Islamic Period: An Historical Outline: D. Gurgān and the Gunbad-i Qābūs," in *A Survey of Persian Art from Prehistoric Times to the Present*, A.U. Pope and P. Ackermann, eds., 6 vols. (London: Oxford University Press, 1939), 2: 967–74; Simone Cristoforetti, "Cycles and Circumferences:

The Tower of Gonbad-e Kāvus as a Time-measuring Monument," in *Borders: Itineraries on the Edges of Iran*, Stefano Pellò, ed. (Venice: Edizioni Ca' Foscari, 2016), 89–116, https://arca.unive.it/retrieve/handle/10278/36051/80030/Cristoforetti-The%20tower%20of%20Gonbad-e%20Kavus.pdf, accessed 27 August 2018, is a detailed study of the architecture and symbolism, and possible function, of this magnificent monument.

23 A comprehensive study of the complex and its architectural history is Roya Marefat, "Beyond the Architecture of Death: The Shrine of the Shah-i Zinda in Samarkand," PhD Dissertation, Harvard University, 1991; idem, "Timurid Women: Patronage and Power," *Asian Art* 6(2) (1993): 28–49, for a summary of her observations; Claus-Peter Haase, "Shrines of Saints and Dynastic: Towards a Typology of Funerary Architecture in the Timurid Period," *Cahiers d'Asie Centrale* 3-4 (1997): 215–27.

24 Hany Hamza, *The Northern Cemetery of Cairo* (Malibu, CA: Mazda Publishing, 2000); Galila El Kadi and Alain Bonnamy, *Architecture for the Dead: Cairo's Medieval Necropolis* (Cairo: American University in Cairo Press, 2007), 171–252.

25 Mohammad al-Asad, "The Muqarnas: A Geometric Analysis," in Gülru Necipoğlu, *The Topkapı Scroll – Geometry and Ornament in Islamic Architecture: Topkapı Palace Museum Library Ms H.1956* (Santa Monica, CA: Getty Center for the History of Art and the Humanities, 1995), 349–59; Ubaldo Occhinegro, "Muqarnas: Geometric and Stereotomic Techniques in Ancient Islamic Architecture: Ceilings and Domes of Mamluk Buildings in Old Cairo," in *Handbook of Research on Visual Computing and Emerging Geometric Design Tools*, Giuseppe Amoruso (Hershey, PA: Information Science Reference, 2016), 549–74.

26 V. Strika and J. Khalil, "Zumurrud Khatun Tomb in The Islamic Architecture of Baghdad: The Results of a Joint Italian-Iraqi Survey," *Annali Istituto Orientale di Napoli* 47(3) (1987): 18–22.

27 Yasser Tabbaa, "The Muqarnas Dome: Its Origin and Meaning," *Muqarnas* (1985): 61–74; expanded in idem, *The Transformation of Islamic Art During the Sunni Revival* (Seattle and London: The University of Washington Press, 2001), 103–36.

28 Sheila S. Blair, *The Ilkhanid Shrine Complex at Natanz, Iran* (Cambridge, MA: Center for Middle Eastern Studies, Harvard University, 1986); idem, "Sufi saints and shrine architecture in the early fourteenth century." *Muqarnas* 7 (1990): 35–49.

29 Christel Kessler, *The Carved Masonry Domes of Mediaeval Cairo* (London: AARP Series, 1976).

30 This is a subject that has garnered some interest recently, see Christophe Bouleau, "Batir une coupole en pierre de taille. La coupole du mausolée de l'émir Khayr Bek au Caire: dessin, construction et décor," *Annales Islamologiques* 41 (2007), 209–28; Barbara Cipriani and Wanda W. Lau, "Construction Techniques in Medieval Cairo: the Domes of Mamluk Mausolea (1250–1517 AD)," in *The Proceedings of the Second International Congress on Construction History, Queens' College, Cambridge University* (Ascot, England: Construction History Society, 2006), 695–716, online http://www.arct.cam.ac.uk/Downloads/ichs/vol-1-695-716-cipriani.pdf, accessed 28 August 2018; Gemma Pinto, "Construction, technique and form in the Circassian Mamluk architecture: the mausoleum of Sultan Qaytbay in the northern cemetery of Cairo," in *The Mediterranean Medina. International*

Seminar, Ludovico Micara, Attilio Petruccioli, and Ettore Vadini, eds. (Rome: Gangemi, 2009), 467–70; Ahmed Wahby and Dina Montasser. "The Ornamented Domes of Cairo: the Mamluk Mason's Challenge," Masons at Work, 2012 Center for Ancient Studies Symposium, the University of Pennsylvania, Philadelphia, 13–14, https://www.sas.upenn.edu/ancient/masons/Wahby-Montasser_Domes_of_Cairo.pdf, accessed 28 August 2018; Bernard O'Kane, "The Design of Cairo's Masonry Domes," Masons at Work, 2012 Center for Ancient Studies Symposium, https://www.sas.upenn.edu/ancient/masons/OKane_Domes.pdf, accessed 28 August 2018; José Carlos Palacios Gonzalo, "Islamic Stereotomy in Cairo," in *Handbook of Research on Visual Computing and Emerging Geometric Design Tools,* 523–47.

31 George Michell and Will Kwiatkowski, *Red Stone: Indian Stone Carving from Sultanate and Mughal India* (London: Sam Fogg Gallery and Francesca Galloway Gallery, 2012). Subhash Parihar, "Early Sufi Tombs in South-Western Punjab: Understanding the Architectural Features," in *Sufism in Punjab: Mystics, Literature and Shrines,* Surinder Singh and Ishwar Dayal Gaur, eds. (Delhi: Aakar, 2009), 303–35.

32 Michael Brand, "Orthodoxy, Innovation, and Revival: Considerations of the Past Imperial Mughal Tomb Architecture," *Muqarnas* 10 (1993): 223–34.

33 Glen Lowry, "Humayun's Tomb: Form, Function, and Meaning in Early Mughal Architecture," *Muqarnas* 4 (1987): 133–48; D. Fairchild Ruggles, "Humayun's tomb and garden: typologies and visual order." In *Gardens in the Time of the Great Muslim Empires: Theory and Design,* Attilio Petruccioli, ed. (Leiden: Brill, 1997), 173–86.

34 Lisa Golombek, "From Tamerlane to the Taj Mahal," in *Essays in Islamic Art and Architecture in Honor of Katharina Otto-Dorn,* Abbas Daneshvari, ed. (Malibu, CA: Undena Publications, 1981), 43–50.

35 Ebba Koch, "The Taj Mahal: Architecture, Symbolism, and Urban Significance," *Muqarnas* 22 (2005): 128–49; idem, *The Complete Taj Mahal and the Riverfront Gardens of Agra* (London: Thames & Hudson, 2006); Wayne E. Begley, "The Myth of the Taj Mahal and a New Theory of Its Symbolic Meaning," *Art Bulletin* 61 (1979): 7–37. For a truly cross-cultural interpretation of the Taj Mahal *avant la lettre* as it were, see R.A. Jairazbhoy, "The Taj Mahal in the Context of East and West: A Study in the Comparative Method," *Journal of the Warburg and Courtauld Institutes* 24 (1/2) (1961): 59–88; Krupali Uplekar Krusche, et al. "History, Morphology and Perfect Proportions of Mughal Tombs: the Secret to Creation of Taj Mahal," *Archnet: International Journal of Architectural Research* 4(1) (2010): 158–78, online https://archnet.org/system/publications/contents/5312/original/DPC2053.pdf?1384790889, accessed 26 August 2018.

36 Ebba Koch, *Shah Jahan and Orpheus: The Pietre Dure Decoration and the Programme of the Throne in the Hall of Public Audiences at the Red Fort of Delhi* (Graz: Akademische Druck-u. Verlagsanstalt, 1988), reprinted in *Mughal Art and Imperial Ideology: Collected Essays* (New Delhi: Oxford University Press, 2001); M.H. Khan Khattak, "Pietra dura: a unique art of decoration in the sub-continent," *Journal of The Pakistan Historical Society* 40(3) (1992): 309–25.

37 Thalia Kennedy, "The Notion of Hierarchy: The 'Parchin Kari' Programme at the Taj Mahal," *International Journal of Architectural Research: ArchNet-IJAR,* 1(1) (Dec. 2013): 105–21. Available at: http://italia-vacance.com/index.php/IJAR/article/view/11, accessed 25 August 2018; Amina Okada, "Fleurs de pierre du Taj Mahal," *Connaissance des Arts* 499 (October 1993): 62–71.

38 Laura Parodi, "The Bibi-ka Maqbara in Aurangabad: A Landmark of Mughal Power in the Deccan? *East and West* 48(3/4) (1998): 349–83; Catherine B. Asher, *Architecture of Mughal India* (Cambridge, UK: Cambridge University Press, 1992), 261–65; Chanchal Dadlani and Yuthika Sharma, "Beyond the Taj Mahal: Late Mughal Visual Culture," in *A Companion to Islamic Art and Architecture,* 2: 1055–81.

39 Edhem Eldem, *Death in Istanbul: Death and its Rituals in Ottoman-Islamic Culture* (Istanbul: Ottoman Bank Archives and Research Center, 2005), 247–89.

40 For the long and bizarre journey of Atatürk's body until its final resting place in Anitkabir, see Christopher S. Wilson, *Beyond Anitkabir: The Funerary Architecture of Atatürk. The Construction and Maintenance of National Memory* (London: Routledge, 2013), 5–22, 65–99.

41 Wilson, *Beyond Anitkabir,* 101–33; Emel Akçalı, "The Ambivalent Role of National Monuments in the Age of Globalisation: The Case of Atatürk's Mausoleum in Turkey," *Borderlands* 9(2) (2010): 1–23, http://publications.ceu.edu/sites/default/files/publications/akcaliataturk.pdf, accessed 27 August 2018.

42 Donald Malcolm Reid, *Whose Pharaohs? Archaeology, Museums, and Egyptian National Identity from Napoleon to World War I* (Berkeley: University of California Press, 2002), 258–98; Yoav Di-Capua, "Embodiment of the Revolutionary Spirit: The Mustafa Kamil Mausoleum in Cairo," *History and Memory* 13(1) (2001): 85–113.

43 Aly Hatem Gabr, "Neo-Pharaonic Architecture in Cairo: A Western Legacy," *Medina Magazine* (1998): 44–51; Ralph M. Coury, "The Politics of the Funereal: The Tomb of Sa'd Zaghlul," *Journal of the American Research Center in Egypt* 29 (1992): 191–200.

44 Kishwar Rizvi, "Religious Icon and National Symbol: The Tomb of Ayatollah Khomeini in Iran," *Muqarnas* 20 (2003): 209–24.

45 Margaret Morton, et al., *Cities of the Dead: The Ancestral Cemeteries of Kyrgyzstan* (Seattle and London: University of Washington Press, 2014).

II. Divergence

The White Mosque (1980)

Architect: **Zlatko Ugljen**
Location: **Visoko, Bosnia and Herzegovina**

Recipient of the Aga Khan Award for Architecture in 1983

The White Mosque serves as the religious and intellectual centre for the community. Its geometrically simple plan encloses a complex, slope-ceilinged, skylit volume that is pure, abstract, sparsely ornamented, and painted white. The archetypal Bosnian mosque has a simple square plan crowned by a cupola and entered by means of a small porch. The White Mosque's plan conforms to the archetype, but its roof is a freely deformed quarter of a cupola, pierced by five skylights, themselves composed of segments of quarter cupolas. The effect is one of confrontation between the elementary plan and the sophisticated hierarchy of roof cones. The principal symbolic elements, mihrab, minbar, minaret, and fountains, have a fresh folk art character subtly enhanced by the avant-garde geometries of their setting. Commending the mosque for its boldness, creativity, and brilliance, the jury found it "full of originality and innovation (though with an undeniable debt to Ronchamp), laden with the architect's thought and spirit, shared richly with the community, and connecting with the future and the past."

— AKAA jury citation

In the summer of 2018, artist Velibor Božović visited the White Mosque in Visoko for the first time. He was commissioned to create a perspective on this Aga Khan Award-winning project through a series of photo-interviews with different individuals that he selected based on their personal or professional relationship to the project. The following piece introduces excerpts of Božović's conversations with the mosque's imams, congregation members, architects, and a filmmaker.

IBRAHIM HADŽIĆ,
imam

The White Mosque was opened in 1980. By that time, I had already been working in a village near Visoko and I remember being present at the Mosque's opening ceremony. There was one barber who lived here; I have forgotten his name but we all called him *Šepo* ("gimpy"), and he was a passionate fan of the soccer club Hajduk from Split. Moreover, he was the soccer referee and we knew each other from games because I used to play too. And when I came to the opening ceremony, because there were some 50,000 people present, he asked me, "Why don't you come to my house and sit at the window?" (his house was just opposite from the White Mosque, facing the stage). He said, "You could sit on the sill and put your legs through the window—I can't offer you anything better." And that is how I got to be at the White Mosque's opening ceremony.

The mosque is mostly visited by individuals studying architecture. We have students coming from Slovenia, from Austria, from Belgrade, from all those schools of architecture. Every year we get at least two to three such visits. Other tourists prefer to go down the street to the Tabačka Mosque because this mosque's problem is the shops out front: they completely shield it from the view. They say that these shops, which allegedly are of Slovenian architecture, were put up on purpose to block the mosque from the view. Some say so. But professor Ugljen designed the complete project, including all structures surrounding the mosque. All of this other stuff should come down and one beautiful project vision should be implemented. We financed it, but the Municipality has encroached upon the site and will never give it back to us.

It is impossible to photograph this mosque.

The people in Visoko would greatly appreciate the opening of the view toward the mosque from this side, that is, tearing down these structures and finding another solution for all those handicraft shops in a manner that would make the White Mosque dominant. The people who come to the White Mosque have grown accustomed to this situation, but a reconstruction should be done, of course, and those basic problems should be resolved. Unless we take down that tin roof, we won't even know what is below it. Look, it had been completed in 1980 and in 1983 it received the Aga Khan Award. In 1983, the people from our community bought the copper and covered it ... From the Aga Khan Award, they paid $30,000 for the metal sheets. And that was when all contact with professor Ugljen ceased, until I came here and we began to talk about reconstruction.

HARIS GORAK,
a member of the congregation

I am a member of the Mosque's Board and my home is in the vicinity. My mother is from Visoko, but I was born in Orašje on the Sava River. I have been living here since 2000, but I also used to come here often as a child because my uncles lived here.

This mosque has a unique character. We have a lot of mosques in the traditional style, and now also in the Arabic style, but this one is unique. It is impossible to discern one particular style, only the style of professor Ugljen. When you enter other mosques, you might see grand chandeliers and other items that decorate the interior, but the beauty of this mosque lies in its simplicity.

What we lack here is the space for women. This mosque did not provide for that kind of setting. Whenever there is a large gathering, there is a problem: we have no designated space. Originally, this was all one single large room, and this part was subsequently made. But we haven't solved the problem of women's space. The mosque belongs to them as well. When there is a large gathering, men come in and women position themselves here and then we have a problem: the situation is not adequate this way; it simply is not. Some women who have been coming here longer know of this problem, but others who are new don't and then they sit in lines here. That is this mosque's problem, and it is a functional problem that should be solved in such a way that every woman, when she enters the mosque, can straight away identify the place that is designated for her.

AMRA HADŽIMUHAMEDOVIĆ,
professor of architecture

I believe that many people share a kind of pride in this place because it is one of the first mosques which, through a more rigorous, architectural approach, strove to find a new form of expression for religious architecture.

The White Mosque is pure modernism. It does indeed represent one kind of modernist expression, or perhaps, late modernism, which strongly resembles Le Corbusier's approach. And such buildings need an empty space; they do not have the sequences typical of Bosnian mosques, for example, which express themselves through sequence.

A big problem with the people in the Islamic Community today is that they want to segregate women. Apparently there is not enough space for women. I suppose that if you asked Mr. Ugljen, the architect, he would say that the space was made for men and women alike. In the Bosnian mosques, the space for women was never separated. When you enter the space, you could once see short partitions, but that was not necessarily a place designated for women. The rule is that men pray in front of women. The space was at times filled with men praying in the front—who, by the way, were always present in fewer numbers in the Bosnian mosques, especially during the Communist era. When the men were busy providing for their families and were not as visible, then it was women who occupied that space. Today, we witness this cultural memory being thrown into oblivion. Or, I might say, some other approach, some other cultural memory has been brought here to shroud that which is Bosnian. If you told my mother, who is 98 years old and who regularly went to a mosque, that there is no space for women in Visoko's White Mosque, she would be astounded: "Do so many people really come to that mosque?" This segregation of women is a completely new phenomenon; it represents the elimination of the Bosnian cultural memory.

EDIN ef. BUKVA,
imam hafiz

I have been here since January 2014. Ever since I came, we have been intensively working on the campaign and preparations for rehabilitation and renovation of the mosque. This applies particularly to this central and main part of the roof truss, which, due to material wear and shelling, has been damaged beyond simple repair. Marks from the rain leaks can still be seen. When it rains, the rainwater is collected in glasses and bowls. However, in the midst of all of that, what might be of interest is the fact that we who pray in this mosque daily are interested even more than the experts in preserving its original architectural form, its uniqueness and value, simply because it belongs not only to us, but, in all modesty, to the world.

At that time, 38 years ago, this mosque was not accepted very well, especially regarding its particular shape. But those of us who had religious education were taught something completely different, namely that the religion itself does not in any way lay down the rules on what the shape of either a mosque's interior or exterior should be like, besides some basic rules, for example that its interior should not be decorated with images. What is interesting about this mosque is that, despite being contemporary and modern in its form—being ahead of its time, even today—it is in certain aspects even more Islamic than those older, traditional mosques, especially regarding the decoration of its interior.

Our mentality is such that we tend not to notice the wealth we have. Even I found out about its value through numerous expert visits I hosted here. I have welcomed here students from Slovenia, the United Kingdom, as well as experts from Rome and elsewhere. In those first contacts I had to improvise. And then, visitors from outside of Bosnia and Herzegovina, including ordinary tourists who came because they had heard about the mosque, inspired me to learn more about the significance of this mosque. We who lived here, except for the experts who studied it, were not aware of the treasure we had.

We have not disturbed anything from the original interior, even now during this rehabilitation and renovation phase. For example, the project requires that the identical carpet to the original one be ordered. However, there is one detail that professor Ugljen asked for, but that could not be fulfilled at that time: this part over there, a pulpit or in broad translation a cathedra, wherefrom the imam addresses the congregation. The professor's request was that it be covered with black leather or fur, which I believe is meant to symbolize the Ka'ba. However, at that time they were unable to find a piece of hide that was large enough. And a few years ago, our mosque's caretaker asked one local leather craftsman to make it and he promised to do so. But in the end, even he could not find the black one, so he brought this grey leather. That is a very small detail, but we will strive to realize it all the same, because the professor wanted it so.

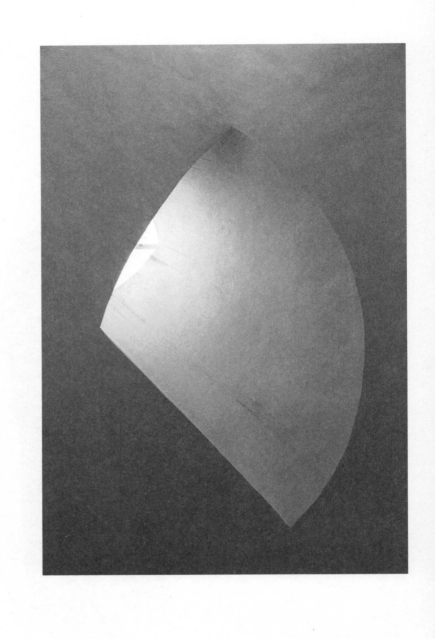

TARIK HODŽIĆ,
film director

My grandfather (Ibrahim Hodžić) wrote his entire life and left behind a great deal of writings and articles for numerous newspapers he had worked for. Among other things, he made a collection of selected religious lectures that were similar in subject and he assembled them in one book named *On Intellectual and Primitive Understanding of Religion and Religious Regulations*. One could say that at that time this book was a bombshell and represented a new view of this subject matter. Generally, we, the people here, have always been difficult regarding religion, or anything else, so a large number of colleagues renounced my grandfather due to some of his views. Even so, the book fared very well. At that time, the preparations for the building of the White Mosque were underway and my grandfather decided to donate all the money he would get. The book passed the censorship in the former Yugoslavia and some 20,000 books were sold. He received the money and went and gave it all for the building of the White Mosque. He wanted in a way to leave something behind.

I remember—I have it recorded—the three ways in which a human being can become immortal according to Islam; it was mentioned during my grandfather's funeral. These three ways are the following: to leave behind a child that will pray to God on your behalf, to leave behind some knowledge that will be of use to others (that was that book), and the third is to give your money for something that will also be of use to others, something that will remain, something that is turned into a charitable endowment—*waqf*. And that has stuck with me ever since. How old was I then, when my grandfather died? I was 16 to 17 years old, and somehow these words really imprinted on my subconsciousness. Every time someone mentions the White Mosque, I somehow remember these words and everything that my grandfather did at that time. I know that he was very happy that such a mosque was built. He liked that it was something out of the ordinary.

As a child, I preferred to go to the White Mosque for some reason. We belonged to the Šadrvan Mosque but I liked going to the White, because somehow to me it seemed larger, although it was not. The Šadrvan Mosque was larger, but it was an optical illusion: the White was bright, it was spacious. I remember there being some sort of green carpeting, and when you looked around you could see some degree of light on all sides. Those are the images I remember today.

There is one story, I don't know if someone has already mentioned it; I think the architect Samit told this story, or maybe Jasmin, I can't remember exactly. But what is interesting is that, at the time when a proposal for what the mosque should look like was being made, one thing tipped the scales. There was one local congregation member who, at one of those meetings, said: "Look guys, when you show me this mosque, to me it doesn't look like a mosque, I don't even like it that much. But there is one thing we have to take into consideration: I took these images home with me and the children saw them. And the children were delighted. It seems to me that this might be some kind of architecture for the future—children understand that better, and our time is slowly passing."

ZLATKO UGLJEN, architect

NINA UGLJEN ADEMOVIĆ, architect

ZLATKO UGLJEN,
architect

When that shell finally came out of the ground—it had been built for 10 years—they said it was all a scam and "we threw our money away," etc. It was the citizens who collected the money at that time; there were no donors. Once it happened, and I was simultaneously working on the Post Office building in Visoko, that while I was on my way to the building site a man stopped me. I realized that I didn't know him and I said, "Excuse me, but I cannot remember you." "Well, there is no need for you to know me, because we all know you. I just want to tell you that all of us who donated money for this mosque to be built would now give even double just to have it torn down."

That mosque will not be accepted despite all the accolades and awards. When that 10-year-long hiatus ended, allegedly—and this I heard from some people from Visoko—an architect from Algeria came to see someone on some private business and inquired about the project and they told him the worst things and how they didn't want to finance it anymore. But he said that the project should be completed and that everything would be all right. And then they also found an Arab investor. I never knew who he was because they stopped communicating with me. I have this photograph from the White Mosque's opening ceremony, which was a sensation in all of Yugoslavia, and Muslims even came from from Kosovo, Macedonia, Slovenia. On the stands there were flags with the five-pointed star and Tito's picture. When this photograph was taken, a Franciscan was giving the speech and there were Arabs and other guests in the back. I was supposed to be there at the stands, alongside the mayor and Reis ("Head of the Muslim Community"), and others. However, I went up on the minaret and watched it all from above. And prior to all that, when the final construction works on the mosque had started again, one old man often came to the site when he knew I would be there, but he never approached me. I remember his last name was Patak. And that went on for over a year. He used to come there and walk around the site, but he never talked to me. And when the opening ceremony came to a close, I went down from the minaret into the mass of people. Suddenly someone took me by the arm and I recognized that man. And then he whispered to me "I came here to ask for forgiveness." To that I could only respond, "Hajji, what would I be forgiving you for?" "Well," he said, "I used to say a lot of bad things about you around the town."

I can't even remember why I gave up the idea of the originally planned, traditional minaret.

And there is one more anecdote I wish to tell you. We got a call from the Commission from Geneva, where the center of the Aga Khan Institution was situated, informing us that they would be coming to Sarajevo and that all of us should then go to Visoko. By that time, the White Mosque had already been in operation for almost three years, so I went two or three days in advance to visit the mosque and see the state it was in. I asked for the mosque to be freshly painted. And when the delegation arrived to Sarajevo, I went to Visoko once again to check whether this had been done. It was evening and I could see that the mosque was indeed freshly painted. Then I went once more the next morning and I saw that nothing was painted. I didn't understand what happened because I had witnessed the previous night that it had been painted. I went to an inn across the street to have a round of rum and then I went back to the mosque. And there was an old man looking through the window of his house, watching me walk around the mosque; he was laughing. He said to me, "There was a rain shower last night and because the paint hadn't dried, it got all washed away." On top of that, it was May 1, a holiday. Everything was closed and we had to find the equipment and workers. But we somehow managed to organize it all and had it painted quickly once again.

NINA UGLJEN ADEMOVIĆ,
architect

I was young then. I was in elementary school when the mosque was being built. I did not know anything about it and it did not interest me at that age. Only when the application for the Aga Khan Award was being prepared at our house, a very demanding application, did it grab my attention. I was then a high school student; I didn't know that I would be an architect. I was still uncertain. I actually wanted to study art history, but there was no such study program in Sarajevo. I also considered design, because there was some talk of them planning to introduce that program. That was the dilemma. But I knew that it had to be some kind of art. At that time, I didn't perceive the White Mosque as a structure at all, or as architecture. To me, it had always been a sculpture because there had been a small model of it on a shelf in my home for as long as I could remember. That is how I perceived it: a sculpture, a sort of decoration in the room.

I remember when I went to Visoko to see the White Mosque for the first time. This was before the project received the Aga Khan Award. When I first entered the space, that was when I comprehended for the first time not only what architecture was, but also what it meant to feel a space. And even today when someone mentions architecture, and when I think of a space, my first association is that first experience entering the White Mosque and catching sight of those two skylights.

Headless, They March On: Cephalophores and Coexistence in Ottoman Bosnia

Amila Buturović

More than a mere spatial juxtaposition of buildings and structures, "architecture of coexistence" implies the presence of forms that allow kinesthetic contact, communication, and interaction. Coexistence thus unfolds as a three-dimensional experience since the trajectories of movement always open up relationally. But what about the architectural forms for the dead, where there is no movement or interactive contact? In order to move away from the conventional two-dimensional perception of the spaces of death, this essay explores the topic of coexistence by looking at the dead as subjects/agents rather than objects/remains, and by highlighting the dynamic between the dead and the living. It focuses on the phenomenon of "cephalophory" and "cephalophores," the head-carrying martyr shrines and grave-markers depicting the solitary warrior-saints of early Ottoman Bosnia. I examine how such enshrined martyrdom releases suffering from its historical particularity, allowing it to be articulated and manifested in inclusive and shared rather than solitary and exclusive ways. Drawing elements from Islamic, Byzantine, and local Slavic hagiographic sensibilities, cephalophoric martyrs inform and affect the practices of memory and rituals across Bosnia's religious boundaries. They are revered by both Christians and Muslims, and help us to expand our discussion of coexistence beyond conventional architectural and spatial forms. Few and never the focal point of "official" religious visitations, these shrines nevertheless form an aspect of living tradition and represent physical anchors for a highly localized but recurring narrative of headless martyrdom that circulates across Bosnia and Herzegovina. They bear both the traces and the potential for hope and striving that are particularly relevant for a region in a post-genocidal period of return, reconciliation, and literal "re-membering."

Space, gravestones, and movement

Henri Lefebvre argues that the systems and modalities of spatialization are always historically conditioned.[1] He addresses the implications which dominant narratives bear on the social arrangement of space in different historical settings and suggests that such arrangements become internalized as a "socio-spatial outlook" which inescapably regulates our expectations, actions, and routines within space. In modern, living societies, that may be easier to study; in premodern societies, especially those encompassed within imperial frameworks, it may be more challenging to establish the trajectories of movement and interaction that constituted a shared socio-spatial outlook.

In the case of the Ottoman Empire, the dominant sources—usually court records—about the imperial social order guide our understanding of interactive spaces, but the local sources are increasingly considered as well. Recently, such micro-histories have proliferated, problematizing the traditional concept of the archetypal "Islamic/Ottoman city" and engaging in a more nuanced examination of how local conditions play out in the formation and growth of urban spaces across the imperial belt.[2] While some of these studies focus on architectural qualities, others pursue historical-cum-anthropological evaluations of city life. In each case, diversity and coexistence—conceived as permutations in architectural styles, cultural hybridity, and the general acceptance of the "other"—challenge the rigid essentialism entailed in the idea of "the Ottoman/Islamic city" and the grand narrative in which otherness is absent or invisible. As new studies restore these minor narratives, a richer and more colorful image emerges of Ottoman urban spaces as multifocal and multilocal formations in which coexistence is signified by architectural and cultural tapestry alike. The narratives, though concurrent, are hierarchically related, revealing the realities of friction within religious, social, gender, and other forms of empowerment and disempowerment, all contributing to a layered socio-spatial outlook.

In Bosnia, the topic of the Ottoman architecture of coexistence has been addressed in historical terms as a piece of the broader imperial puzzle, but also discursively as a way to argue against recent representations of Bosnia as a place of ancient ethnic hatreds that galvanized the violence, war, and genocide in the 1990s.[3] The textured spaces of mingling and competition captured in the architecture of Bosnian cities and towns, associated not only with the houses of worship but also marketplaces, residential quarters, hospitals, and so on, testify to a complex, bustling world that lasted for centuries. Alarmingly, that world has now been greatly endangered in the aftermath of the 1992–95 ethnic cleansing with the entrenching of discrete political entities along ethno-religious lines. In fact, Ottoman Bosnia epitomizes well the heterogeneity and simultaneity of space which most scholars now underline as space's main feature. As Doreen Massey suggests, all space, through social action, is open to plural meanings and concurrent possibilities.[4] The outcome of different orientations, movements, and relations within space ascertains a continuous production of its meaning. Extending this proposition toward the spaces of death and the stories they can tell, we encounter new possibilities to discuss the modalities of coexistence in Bosnia, as well as a denial thereof that has periodically resulted in violence, even genocide, and that is also poignantly inscribed in the region's deathscape.

In the Ottoman empire's administration of space, the dead needed to be buried *extra muros*, outside of city boundaries, except those who for various reasons, often of social and religious eminence, were laid in the *hazire*, or the mosque yard.[5] In Bosnia, the precinct of the mosque is referred to as *harem*, the sacred ground that intimates a privacy of relations with the deceased, where individuals of note are commonly buried. Common folk lay in the cemeteries at the outskirt of towns although, in time, as the urban space expanded, they became incorporated into parks or were bulldozed over to yield new urban structures.

This practice of burying the dead away from human settlements was not introduced by the Ottomans: the most common burial tradition in mediaeval Bosnia associated with the *stećak* monoliths favored the disposal of the dead in distant mountainous locations commonly inaccessible to everyday movement. The consequence of this overlap in pre-Ottoman and Ottoman rituals is a spatial continuity of funerary architecture which can still be found in many parts of Bosnia and Herzegovina where the *stećaks* lie side by side with Islamic and Christian gravestones, and in certain cases with the Jewish stones. While mixing the living and the dead in the same space may have been a taboo, mixing the dead was not (Fig. 1).[6]

The spatial arrangement of the dead across Ottoman Bosnia thus inscribes the historical diversity of religious life and persists to date. As mentioned, early Ottoman gravestones were placed in close proximity to each other, attesting to a social intimacy despite widespread conversions, primarily to Islam, and the change in the religious fabric. In the early eighteenth century, however, we witness more differentiated funerary representations on the tombstones in response to a sharper administration of

Figure 1. Mixed burial stones at the cemetery in Žunovi, Sokolac

the *millet* system of religious grouping. A similar shift can be observed in form: whereas the tombstones of the fifteenth and sixteenth centuries were shaped in similar styles, distinctive features—Catholic and Orthodox crosses, Jewish slabs, and Muslim turbans—appear bolder in the later period of the Ottoman rule. Their presence in the landscape continues to tell a story of coexistence, but in a static, two-dimensional way.

It is in the reconfiguration of the spatial status of the dead that the conundrum of their immobility can be addressed. The dead are not always a fixed, unchangeable otherness. Rather, they can have an agency to act in ways that instigate movement of the living and recalibrate their spatial outlook. Howard Williams suggests that the remains "provide an agency to affect the experience and actions of mourners and evoke memories of the past, rather than serving as a static and passive set of substances manipulated and disposed of by the mourners to serve their sociopolitical ends."[7] The dead, in other words, can maintain an affective social presence with a lasting impact on the way they are remembered and can enhance coexistence through rituals and narratives, synchronically and diachronically, that engage communities and groups across ethnic and religious lines. Examples of such active presence in Bosnia vary in consistency, intensity, inclusiveness, and location, but their relevance for coexistence is worthy of consideration. Let us examine the case of headless martyrs.

Cephalophory and the marking of interactive space

Cephalophory is a reference to head-carrying martyrdom. In Bosnia and Herzegovina, this phenomenon is commonly associated with solitary shrines scattered across the landscape, often in spatial disconnect from cemeteries or urban formations. Massive and imposing, and usually topped with a turban, cephalophoric gravestones are rarely inscribed, containing only occasional dates and figural representations. With few exceptions, we do not know who erected them but their form suggests a highly localized style and points to similarities with other slabs. Referred to by some historians as the tombstones from the period of *feth* (conquest), these slabs are commonly dated to the late fifteenth, early sixteenth century and popularly referred to as *šehitski nišani,* or martyrs' tombstones. At times, such tombstones appear in clusters and are referred to as *svatovski nišani,* or wedding martyrs, and are remembered by Christians and Muslims in a different type of legend. Since the epigraphic document on the shrines is absent and there is a lack of written sources or association with religious or political elite, the knowledge of this martyrdom is transmitted primarily through local ritual and narrative traditions.

The motif of a head-carrying saint is not unique to Bosnia. Regionally, it appears in both Christian and Muslim lore across the Balkans and often relates to individuals revered by both Christians and Muslims. Sometimes they evoke connections with popular Sufi practices but do not directly relate to them.[8] More broadly, the trope of severed heads spans literary and religious imagination around the world with a broad symbolic potential: the Tantric goddess Chinnamasta is a cephalophore, depicted in an extreme form of the divine feminine as holding a bloody sword in one hand and her head in the other. In ancient Greece and Rome, the motif dramatizes violent encounters between heroes and anti-heroes and is deployed to shock the audience.[9] Christian religious imagination also uses the motif: Saint-Denis, the patron saint of Paris, is perhaps the best-known example in Western Christianity. In Islam, the trope is less common but appears in interesting variations: the beheaded Sufi master al-Hallaj becomes the central metaphor for self-transcendence in *Bisar-name* (the Headless epic); in *The Arabian Nights,* doctor Duban is a talking head; and the seventeenth–century poet Sarmad of Sindh, once decapitated, utters the full declaration of faith. In all cases, disembodied heads become animated and speak in truth and clarity, having grasped the unknown.

The detachment from the original body provides a liminality that results in a comprehension of the world and virtue that transcend historical conditions and human limitations. Experience of death is superimposed over the finality of life. Violence creates a purpose. New knowledge is acquired and produced. This interplay between two states of existence, one as a common mortal and the other as immortal martyr, keeps the subject within history and outside of it, allowing him/her to remain bound in space but elevated to higher grounds of knowledge and morality. In the Bosnian tradition, the stories of cephalophoric martyrs are present and narrated in local hagiographical tradition and are retold through an interplay of religious and secular motifs, military and lay experiences, and include both male and female protagonists. Notably, the motif is not present in urban lore, which partly explains its absence from the local Jewish culture that took roots in urban centers in the sixteenth century. Bosnian cephalophory offers an eclectic repertoire that draws on several sources: Byzantine Christianity, Islamic tradition, and the local Slavic-Bosnian notion of *dobri* (the good ones). Its eclecticism in form and content gives it metonymic force, it helps cement a sense of community fragmented by violence, consolidate a relationship with the otherwise anonymous graves, and assign a new meaning to the landscape where these graves seem randomly embedded.[10] Most importantly, it is in the animation of stories and rituals that narrative and spatial movement is channeled and the connective threads of historical coexistence reaffirmed.

Stories and rituals

In the basic storyline drawn from military martyrdom, at a brutal and exhausting battle, a heroic warrior is decapitated by a mortal blow of the enemy sword and his/her severed head rolls away. The hero staggers but does not relent; collecting their head, the hero carries on killing more enemy soldiers. Death is refused. Eventually, s/he slows down and walks away through the battle line to a seemingly random spot where s/he finally collapses, the head clutched in the hand. This location becomes the final resting ground from which a spring of water spontaneously gushes forth, a tree grows or a shrine emerges. The same narrative progression informs non-military renditions, with a comparably intense emphasis on suffering caused by decapitation; the refusal to die; the liminal period when the walking dead defiantly enacts his/her own pilgrimage; and the transformative apex where the head is laid, the shrine spontaneously erected, and the martyr freed from somatic violence to become a saint and healer. The cephalophore's arrival/death and exit/rebirth merge the profanity and reverence of life.

   Like their Byzantine counterparts, Bosnia's earliest cephalophores are military martyrs: they die in battles and, continuing to wreak damage on enemy soldiers, they retain control over their own death. Cephalophoric military heroism is a well-developed motif in Byzantine Christianity where it forms the cultural backdrop of warrior-saints, for whom combating the enemy constitutes a spiritual and worldly mission, and culminates with the recruitment into the celestial army (Walter 2003). In contrast to their Byzantine counterparts, Bosnian cephalophores do not leave relics for ritual veneration and celebration. Rather, their memory is materialized in stone but consecrated through stories and rituals that involve visitations, healing, and receiving blessings.

   Furthermore, unlike Byzantine warrior-saints of Christendom, Bosnian heroes variably fought for the Ottomans or against them. Their political siding seems of little relevance. In Kozarac near Prijedor, for example, he was a Muslim fighting non-Muslims. In Turovi near Sarajevo, he was a Muslim but fighting an unjust Ottoman governor (Fig. 2). In Ostružnica near Fojnica, the soldier fought with the Bosnian army against the Ottomans before being struck down. The rolling head revealed a long tress of hair—the cephalophore was a young woman. The year chiseled into her gravestone is 1171 AH/1757 CE, which is not necessarily the date of her death (Fig. 3). Incongruity in dating is common, as for example in the Kozarac shrine that bears the following inscription: "Lord, this is a martyr's shrine. God makes him into the manifestation of His Glory. He fought for some time heroically, then came to this spot carrying his

Figure 2. Female cephalophoric shrine in Ostružnica, near Fojnica, dated to 1171 AH/1757 CE

Figure 3. Male cephalophoric tombstone in Turovi, near Trnovo, no date

Figure 4. Male cephalophoric turbe/shrine in Kozarac, near Prijedor, dated to 1125 AH/1713 CE, inscribed

own head. May Muhammad pray for him. Lord, receive this as our gift on behalf of all martyrs and in the name of our Prophet Muhammad. We thank the Lord, the Creator of this world. This tombstone was erected by the noble captain of Kozarac, Mehmed Bey. The Year 1125AH/1713CE."[11] (Fig. 4)

Bosnian cephalophoric narratives also include non-military legends that similarly have a divine shelter follow from a decapitation. This acknowledges a broader range of experiences, acts, and gestures making the motif more inclusive and constitutive of a shared socio-spatial outlook. What follows are three narrative examples from different parts of Bosnia, each one violent, dramatic, and evocative.

Story 1:

In his 1908 book on Mostar, the Austrian journalist Robert Michel records the following:
"By the main mosque on the river bank lies a *dobri*. His story dates to the eighteenth century. When the news of an Austrian military incursion reached Mostar, a man was shaving in his store. Hearing the news, he rushed out, his face only half shaved, swinging his walking stick ferociously and summoning his fellow Mohammedans to rise against the Austrians. He then disappeared from the face of the earth. At the moment when he was swinging his stick, the Austrians all the way to Banja Luka felt pangs of pain as if whipped. Many years later he was spotted at a hill overlooking Mostar carrying his severed head under the armpit down into the market. He walked over the Čejvan-Pasha mosque and disappeared into the earth. A shrine/*turbe* was erected on that spot that became a pilgrimage site for both Muslims and Christians to burn candles at their respective holidays."[12]

Story 2:

An eighteenth-century Latin chronicle, *Liber memorabilium parochiae Vetero Gradiscanae* [Memory Book of the Gradiška Parish], about the parish priests and religious officials of the border town of Gradiška (Berbir fortress), includes a note on an author of prophecies and ecstatic utterances, an odd dervish by the name of Gaibija, entitled "Sepulcro magni prophetae Gaibia." It says that the Christians regarded Gaibija as a great healer who cured the plague. Many a foreigner traveled to the Balkans by boat along the Sava river to pray at his grave. According to the Chronicle, all Gaibija's predictions came true. One pleasant evening, he walked across to the Slavonian (Croatian) side of the river to enjoy the view from the park. As he sat by the bank, a group of drunken Ottoman soldiers attacked him and beheaded "the filthy dervish with much pleasure," as they later boasted to the judge. The next morning, the fortress commander issued an order to have Gaibija's body retrieved and buried on the Bosnian side. The night after the burial, the guard of the northern gate spotted an apparition walking on the river as though it was on land, carrying his head under the armpit. As the moon rose, the guard took a good look at the severed head and noticed its complexion was wax pale, its eyes wide open and shiny in the moonlight, looking at once threatening and saintly. This ghastly creature walked calmly across the river toward the spot where a couple of days earlier the old dervish had been beaten and beheaded. The creature was Gaibiya's ghost. The next Friday, as per the commander's orders and under the pressure of the saint's keen followers and general populace, his remains were transported to the location of his death and, with the approval of the Austrian authorities, a shrine was erected at his grave.[13]

Story 3:

One sunny day, in a village near Tuzla, a beautiful Muslim maid walked down to the river to wash clothes. Oblivious to her surroundings, with feet submerged in the river and the *shalwars* rolled up to expose her calves while she lathered up the clothes, she sang love songs in a sweet, tender voice. From a distance, an Austrian soldier, lured by her voice and mesmerized by her beauty, sneaked over and demanded a kiss. Startled, she refused and screamed, but he forced himself on her. In self-defense, the girl hit him with the laundry mallet, which sent the soldier into a violent rage. In a swift motion he pulled out a knife and cut off her head with a sharp slash. The head rolled over onto the ground, stunting them both in horror. Defiant, the girl picked up the head and walked proudly back to her village where she collapsed onto the ground, her head tightly held in her arms. A shrine emerged at the very spot where she lay her head, becoming a holy ground for both women and men to pray for good fortune and health.[14]

Despite their differences, the three stories, like military ones, are tragic but do not end in tragedy. Life continues through death, or starts again. Where the physical universe cannot accommodate a headless body, the universe of martyrdom creates space for its affirmation. Decapitation creates a portal to defy the savagery of human act with a triumphant catharsis after suffering. We are invited to reflect and imagine the possibility of individual and social salvation in new terms. Disfigured martyrs challenge the notion that bodily integrity is necessary for a meaningful selfhood, sending a productive message of communal healing through the idea of truth and regeneration after dismemberment.

As they utilize local tropes and symbols, the shrines set the stage for inclusive moral lessons and ritual participation across religious divide. In Kozarac, until the 1992–95 war, both Muslims and Christians attended to the cephalophoric shrine with offerings and supplicatory prayers. In Ostružnica, the cephalophoric female martyr gives blessings and heals women of all walks of life and religious background (the ritual scraping of the stone is clearly visible). In Turovi, the shrine is visited during various festivals, rites of passage, and commemorations, by locals and tourists alike. The idea of perseverance in the face of calamity puts on hold the fear of death and channels the drama of brutal bodily fragmentation into a virtuous, purposeful existence. The common thread then is that decapitation, the metaphor for the most extreme assault on individual and collective integrity, can be scrambled into alternative, and much better beginnings and continuities.

Notably, there is a spatial component to this reconfiguration. As mentioned earlier, while the relics are not commonly found at the Bosnian shrines, the spot where the decapitated head falls allegedly results in a miraculous geological event: a spring bursting from dry soil, a creek turning into a torrential waterfall, a barren spot transforming into a lush shrub. This productive, transformative power of the narrative is likewise naturalized and embedded in the shared landscape, anchoring martyrdom to a specific location. Moreover, cephalophoric heroes are not bestowed a thaumaturgic function like Sufi saints or the local *dobri* who appear in dreams and visions.[15] They no longer travel after their dramatic journey. To profit from their grace, you go to them; they do not come to you.

In his critique of the way human spatiality is reductively discussed, Larry Shiner suggests that space is primarily a lived environment in which movement is the defining characteristic. Because "we are not in space as shoes are in a box," Shiner concludes that, as compared to the homogeneity and indifference of geometrical space, lived space is heterogeneous and discontinuous. It is tied to human aims and meanings; its orientations and places are interlaced with symbolic associations. space is less a matter of "positions" than of "situations," of intersecting coordinates than of "sites." As the encompassing habitat of human life, where distance, direction and place are determined by valuation and purposive movement, lived space is permeated with human significance.[16]

In Ottoman Bosnia, coexistence has been documented in numerous ways across urban centers, but it also existed in the remote countryside. Because everyday life there is hard to investigate through official historical sources, it is important to reach out to rich oral and material heritage to supplement our gaps in knowledge. Cephalophory is one example. It has impregnated the landscape of coexistence with the idea that violence and sacrifice, forced at times for lofty ideals and at others for personal integrity and honor, is a shared reality regardless of one's social place or religious background. The landscape becomes the connective tissue between the physical and cosmic loci of meaning, which the living trespass through the "purposive movement" of self-validation. Because cephalophoric martyrs highlight the capacity of receiving divine grace in the moment of ultimate bodily violation, they both confirm and outmatch human limitations, but keep the narrative and ritual potency of their experiences grounded deeply in the Bosnian soil. Elevated from the constraints of their historical moment, their life thus becomes a morality tale, twice-lived and many times retold. In cultural terms, this enables the communities living around such shrines to participate, inherit, and renew ties with their history and land. Commemorating sacrifice above and beyond the particular cause for which the martyr suffered offers the miraculous possibility of shared salvation, a coexistence in life as much as in death.

1 H. Lefebvre, *The Production of Space*, D. Nicholson-Smith, trans. (Oxford: Blackwell Publishers, 1991).

2 H. Watenpaugh, *The Image of an Ottoman City* (Leiden: E.J. Brill, 2004); E. Eldem et al., *The Ottoman City Between East and West* (Cambridge, UK: Cambridge University Press, 1999); U. Freitag et al., *The City in the Ottoman Empire* (Abindgdon: Routledge, 2010); M. Mazower, *Salonika: The City of Ghosts* (New York: Vintage, 2006).

3 See A. Handžić, "O formiranju nekih gradskih naselja u Bosni u XVI stoljeću - uloga države i vakufa [Development of towns in Bosnia in the 16th c. - the role of the state and religious endowments]," *POF* 25 (1975); A. Handžić, "O ulozi derviša u formiranju gradskih naselja u Bosni u XV stoljeću [The role of dervishes in the formation of towns in Bosnia in the 15th c.]," *POF* 31 (1981); S. Schwartz, *Sarajevo Rose: A Balkan Jewish Notebook* (London: Saqi Books, 2005); N. Malcolm, *Bosnia: A Short History* (New York: NYU Press, 1994).

4 D. Massey, *For Space* (London: Sage, 2005).

5 E. Eldem and N. Vatin, *L'épitaphe otomane musulmane, XVIe-XXe siècles* (Paris: Peeters, 2007), 10–15.

6 A. Buturović, *Carved in Stone, Etched in Memory* (Farnham: Ashgate, 2015), 125.

7 H. Williams, "Death Warmed Up: The Agency of Body and Bones in Early Anglo-Saxon Cremation Rites." *Journal of Material Culture* 9(3) (2004), 265–67.

8 V. Yankova, "Светци-воини. Балкански легенди за светци кефалофори/Martyrs-Warriors: Balkan Legends of Saints Kefalofori." Ethnocultural Interactions (2005).

9 B. White, "A Persistent Paradox," *Folklore* 83(2) (1972).

10 Buturović, *Carved in Stone*, 52–53.

11 M. Mujezinović, *Islamska epigrafika Bosne i Hercegovine* [Islamic Epigraphy of Bosnia and Herzegovina] (Sarajevo: Sarajevo Publishing, 1998), 3: 43.

12 R. Michel, *Mostar*, 1908 (Sarajevo: Dobra knjiga, 2006), 123–24.

13 F. Hadžibajrić, "Risala Šejha Mustafe Gaibije [Treatise of Shaykh Mustafa Gaibi]," *Anali Gazi Husrev-begove biblioteke* 4 (1976); M. Kostić, "Gaibijino Turbe kod Stare Gradiške [Gaibi's turbe near Stara Gradiška]," *Narodna Starina* 13 (1934); M. Huković, "Gaibija, šejh Mustafa - mistik i buntovnik [Sheikh Mustafa Gaibi - a mystic and rebel]," *POF* 41 (1991).

14 V. Palavestra, *Historijska usmena predanja iz Bosne i Hercegovine* [Oral Histories from Bosnia and Herzegovina] (Sarajevo: Buybook), 2004.

15 A. Hangi, *Život i običaji muslimana u Bosni i Hercegovini* [Lifestyle and customs of the Muslims of Bosnia and Herzegovina] (Sarajevo: Naklada Danijela Kajona, 1906), 305.

16 L. Shiner, "Sacred Space, Profane Space, Human Space," *Journal of the American Academy of Religion* 40(4) (1972), 429.

Bosnia and the Destruction of Coexistence
Helen Walasek

When outright warfare erupted in Bosnia and Herzegovina in April 1992 following its declaration of independence from Yugoslavia, it appeared to be driven by claims for ethnoreligious separatism. Yet few now consider the 1992–95 Bosnian War a religious or ethnic conflict, but rather the horrific outcome of a political project and a race for territory. Nevertheless, perceived ethnonational differences and the past were extensively mobilized by those driving the conflict, binding religion tightly to ethnic identity and inciting fears of an existential threat, from Islam and Muslims in particular.

As Yugoslavia began to disintegrate, after first Slovenia, then Croatia declared independence from the federal state, the wars of the 1990s were the culmination of years of nationalist rhetoric and propaganda pouring out of Slobodan Milošević's Serbia, backed by the might of the Yugoslav People's Army (JNA) and brutal paramilitary units. It was in Bosnia's neighbor, Croatia, that cultural property first came under attack, most infamously when the Old City of Dubrovnik, a UNESCO World Heritage Site, was bombarded by JNA forces and its Montenegrin allies in 1991.

In Bosnia and Herzegovina, secessionist Bosnian Serbs led by Radovan Karadžić, supported by Serbia, had long been working toward the division of the country on ethnonational lines. But Bosnia was a demographic patchwork of three principal ethnonational groups (Bosnian Muslims/Bosniaks, Bosnian Serbs, and Bosnian Croats) that would be impossible to separate without violence.[1] By the beginning of 1992, JNA heavy artillery was entrenched on the mountains overlooking Sarajevo, the country's capital, waiting for a signal to be called into play.[2] That signal was not long in coming after the country's declaration of independence, as JNA troops and Serb paramilitaries swept in from Serbia to help Karadžić and his supporters implement their long-held plan to create a separate Republika Srpska where Serbs and their cultural-religious identity would dominate. Sarajevo, hated symbol of Bosnia and Herzegovina's pluralism, was now a target and the siege of the city began.

But far to the south, a portent of the onslaught Bosnia was to face had come months before as JNA troops made their way to attack Croatia. On 1 October 1991, the small Croat-majority town of Ravno in southern Herzegovina was heavily damaged (including its Catholic church) and its inhabitants killed or expelled by JNA forces and Montenegrin reservists moving toward Dubrovnik—a date some say marks the real start of the Bosnian War. Yet one week earlier, on the night of 23–24 September, assembling JNA reservists had shot at the minaret of the historic Ljubović Mosque in the village of Odžak in eastern Herzegovina and detonated explosives inside.[3]

Here were foreshadowed the twin horrors of ethnic cleansing and the intentional destruction of religious and cultural property that was to be the greatest destruction of cultural heritage in Europe since World War II. These were among the defining features of the 1992–95 Bosnian War, a war that rapidly spun into the most violent of the conflicts that accompanied the break-up of Yugoslavia during which more than half the population of 2.2 million became refugees or were internally displaced, around 100,000 were killed, tens of thousands were interned in concentration camps, tortured or raped, and thousands of monuments of cultural or religious importance were destroyed or badly damaged before the final ceasefire.

Ethnic cleansing and destruction

Ethnic cleansing and the destruction of cultural and religious property were inextricably linked. The violent removal of structures that visibly marked the long historic presence of the groups targeted for expulsion (most often, though not entirely, Bosnia's Muslims) was a central part of the aggressive campaigns to carve out monoethnic spaces. This was the forcible elimination, not only of the living, unwanted "Other," but of the built evidence of their deep-rooted presence in a locality—the eradication of a group and the symbols of its identity, and the obliteration of a cultural landscape that was testimony to centuries of coexistence.

While the conflict first pitted separatist Bosnian Serbs against the internationally recognized government of Bosnia and Herzegovina, it did not take long for secessionist Bosnian Croats, egged on by Croatia, to turn on their former allies. After the Vance-Owen Plan of January 1993 proposed the division of Bosnia and Herzegovina into ethnically segregated provinces, the forces of the Croatian Defence Council (or HVO) moved to claim territory for an ethnically homogenous Croat statelet of Herceg-Bosna with Mostar as its capital.[4] The removal of Bosnian Muslim populations from Croat-held lands was crucial to their plan.[5] Once again, ethnic cleansing was accompanied by the destruction of both Muslim and Serb religious and cultural heritage.

Global condemnation followed attacks on iconic monuments like Sarajevo's Austro-Hungarian-era National Library (*Vijećnica*) in August 1992 by Bosnian Serb artillery, and Mostar's sixteenth-century Ottoman Old Bridge (*Stari Most*) in November 1993 by Bosnian Croat forces. Yet the most extensive destruction took place far from the gaze of the international media. It was in small towns and villages and isolated rural settings where secessionist forces waged violent campaigns of ethnic cleansing across huge swathes of territory that the destruction of religious and cultural property went hand in hand with multiple atrocities and human rights abuses. Here was a determined assault on the material evidence of a long-lived heterogeneity, transforming a visibly diverse cultural landscape into an apparently historically monoethnic domain, where in 1993 the mayor of Bosnian Serb-held Zvornik could declare of the once Muslim-majority town: "There were never any mosques in Zvornik."[6]

The buildings attacked were overwhelmingly religious and overwhelmingly Muslim or Ottoman: out of a prewar total of 1,144, almost 1,000 mosques and other Islamic religious structures were destroyed or damaged.[7] Around 233 Catholic and 70 Orthodox churches (including monasteries) were also destroyed or badly damaged.[8] It was destruction that, for the most part, was entirely intentional and took place far from the frontlines, most often during the forced expulsion of specific communities.

In Sarajevo and Mostar, home to important archives, libraries, museums, and research institutes, structures that symbolized a historically diverse pan-Bosnian identity were targeted as architectural expressions of the country's pluralism and holders of its cultural memory. Institutions like Sarajevo's Oriental Institute, with its rich collections of Islamic and Jewish manuscripts and Ottoman cadastral registers, was bombarded with incendiary shells and its collections set ablaze, while buildings all around it survived.

It did not take long for victims and observers alike to see how systematic and deliberate these attacks on Bosnia and Herzegovina's cultural and religious heritage were. Jan Boeles of the European Community Monitor Mission (ECMM) told journalist Robert Fisk:

> You have to understand that the cultural identity of a population represents its survival in the future. When the Serbs blow up the mosque of a village and destroy its graveyards and the foundations of the graveyards and mosque and then level them all off with a bulldozer, no one can ever, ever tell this was a Muslim village. This is the murder of a people's cultural identity.[9]

Nihad Čengić, a Bosnian conservator and a member of Sarajevo's Office for the Protection of Cultural Property, asserted in 1993: "How do you destroy a people if you can't kill them all? You destroy all the materials which proved their existence. That's why mosques are being destroyed. That's why the Oriental Institute was destroyed. They're destroying these things to reconstruct history ..."[10]

Professor Cherif Bassiouni, the international criminal lawyer who headed the United Nations (UN) Commission of Experts appointed to document and investigate the atrocities taking place during the conflicts in the former Yugoslavia, was convinced that neither the ethnic cleansing nor the destruction of cultural and religious property were random acts, but the implementation of a policy made at leadership level.[11] It was the work of Bassiouni and his team that led in 1993 to the formation of the International Criminal Tribunal for the former Yugoslavia (ICTY) by the UN Security Council.[12] The ICTY's jurisprudence was to make a distinctive contribution to the prosecution of crimes against cultural heritage, particularly in establishing that the deliberate destruction of structures which symbolize a group's identity was a manifestation of persecution and a crime against humanity.[13]

For this was not the equivalent and mutual destruction of cultural heritage by all three principal warring parties in the conflict. More than twenty years of war crimes investigations and assessments have determined that the greatest part of the deliberate destruction of religious and cultural property took place during campaigns of ethnic cleansing, the primary perpetrators of which were Bosnian Serb forces and their allies (which controlled 70 percent of the territory of Bosnia and Herzegovina), followed to a lesser extent by Bosnian Croat separatists.

It was typical of Bosnia and Herzegovina, most strikingly in small towns, to find a Catholic church, an Orthodox church, and a mosque (and sometimes a synagogue) within eyeshot of each other. Now these proofs of a lived coexistence were being violently eliminated. The particular targeting of minarets and their removal from the landscape was noted as "... a kind of architectural equivalent to the removal of the population, and visible proof that the Muslims had left."[14] With one exception,[15] not a single minaret on a functioning mosque was left intact on territories occupied by Bosnian Serb forces by the end of the war, and the transformation of the landscape was often completed by what has been called the "linguistic cleansing of toponyms" to more "Serbian" place names.[16]

While many of the recently built village mosques that were destroyed were perhaps of little architectural value, they were almost always of ancient foundation, and arguably may have held important movable heritage such as manuscripts and carpets. But some of Bosnia and Herzegovina's

Figure 1. An old postcard of the sixteenth-century Ferhadija (or Ferhat-paša) Mosque, Banja Luka

most significant Ottoman monuments were also obliterated. In Banja Luka, de facto capital of Republika Srpska, where there were no military operations at any time, between April and December 1993 fifteen mosques, twelve of them listed national monuments, including the famed Ferhadija, a domed sixteenth-century mosque that stood at the very heart of the city, were systematically blown up, along with other examples of the city's Ottoman heritage, like its ancient clock tower (Figs. 1 and 2).

In the small town of Foča stood the Aladža Mosque, one of the most important examples of classical Ottoman architecture in southeast Europe, renowned for its exquisitely painted interior. Some of the worst atrocities of the war were committed against Foča's Muslims by Bosnian Serb forces and their allies, and all the town's mosques had been attacked. Finally, on the night of 2–3 August 1992, months after opposition to the town's takeover had ended, the Aladža was demolished in a huge explosion.

In rural settings or on the outskirts of towns, the ruins of destroyed structures were often left to crumble, the stones lying where they had fallen. But in town and village centers remains were bulldozed, debris trucked away and dumped and sites leveled so not a single trace of the structures could be seen. The sites of what had once been sacred buildings went on to be used as parking lots, for markets and garbage dumpsters, or left as rubbish-strewn spaces.

The perpetrators of these attacks were not afraid to openly voice the aims behind the destruction: to permanently remove from the landscape the material evidence of the expelled communities' historic roots on the territory and to discourage those who survived expulsion from ever returning.

Figure 2. Citizens of Banja Luka stare at the remains of the Ferhadija Mosque after it was deliberately blown up with explosives in the early hours of 7 May 1993. The minaret survived the first attempt at demolition but was blown up the following day. The *turbe* (mausoleum) of the mosque's founder, Ferhad-paša, still stands on the far right; it was blown up later in the year on 15 December. The offices of the Islamic Community can be seen in the background.

Testifying at the ICTY, Milan Tupajić, wartime chief of the Bosnian Serb-held municipality of Sokolac, spelled this out when he described how, over a few days in September 1992, all the mosques in his area were demolished. Asked why he thought the mosques had been destroyed, Tupajić explained: "There's a belief among the Serbs that if there are no mosques, there are no Muslims and by destroying the mosques, the Muslims will lose a motive to return to their villages."[17]

When the war was over

The signing of the Dayton Peace Agreement brought the war to an end in December 1995. Underpinning the peace treaty was the hope of reversing the effects of ethnic cleansing and restoring Bosnia and Herzegovina's prewar pluralism. But while the treaty guaranteed the right of refugees and the displaced to return to the localities from which they had been forcibly expelled, it also marked the division of Bosnia into two entities, the Federation of Bosnia and Herzegovina (the so-called Muslim-Croat Federation) and Serb-dominated Republika Srpska, with sweeping political powers at entity level that worked against this aspiration.

Now a new battle began as the ethnically cleansed started to return and restore their shattered communities. In places where returnees were called "minority returns," return could be fiercely and sometimes violently contested. Here, rebuilding meant not only rebuilding homes, but asserting the right to a visible presence in the public space, including the reconstruction of the built markers of identity, in the face of obstruction, threats, or worse from hardline nationalist local authorities and their supporters. But reconstructing the symbolic markers of community identity became almost an imperative for returnees, closely bound up with restoring feelings of security and home—a need to restore a cultural environment which had been so abruptly destroyed and was now a landscape of empty spaces or ruins. Here, rebuilding the heritage became a struggle for justice and human rights.[18] (Figs. 3 and 4)

Figure 3. Coming home: the leveled site of the Krpića Mosque in Bijeljina in 2000 with parked cars, communal garbage containers, and small kiosks.

But rebuilding could also be an act of remembrance and bearing witness, of ensuring that the rewriting of history by the perpetrators of ethnic cleansing did not hold. In the early 2000s, a fundraising campaign to rebuild destroyed mosques in Republika Srpska called on Muslims not to abandon their "cultural and religious traces in the region" and urged them to be persistent in preserving their heritage and identity.[19]

The need to reestablish a visible Muslim presence in the landscape led to the building of what have been called *memorial mosques,* reconstructed in the absence of any Muslim returnees.[20] One was the seventeenth-century Avdić Mosque in the devastated Muslim village of Plana that sits to the north of Bileća, still a stronghold of support for convicted Serb war criminal Vojislav Šejšel. With its distinctive square minaret, the Avdić Mosque is believed to have been constructed by Christian builders from Dubrovnik. Donations to reconstruct the mosque came from around the world and it was formally opened in August 2013. Yet when the author visited Plana in 2015 not a single person lived in the devastated village and its houses remained roofless shells. Only the recent dead had returned, buried in the graveyard beside the mosque.

Nevertheless, Bosnia and Herzegovina's former pluralism and a belief in coexistence has survived, if severely challenged. During the conflict the Bosnian government—often labelled as "Muslim"—proscribed attacks on Christian sacral structures and actively protected them. This, and the generally

Figure 4. Coming home: the site of the mosque at Modrička Lug. Imam Osman ef. Mulahuseinović holds a photograph of the structure before its destruction in front of the remains of the mosque in June 2001.

respectful attitude of Bosnia's Muslims to the sacred structures of other faiths was noted by Colin Kaiser, who spent years recording the heritage destroyed during the Bosnian War.[21] In central Sarajevo, churches and monasteries remained intact,[22] as they did in Muslim-majority towns like Visoko, Bihać, Gračanica, and Tuzla. In places like Sanski Most and Bosanska Krupa, where occupying Bosnian Serb forces had destroyed mosques and Catholic churches, Orthodox churches remained intact when Bosnian Army troops retook the town in 1995.[23]

That notable exception to the assault on Muslim structures in territory held by Bosnian Serb forces mentioned above was in the village of Baljvine, whose Bosnian Serb residents actively protected their Muslim neighbors and saved the mosque from destruction. Even today, a lived coexistence continues in Baljvine.[24] But although the expelled have returned to many places, their numbers are small and most have not. While scores of cultural and religious structures have been (and still are) being rebuilt, they are often mosques and churches without parishioners. In June 1992, the Serbian Orthodox church of the Assumption of the Holy Mother of God in the Croat-majority town of Livno in western Herzegovina was set on fire; the majority of its parishioners had already been expelled or fled. Yet parishioners had not wanted to remove the church's important collection of Italo-Cretan icons. Now under threat, they were rescued by the local Catholic priest, Fra Marko Gelo, and taken to the nearby Franciscan Monastery of Gorica where they were stored throughout the war. Today, the Orthodox church has been repaired, a priest has been appointed, and the icons returned. However, in common with many of Bosnia's expelled communities, few of Livno's Serb residents have returned.[25]

Another effect of ethnic cleansing had been observed by Colin Kaiser: while it was clear that the removal of the "Other" and the obliteration of their built heritage was an attempt to destroy the identity of the forcibly displaced, it also changed the identity of those who remained, creating a people without the experience of having lived with someone different from themselves.[26] On the occasion of the opening of the reconstructed Ferhadija Mosque in 2016, twenty-three years after it had been destroyed, journalist Gordana Knezević wrote how she had met a girl from Republika Srpska in Prague, a girl born after the war. The young woman asked: "Is it true that people of different ethnic groups lived together in Bosnia before the war?" For Knezević her question "was a disheartening reminder of the successes of wartime ethnic cleansing and the reality of Bosnia's postwar ethnic divides." Yet Knezević ended on an optimistic note: for her, the opening of Ferhadija was a sign of hope, one of those rare moments when she believed "that Karadzic and his like—who sowed the seeds of hate and violence— had not won the war."[27]

1 Muslim was a term of "nationality" (rather than religion) in Yugoslavia. Many Bosnian Muslims now choose to call themselves Bosniak as a national group; Bosniaks, Serbs, and Croats are now Bosnia and Herzegovina's three main "constituent people" enshrined in the country's constitution written into the terms of the Dayton Peace Agreement. Bosnia and Herzegovina's 1991 census showed that Muslims formed 43.47% of the population, Serbs 31.21%, Croats 17.38%, Yugoslavs 5.54%, and Others 2.4%.

2 Richard Caplan, *Europe and the Recognition of New States in Yugoslavia* (Cambridge, UK: Cambridge University Press, 2005), 123; Christopher Bennett, *Yugoslavia's Bloody Collapse: Causes, Course and Consequences* (New York: New York University Press, 1995), 185.

3 The Ljubović Mosque was almost totally destroyed in June 1992.

4 Herceg-Bosna ceased to exist on the signing of the Washington Agreement in March 1994, which ended the fighting and created the Federation of Bosnia and Herzegovina, the so-called Muslim-Croat Federation. During the conflict, however, the separatists received substantial support from Croatia and the Croatian Army. HVO (*Hrvatsko vijeće obrane*), or Croatian Defence Council, was the military force of Herceg-Bosna.

5 Few Bosnian Serb residents remained by that time and had either fled or been expelled.

6 Carol J. Williams, "Serbs Stay Their Ground on Muslim Lands," *Los Angeles Times*, 28 March 1993. http://articles.latimes.com/1993-03-28/news/mn-16253_1_bosnian-serb.

7 According to the figures of the Islamic Community of Bosnia and Herzegovina. See "Dan Džamija," 6 May 2015, http://www.islamskazajednica.ba/vijesti/aktuelno/22237-dan-dzamija. Of course, many religious structures with no architectural or historic value were also destroyed as part of the same processes.

8 András Riedlmayer, personal communications, 22 July 2013.

9 Robert Fisk, "Waging War on History," *The Independent*, 20 June 1994.

10 Bill Schiller, "Bosnian Artists Save Heritage Treasures," *The Toronto Star*, 15 May 1993, A10.

11 Mike Sula, "On Top of the World," *The Chicago Reader*, 4 March 1999, http://www.chicagoreader.com/chicago/on-top-of-the-world/Content?oid=898556.

12 The ICTY was based in The Hague. Its work ended in 2017 and its outstanding prosecutions are being carried out by UN-established International Residual Mechanism for Criminal Tribunals (MICT or "the Mechanism"). See http://www.icty.org/ for more information on its work.

13 Serge Brammertz, Kevin C. Hughes, Alison Kipp, William B. Tomljanovich, "Attacks Against Cultural Heritage as a Weapon of War: Prosecutions at the ICTY," *Journal of International Criminal Justice* 14(5) (1 December 2016): 1143–74.

14 Colin Kaiser, *Report on Destruction of Cultural Property 09-Jul-02*, ICTY Krajišnik Case No. IT-00-39, 4, available at http://icr.icty.org/.

15 The exception was the village of Baljvine. See Marija Arnautovic, "Bosnia: The Village Where Hate Never Triumphed," *Institute for War and Peace Reporting*, TRI Issue 642, 10 April 2010.

16 "Renaming Fashion," *Transitions Online*, 12 April 1993. See also Associated Press Report: "Serbs Would Change Name of Sarajevo," Associated Press [online], 10 November 1992; Dusko Doder, "Warring Bosnia factions practice linguistic cleansing of geographic names," *Baltimore Sun* [online], 4 May 1993.

17 *Krajišnik*, Case No. IT-00-39-T, Tupajić, 29 June 2005, 15431. Available at http://icr.icty.org/.

18 Helen Walasek, "Domains of Restoration," in *Bosnia and the Destruction of Cultural Heritage* (London: Routledge, 2015), 205–258.

19 See "Ramazanska akcija prikupljanja novca za obnovu džamije u Pridvorcima kod Trebinja," *Bošnjaci.Net*, 14 August 2010, http://bosnjaci.net/prilog.php?pid=3858.

20 See Azra Akšamija, "Our Mosques Are Us: Rewriting National History of Bosnia-Herzegovina through Religious Architecture," (PhD diss., Cambridge, MA, Massachusetts Institute of Technology, 2011). See also Richard Carlton, *Restoring and Preserving Cultural Property in Post-conflict Bosnia and Herzegovina*, Conference presentation at Chartered Institute for Archaeologists (CIfA) Conference, Newcastle, 20 April 2017.

21 Colin Kaiser was a former director of ICOMOS, a consultant for the Parliamentary Assembly of the Council of Europe consultant, and later the UNESCO representative in Bosnia and Herzegovina.

22 Apart from damage caused by Bosnian Serb shelling.

23 See Helen Walasek, *Bosnia and the Destruction of Cultural Heritage* (London: Routledge, 2015), 63–65.

24 Dragan Maksimović, "Bošnjaci i Srbi u selu Baljvine: Jedna duša, dvije nacije," *Deutsche Welle*, 21 October 2017.

25 Walasek, *Bosnia and the Destruction of Cultural Heritage*, 78–79.

26 *Blaškić* Case No. IT-1995-14-T, testimony, 16 July 1998, ICTY 10634. Available at http://icr.icty.org/.

27 Gordana Knezevic, "In Banja Luka, A Mosque Rises from the Rubble." *Radio Free Europe/Radio Liberty*, 5 May 2016, http://www.rferl.org/content/balkans-without-borders-banja-luka-mosque-reopened/27717823.html.

Mosque First: Coming to Terms with the Legacy of Abuse in Bosnia Through Heritage Restoration

Amra Hadžimuhamedović

Responding to the call of home through mosque reconstruction

This essay explores how Bosnian Muslim religious spaces—landscapes and architecture—both reflect and influence post-Dayton Bosnian life, that is, the country's new reality following the signing of the Dayton Peace Accord in December 1995, which put an end to more than three years of ethnic cleansing and systematic destruction.[1] Once the war against Bosnia had stopped, its victims sought the right to go back home.[2]

This was not just their right to physical return, but even more the right to restore the familiar images of their homescape. "Homescape" in this essay stands in for the necessarily complex explanation of a people's positive emotional attachment to their place of origin or living, which inevitably influences every human individual's identity, mentality, and perception of the world in a dialectic with its changing social environment. Multiple layers of the term can be very closely translated by the Bosnian word *zavičaj*.[3] Reconstructing the mosque in their place of return was considered a central symbol of such a reclaimed home, a testament to their place in the world, and their right to public expressions of identity.

The reconstruction of mosques in those areas of Bosnia where crimes of genocide and ethnic cleansing were carried out is a significant resource both for restorative justice and for restoring trust between war-divided groups and individuals. Here, I will look at some examples of how, even for those who are not themselves Muslims, reconstructing damaged mosques can be a meaningful part of the process of overcoming insecurity, desecration, and dispossession. These are often individuals who stood silently by, passively participating in the rituals of mosque destruction intended to cause a final break in the web of connections linking them and Muslims. The impossibility of fully alienating them from the exiled community has come to be symbolized through a variety of popular folk legends.

A Muslim survivor, Eso,[4] has testified to the fear, powerlessness, discomfort, and insecurity he witnessed among the Bosnian Orthodox[5] in the face of Serb crimes in the early days of the war, in 1992, in the southeastern Bosnian town of Foča, as well as of the wholesale involvement of all the government, military, and civil apparatuses of the occupation authorities:

> I was there when the Nazor mosque was burned down. The Serbs gathered in the laneway beforehand and watched. I don't remember noticing anyone going crazy or any singing. For the most part, there were concerned faces. There was a fire engine by the roadside, to ensure none of the houses caught fire. There was a lot of smoke coming out of the minaret, but it was the mosque that was burning.[6]

Thanks to the policies of "ethnic purity," these Orthodox Christians found themselves placed by automatic ethnic association on the side of those who had planned, executed, and overseen the destruction—those who had designated destruction of the mosque their "final solution."[7] For them, as individuals who themselves neither engaged in nor celebrated the act of destruction, reconstruction of the mosque offers, first and foremost, a chance at emancipation from being labelled with responsibility and guilt for the crime of ethnic cleansing. Moreover, reconstruction of the mosque represents a reestablishment for them too of a key reference point in the shredded mental map of their homescape.

They too have been deprived of their homescape by the ethnic cleansing of others. Their loss is contained in two key physical negative aspects of their life-landscape: emptiness and absence.

The areas of emptiness encroach upon *lived-space*,[8] standing in for places that were of central importance to the physical structure of the settlement. Such absences have a direct impact on our human senses and change the regime of space-determined-by-sensibilities to the point of rendering it unrecognizable. This is something that Ludwig Binswanger, a pioneer of existential-phenomenological psychology, long ago defined within psychopathology, terming it *gestimmter Raum,* which has been translated in various English publications as "tuned space,"[9] "thymic space,"[10] or "inclined space."[11]

Both emptiness and absence tend to destroy what Bosnians call *komšiluk,* or neighborhood-as-community, a major factor in Bosnian cultural landscapes. Cultural anthropologist Cornelia Sorabji, who has widely published on Bosnian tradition and social relations, uses a dual designation—physical structure and interpersonal relations within space—to show how *komšiluk* operates as a regulated system of inter-confessional relations by which tolerance is maintained through various forms of intangible and tangible heritage.[12]

The demand that mosques be reconstructed was thus conceived as a first step in coming to terms with the legacy of ethnic cleansing. Such reconstruction as has been possible has generally happened through either the erection of new buildings or the restoration of destroyed ones. Any return on this basis has faced challenges in the form of unresolved questions and mixed feelings over what life will bring and personal trauma regarding reconciliation and justice, and the dialectic of topophilia and topophobia—both of which serve to frame the longing for the homescape.

Filling the emptiness that appeared when the mosques were destroyed with familiar forms, content, users, and customs offers the hope of a return to stability, which is sorely needed by all those whose homescape has been stripped away in one way or the other. Neither return nor the loss of one's homescape, however, is a simple matter: it can be symbolic, physical, formal, and existential.

When I discuss symbolic return in this text, I am referring to the restoration of the homescape to those who never had to leave it—generally either Orthodox Christians or Catholics—but who nonetheless are subject to nostalgia and a sense of loss and placelessness when facing the emptiness and absences that haunt the ruins that surround them.

When I talk of physical return, I mean the process by which refugees and displaced persons themselves come back to their homes or what are now just their houses in a profoundly altered reality.

Formal return means restoring rights that the expelled were stripped of during the war—primarily, the right *to dwell,* as defined by the Otto Friedrich Bollnow, one of the founders of spatial and architectural anthropology.[13] First and foremost, it includes protection of life, integrity, and home, as well as the right to move, work, and express oneself in public space.

Existential return depends on formal return and comes about only after a reciprocal relationship has been established between the individual and the homescape, regardless of whether or not an actual physical return takes place. It is the active connection forged between the individual's complex existence and a given cultural landscape that constitutes the return. And this cultural landscape comes to ground their identity, just as the landscape grounds their spatial and temporal sense of the world. Existential return is not just a method of establishing stability in the world for people forced from their homes, of which they have intimate memories and abiding images, but also for those who were children or perhaps even unborn at the time they were deprived of their rights to a home, and who have therefore built up their own pictures of that lost homescape out of the stories and the testimony of the community they belong to. There are two highly relevant spatial determinants of the homescape in these images and stories—the mosque (or an equivalent building of focal or central significance) and the home. In this imaginary homescape, both the mosque and the home are unchanging in their form—only as such can they signify the unique relationship that determines their identity.

Existential return is a complex process, necessary both for individuals and communities, particularly in helping them carry the burden of their nostalgia. Nostalgia born out of the violent stripping-away of the right to a home/homeland/homescape is special. It is a more profound form of nostalgia, bound up with the meanings of the words sacrifice and injustice. The linear epistemological framework within which the past remains irrecoverable as a whole[14] has the consequence that any reconstruction of destroyed cultural heritage may always be questioned as founded on an impossible method of re-establishing something lost. It thus becomes insufficient for redemption from a state of nostalgic sacrifice or for any form of approach to justice. Existential return requires symbolic anchors within the homescape, so that reconstruction of precisely those forms of mosque that were destroyed at the time of the forcible separation of people from their homescape can come to represent a tangible manifestation of the hope that at least some parts of the nostalgic past are retrievable.

Upside down: deeply buried minarets

After the destruction, the remnants of the Bosnian mosques were transported away to be thrown into the beds of rivers and lakes and rubbish dumps or, in some cases, buried in the ground alongside the bodies of murdered Muslims. The more important the mosque in the mental maps of those who had lived around it, the more the process of destruction took on the shape of ritual.

In the summer of 2004, parts of the sixteenth-century Aladža Mosque in Foča were found during the excavation of a mass grave. The finely decorated and lavishly colored blocks loomed forth from the seven-meter-deep pit. The Aladža Mosque was built in 957 AH (1550/51 CE) and dynamited on 2 August 1992, St. Elijah's day, a festival celebrated by both Muslims and Orthodox Christians in Bosnia in parallel.[15] The destroyers followed the pattern of a "destruction liturgy" that exploited the sacred calendar and components of the biblical rituals of consecration by blood to achieve "purification" not only of the land but of all forms of collective memory after the Muslim population had all been killed or expelled.

Other cases of covering over human corpses with the rubble of destroyed mosques have been pointed out by András Riedlmayer in his evidence to hearings in the Karadžić case. He made particular mention of the cases of the Savska (Atik) mosque in Brčko and the mosque at Novoseoci, Sokolac.[16] Details of this co-burial procedure have also been reported by a witness from Brčko:

Figure 1. Fragments of Aladža Mosque (16th c.), which was destroyed on 2 August 1992, excavated from a mass grave in Foča on 25 August, 2004.

[…] Once the pit was full, the Serbs brought a frontend loader to the site and covered it with dirt, then with the ruins of the Brčko mosque, and another layer of dirt. The grave was then rolled flat and grass was planted. The witness estimated that there were 200 or more bodies at this location.[17]

Bosnian mass graves typically "contain many bodies, often jumbled up and incomplete, of the individuals who were murdered."[18] The buried fragments of the mosques were treated in the same way—the remains were thrown into several different places and so never complete. The horrific landscapes of these invisible, buried, scattered pieces of heritage and of people are now imprinted into Bosnian memoryscapes.

The Aladža Mosque is just one of more than a thousand Bosnian Mosques destroyed that summer in 1992 (Fig. 1). It was one of the best researched and documented sixteenth-century buildings in the Balkans.[19] The same social symbolism that places the mosque at the very center of human and personal histories also attached to its construction, use, destruction, and virtual existence post-destruction, both inside and outside Foča. Its high symbolic value in Bosnian memoryscapes is reflected in narratives and in the transmission of personal experiences. Each of these narratives is a myth-forming combination of reality and imagination. This is not least because the reality was so intense, unimaginable, and unbearable that it has made the surreal seem equally possible.

According to a surviving folk tradition about the building of the Aladža mosque, "God opened up the quarry and showed them where to look for the stone."[20] One morning after they had finished the masonry on the dome the builders had discovered, a little to the right of the mosque doors, they noticed a massive black stone "that angels had brought down to the place by their own hands," which then became a place of visitation and supplication by women.[21] Its founder had foreseen the mosque's destruction and ordered that a semiprecious stone be built into the *mimbar* to finance the future rebuilding of the mosque.[22] These and similar legends about the Aladža mosque lent it the aura of a blessed and powerful space. It was erected by Hasan Nazir, an influential official at the Sultan's court, as a thanks-offering for returning to the home he had left as a young man.[23]

According to Milidrag, an Orthodox who was fifteen years old when the mosque was destroyed and then lived in a house beside the mosque:

> As children, we enjoyed sitting with the old imam beside the *šadrvan* [fountain], listening to stories and eating fruit from the nearby house where he lived. I climbed the minaret as a child, up the steps, any number of times. With it, a part of our childhood went too.[24]

Although the Bosnian mosques were heterotopic places in urban structures, they also served to maintain openness and inclusiveness—children, women, and men spent time and prayed in a common place, without any form of separation device, separate entrances, or segregation. Their position and form in urban landscapes was not imposing. These ideals of the traditional Bosnian mosque have, however, been betrayed in post-Dayton Bosnian mosque construction practices.

The *adhan* filling the horror of the void

Those who survived the massacres in Foča continue to repeat a story that the call for prayer would echo from the vacant site of the destroyed Aladža mosque. This story reached Sarajevo immediately after the destruction. It was mentioned in a June 2018 interview with Salem Ćemo.[25] Most of my interlocutors from Foča have repeated the story in one way or another.[26]

Lutvo tells the story of a Bosnian Serb woman from Foča who visited him in his office in October 2000 and entrusted him with the secret that she had heard the *adhan* coming from the site of the Aladža mosque on three successive evenings, starting on 2 August 1992. She lived close to the site and, through her confusion and horror, noticed that her neighbors were also behaving as though they too had heard it.

Semira, who was seventeen when she escaped Foča in May 1992, tells the story that Serbs tried to destroy the Aladža mosque several times using machines. She describes how her older neighbor, Munira, would pass the site of the mosque every day on her way to the prison where her husband had been detained, and witnessed that every time they tried to begin their work of destruction, the *adhan* would reverberate off the walls and the machines would mysteriously stop.

Although I have not been able to locate an individual claiming direct personal experience of the *adhan,* the legend and the burial method both make clear the symbolic halo of the mosque in Bosnian cognitive maps and how it extends beyond the merely physical. The surreal sound of the *adhan* issuing from the void, from the ground that cannot hide its secrets; it reminds one of the popular Southern Slavic folk tale of the secret of Emperor Trojan's goat-ears, which, buried in the ground as a whisper, eventually found their way out as music from a flute made from a reed that grew in that very ground.[27] This could be interpreted as the fear that the ground itself would report on the mosques and Muslims interred within it.

No such legend of an *adhan* holding vigil in a homescape has been recorded elsewhere. The powerful *adhan,* with its intangible, non-destructive nature, has become a symbol not only of the Muslim community's presence but also of shared hope and a comforting intimation of survival.

Bearing in mind that no minaret on the territories controlled by the Serbs survived the war intact,[28] one can understand that existential return only becomes possible when "the sound of the evening muezzin drifts across the valley—once intended never to be heard here again."[29] There can be no doubt, the mosque—its visibility expressed through the minaret and its function expressed through the regularity of the *adhan*—is the first thing that must be put back in place when conflict resolution has been achieved and a return process starts.

While Annexes 7 and 8 of the Dayton Peace Accord provide a framework establishing the link between the return of people and the restoration of heritage, the decision-making process regarding methods, forms, and materials has been complex and always entailed risk for the sustainability of peace. The stake-holders have diverse interests and agendas: the Islamic Community, as an institution, holds the property rights; the local community of Muslims links the mosque with its homescape and the right to existential return; experts have views on authenticity and integrity; donors mirror their own diverse policies through their aid; the local authorities often continue to pursue ethnic cleansing policies and obstruct both the restoration of mosques and the return of the expelled; developers consider mosques non-productive and consequently bottom of the priority list in postwar recovery; and many more.

The following sets of dilemmas have been introduced into the process: whether to rebuild the mosque or look for the archaeological remains of older layers, which would then have to be presented; whether to rebuild the mosque or to memorialize the void; whether to rebuild the mosque or replace it with a new development; whether to restore the mosque as it was or to erect a new, modern, and possibly larger one. The only truly inclusive stakeholder has been the community of returnees. Donors, experts, owners, and authorities can fulfil their role in the peace-building process only if mosque rebuilding serves the returnees' need to come to terms with the legacy of past abuses and loss of *zavičaj.* The returnee community needs visible signs of their connection with the place to be restored, preferably by themselves.

Collecting the scattered and gathering the dispersed

The reconstruction of destroyed mosques in Bosnia begins with a gathering up of their remains or fragments. When the Croat military forces destroyed four mosques in the center of Stolac, a small historic town in the south of Bosnia, in August 1993, after all its Muslims had been expelled or confined to concentration camps, Emir managed to save himself by fleeing. He walked for days over the hills, covering the more than 150 kilometers between the various armies, en route to Sarajevo, which was then under siege. By some miracle he managed to get into the town from which everyone else was trying to escape. In his backpack, he was carrying a stone from the destroyed Čaršija mosque (1519) in Stolac. That day, Emir set down the stone on a desk in an office in the Government of the Republic of Bosnia and Herzegovina and bore his witness to the suffering of the people and the destruction of the mosques as inseparable phenomena. It was the day when the planning to restore the mosque began.

It would only be in August 2001, eight years after its destruction, that systematic collection of the remains of the Čaršija mosque actually became possible. Emir was one of those who dug it out, stone by stone, from the earth, pulled it from the riverbed, and from the garbage dumps. The area of the Čaršija mosque in the deserted town to which return was not allowed became an area for a divided and scattered people to gather and for the collection of discarded fragments. The Catholics of Stolac, those at least who had never fully acquiesced in the forcible separation from their neighbors, their homescape, and so their mosques by the automatic action of religious designation and ethnic affiliation, guided the returnees to the places where the mosque fragments had been disposed of. Those fragments were then, without fixing or hiding the traces of the violence committed against their original workmanship, built into the reconstructed mosque using the method of *anastolysis*. This was a work of cultural memory, in which the scars of destruction and suffering were turned into additional features bearing symbolic and historic value.

After the destruction of the Aladža mosque, there were no more Muslims in Foča. The explosion had scattered the bits and pieces of the mosque across the surrounding trees and into the riverbed of the Ćehotina. After the demolishers had transported its remnants from the site of the Aladža and dumped them in two locations—one part buried in the earth with the bodies of murdered Muslims, the other dumped in the river alongside—it would be children, Orthodox Christian children, who began the process of gathering up the remains. According to Milidrag:

> We, as children, used to gather up the stones from the Ćehotina. We kept them, the fragments, in a burnt-out house. There were some volunteers from Nikšić [a town in Montenegro], there, close by. And one morning, it all just disappeared. Just like they did.

Between this childish attempt to save at least the fragments of memory and a thorough official program of excavation, documentation, and storing of the stones of the Aladža, some thirteen years would pass. The process of re-establishing the mosque took twenty-seven years, from destruction to reconstruction.

Milidrag visits the site, every time he goes to Foča. The reconstructed Aladža mosque can never restore to him that part of his childhood he lost with its destruction, but it does fulfil the hope that his son can climb the steps of the newly erected minaret and share its courtyard with Muslim companions. Semira escaped Foča twenty-seven years ago. "I don't go there. The smell of blood hangs in the air." Asked whether she will go, once the Aladža mosque has been fully restored, she says "I would like to. There is something that draws me, still."

Nowhere that a mosque was not first reconstructed has seen any proper return of expelled Muslims. The reconstruction of the mosque surely has no power to fill the emptiness and absences in Milidrag's and Semira's homescape, but on 4 May 2019, on the day that the mosque is to be reopened, they will both find a common ground to return to, even if only in virtual fashion.

Teams of volunteers, students from all round Bosnia and young returnees, worked on gathering, identifying, and documenting the fragments of the Čaršija mosque in Stolac between 2001 and 2003. In 2002, students from Sarajevo University and from the University in Trieste worked on the same task at the Handanija mosque in Prusac. In the summer of 2005, students from Sarajevo and Banja Luka saved and documented the fragments in remains of the Aladža mosque and the Mehmed-paša Kukavica mosque in Foča. In 2006, the same approach was applied to restoration of the church of St Nicholas in the village of Trijebanj near Stolac, the Ferhadija mosque in Banja Luka, and the Church of Saints Peter and Paul at Ošanići near Stolac. Children from primary and secondary school have had classes in their cultural heritage and their universal and binding values in places where mosques and churches were once destroyed.

This process has, above all, secured the building of bridges between young people from war-torn communities. Teaching about conservation methods, transferring the secrets of traditional materials and techniques for working them from old masters to future experts, these processes have been just as important as the physical reconstruction of the destroyed heritage, or even the excitement of returnees empowered to set reconstruction of their cultural memory against acts of exclusion, ethnic cleansing, and humiliation.

It was from this spontaneously developed approach that the International Youth and Heritage Summer School in Stolac grew. It is one of the most important projects for the integration of heritage into the process of promoting knowledge and cultural values as a basis for peace. More than a thousand young people from all round the world have participated in the International Youth and Heritage Summer Schools, engaging in community service, intercultural dialogue, and the revival of traditional crafts, working on restoration projects on vernacular buildings destroyed during the war and on restoring traditional carpets, books, pictures, as well as learning about traditional knowledge and customs. This has resulted in the establishment of a peace network based upon universal values and universal responsibilities for preserving those values (Fig. 2).

The methodological approach established through reconstruction of the Čaršija mosque in Stolac has become a template incorporated into all the decisions of the Commission for the Preservation of National Monuments of Bosnia and Herzegovina and most projects to reconstruct Bosnian heritage.

Figure 2. Encounter of students of the International Summer School Youth and Heritage at the site of reconstructed Ćuprijska Mosque in Stolac.

It is set out in a statement of principle included in every decision passed for the protection of war-damaged or destroyed Bosnian cultural heritage.

Reconstruction, as a method for re-establishing damaged or destroyed built heritage in the same form and place and from the same or equivalent materials, with maximum possible use of original remains, has, since the beginning of the twenty-first century, increasingly been the subject of expert debate. The claim is not uncommonly put forward that such reconstruction cannot establish its legitimacy on the basis of any internationally accepted doctrine, a claim often supported by inappropriate citation of Article 15 of the Venice Charter, which rules out reconstruction a priori in the case of archaeological excavations. In Bosnia, however, the application of the Venice Charter in projects dealing with the postwar protection of heritage is based upon the position that the voids and ruins created by contemporary wartime destructive activity are not excavations, but "the sites and remains of destroyed monuments." Destroyed monuments can be re-established on the basis of Article 9 of the Venice Charter, so long as the necessary documentation exists as to their previous condition and reliance on speculative guesswork is avoided by applying highly specialized procedures. Dozens of the mosques destroyed during the war against Bosnia have thus been reconstructed in accordance with their last known incarnation (Fig. 3).

Figure 3. Four reconstructed Mosques in Stolac serve as a common ground for students of the International Summer School Youth and Heritage while they establish bridges of dialogue and knowledge-based mutual respect.

The nearly two decades since the Bosnian reconstruction strategy was established have seen new waves of the destruction of cultural heritage as a target of warfare worldwide, in Syria, Iraq, Yemen, Libya, Mali, and other places. Reconstruction has therefore become a keyword in contemporary international doctrine and practice, and the Bosnian experience has been a significant and inevitable touchstone guiding international rules.

Conclusion

The reconstruction of Bosnian mosques was a necessary first step after the war in coming to terms with the legacy of ethnic cleansing. Reconstruction has only been possible by erecting new buildings or restoring destroyed ones. The Islamic Community in Bosnia and Herzegovina reported in April 2018 that 1,175 mosques had been restored, while 841 new religious buildings had been constructed.[30]

New religious buildings assume the role of filling out the emptiness. This emptiness was caused not just by the massive destruction of mosques by Serb and Croat military and paramilitary forces between 1992 and 1996, but also by the catastrophic events that devastated the lives of individuals and communities. While the new mosques (built post-1995) are an expression of social confusion and bewilderment and generate constant tension, competition, and rivalry, the alternative of restoring traditional knowledge of the universal sacred language of symbols, whether read in the forms of nature or inscribed as implicit meaning in the forms of traditional Bosnian Muslim architecture, has offered a landscape of reconciliation and of recovery from past abuses.

The healing power of the process of restoring the Bosnian mosques is based on the notion of heritage in Bosnian Muslim society. The Bosnian Muslim reception of their own heritage has been traditionally embodied in places, their names, traditions, and memories linked with their history. The form and substance of Bosnian mosques has been perpetuated through a process of constant gradual adaptation and development. These historically imperceptible changes have kept heritage sites alive and sustained collective memory. The trauma in Bosnian townscapes caused by war passed beyond the limits of those towns' ability to assimilate change, at least until major significant features were restored.

The restoration of Bosnian mosques, based upon respect for the authenticity of their location, form, and position in urban physical structure, has revived a major paradigm of historic Bosnian landscapes—the dialectic of unity and diversities as an indispensable ideal of Bosnian existence.

1   "Ethnic cleansing" has been often contested as a euphemism for severe crimes against humankind. Hagan and Haugh tell us that this euphemistic perception of "ethnic cleansing" as a social healing act can be traced to "the burning tradition" in Balkans. See John Hagan and Todd J. Haugh, "Ethnic Cleansing as Euphemism, Metaphor, Criminology and Law," Chicago-Kent College of Law, January 2011, http://scholarship.kentlaw.iit.edu/fac_schol/297.
The definition given by Bassiouni and the group of experts in a UN document in 1994, based on their insight into crimes in Bosnia, is considered a step away from euphemism toward a metaphor of incrimination: "… a purposeful policy designed by one ethnic or religious group to remove by violent and terror-inspiring means the civilian population of another ethnic or religious group from certain geographic areas." See the *Final Report of the Commission of Experts Established Pursuant to Security Council Resolution 780* (1992), United Nations, 1994.
The definition has been more recently widened in the academic discourse on ethnic cleansing linked with the Bosnian case to include the removal of all traces bearing witness to the existence of a group, as stated in the International Tribunal for the Prosecution of Persons Responsible for Serious Violations of International Humanitarian Law Committed in the Territory of Former Yugoslavia since 1991's judgement on Radoslav Krstić, "… one may also conceive of destroying a group through purposeful eradication of its culture and identity resulting in the eventual extinction of the group…" Case No. IT-98-33-T, Prosecutor v. Radislav Krstić, 2 August 2001, http://www.icty.org/x/cases/krstic/tjug/en/krs-tj010802e.pdf.

2   The word "Bosnia," as the historical name of a land whose administrative name today is *Bosna i Hercegovina* (Bosnia and Herzegovina), will be used in this text, as will adjectives that derive from it. The name Bosnia and Herzegovina will be used only in cases when it forms part of a formal title of an institution, a legal act, or other kind of document.

3   On *zavičaj* see Hariz Halilovich, *Places of Pain: Forced Displacement, Popular Memory and Trans-local Identities in Bosnian War-torn Communities* (Oxford, New York: Berghahn Books, 2013).

4   The names of some of the interlocutors have been changed in the text, given the continued risk involved in speaking out, both for themselves and their families, except in cases where the interlocutors themselves preferred for their names to be used. The conversation on the destruction of the Foča mosque conducted with a Muslim from the town, who is referred to pseudonymously in the text as Eso, was possible thanks to Kenan Sarač, 1 October 2018.

5   The Orthodox (*pravoslavni* in Bosnian) is used to denote the Eastern-Orthodox Christians in Bosnia who belong to the Serbian Orthodox Church.

6   The Nazor mosque is mentioned, as is the sixteenth-century mosque of the Defterdar Memišahbey. It was one of the seventeen mosques in Foča. It was destroyed in the summer of 1992. The interview makes clear that destruction of the mosque was organized by the Serbian military and that all the municipal wartime structures were involved. The fire brigade was instructed not to put out the fire while the mosque was burning, but to ensure that it consumed only the target of ethnic cleansing.

7   The "Final Solution" (*Endlösung* in German) is a phrase whose semantics are derived from a memorandum dated 31 July 1941, in which Hermann Goering used it in instructing a chief of the SS security service on how to deal with "the Jewish question." The strategy of Serb nationalistic ideologists to deal with the "Muslim Question" in Bosnia, implemented by the Serb armed forces, had all the characteristics of coming to a "final solution," leaving no Muslims and few traces of their existence in the territories planned to become the part of the new Greater Serbia. See "Goering orders Heydrich to prepare for the Final Solution," A&E Television Networks, first published 5 November 2009, last updated 20 February 2019, https://www.history.com/this-day-in-history/goering-orders-heydrich-to-prepare-for-the-final-solution.

8   The concept of lived-space is borrowed here from the German philosopher Otto Friedrich Bollnow, who argues that humans are determined by space as much as by time. The lived-space is expressed through reciprocal relation between humans—their origin, culture, tradition, history, feelings—and physical space. These relations are constituted through orientation, foci, and distances, for instance, where home and mosque determine focal points and provide a known structure of place to those who consider it their homescape. See Otto Friedrich Bollnow, "Lived-Space," *Philosophy Today* 5 (1961): 31–39.

9   Filip Mattens, "From the Origin of Spatiality to a Variety of Spaces," in *The Oxford Handbook of the History of Phenomenology*, ed. Dan Zahavi (Oxford: Oxford University Press, 2018), 558–79.

10 Stefano Besoli, "On the Emergence of Thymic Space in Ludwig Binswanger," in *The changing faces of space*, eds. Maria Teresa Catena and Felice Masi (Berlin: Springer, 2018), 35–57.

11 Bollnow, "Lived-Space."

12 The word *komšiluk* designates a cultural element of Bosnian identity. In English, it may be translated, albeit with insufficient semantic depth or reach, as "neighborliness" and/or "neighbor-hood." See Cornelia Sorabji, "Neighborhoods Revisited: Tolerance, Commitment and Komšiluk in Sarajevo," in *On the Margins of Religion*, eds. Francis Pine and João de Pina-Cabral (Oxford: Berghahn Books, 2008), 97–112.

13 Bollnow, "Lived-Space."

14 James Phillips, "Distance, Absence, and Nostalgia," in *Descriptions*, eds. Don Ihde and Hugh J. Silverman (Albany, New York: SUNY Press, 1985), 64–76.

15 Safet HadžiMuhamedović, "Sincretic Debris: From Shared Bosnian Saints to the ICTY Courtroom," *Ethnoscripts* 20(1) (2018): 79–109.

16 András J. Riedlmayer, "Destruction of Cultural Heritage in Bosnia and Herzegovina, 1992-1996: A Post-War Survey Of Selected Municipalities. Expert Report commissioned by the International Criminal Tribunal for the Former Yugoslavia," ARCHnet (website), Aga Khan Trust for Culture and the Aga Khan Documentation Center, accessed 28 September, 2018, https://archnet.org/publications/3481. See also Mort Rosenblaum, "41 Muslims Finally Buried in Bosnia," *AP News*, 5 November, 2000, accessed 23 September 2018, https://www.apnews.com/82f5d4b27610f697a14dfcbb05fab936.

17 Mahmoud Cherif Bassiouni, "Final Report of the UN Commission of Experts established pursuant to SC Res. 780 (1992), under the direction of M. Cherif Bassiouni," 1994, accessed 21 September 2018, http://www.siracusainstitute.org/portal/wp-content/uploads/2017/01/Final-report-of-the-Commission-of-Experts-on-former-Yugoslavia-1993-94.pdf.

18 Mark Skinner, Djordje Alempijević, and Marija Đuric-Srejić, "Guidelines for International Forensic Bio-archaeology Monitors of Mass Grave Exhumations," *Forensic Science International* 134(2/3) (2003): 81–89.

19 See for example Andrej Andrejević, *Алаџа џамија у Фочи* (Belgrade: Institut za Istoriju Umetnosti Filozofskog fakulteta, 1972); Mehmed Mujezinović, "Autogram Evlije Čelebije u trijemu džamije Aladže u Foči," *Naše starine*, no. 4 (Sarajevo: Zemaljski zavod za zaštitu spomenika kulture i prirodnih rijetkosti N.R. Bosne i Hercegovine, 1957), 291–93; Zdravko Kajmaković, "Konzervatorsko-restauratorski radovi na ornamentima Aladža džamije u Foči," *Naše starine*, no. 7 and 8 (Sarajevo: Zavod za zaštitu spomenika kulture S. R. Bosne i Hercegovine, 1960), 113–28; Alma Simić, *Aladža džamija u Foči, zaštita i obnova u kontekstu urbane jezgre, master thesis* (Zagreb: Sveučilište u Zagrebu, Arhitektonski fakultet, Poslijediplomski znanstveni studij Graditeljsko naslijeđe, 2003).

20 Miron Zarzycki, Ewald Arndt, and Đorđe Stratimirović, "Aladža-džamija u Foči," *Glasnik Zemaljskog muzeja u Bosni i Hercegovini*, no. 2 (Sarajevo: Zemaljski muzej Bosne i Hercegovine, 1891), 103–15, 107.

21 Ibid., 110.

22 Ibid.

23 Ibid., 106.

24 Milidrag Davidović insisted his name be used in the text. Conversations with him were conducted on several occasions during the reconstruction of the mosque.

25 "Aladža džamija u Foči: I kada je bila srušena, iz njenog pravca se razlijegao ezan," Akos.ba (website), 13 June 2018, accessed 11 November, 2018, https://akos.ba/Aladža-dzamiji-u-foci-i-kada-je-bila-srusena-iz-njenog-pravca-se-razlijegao-ezan/.

26 Božo Vrećo, archeologist and singer from Foča; Kenan Sarač, writer from Foča; Lutvo Šukalo, postwar Muslim president of the Municipality Council in Foča; Semira (pseudonim), a displaced person from Foča who lives in Sarajevo.

27 "The Goat's Ears of the Emperor Trojan," in *The Violet Fairy Book*, ed. Andrew Lang [1901], Gutenberg EBook, last updated 16 December 2016, http://www.gutenberg.org/files/641/641-0.txt.

28 See "Hearing - Prosecution Case in chief - Riedlmayer, Andras Expert witness - destruction of cultural heritage in BiH," UN International Criminal Tribunal for the Former Yugoslavia (website), 9 December 2011, accessed 5 September 2018, http://www.icty.org/en/content/karadzic-trial-hearing-list.

29 Ed Vulliamy, "Bringing up the bodies in Bosnia," *The Guardian*, 6 December 2016, accessed 22 September 2018, https://www.theguardian.com/world/2016/dec/06/bringing-up-the-bodies-bosnia.

30 Mirsad Kalajdžić, head of the Department for standardization and evidence in Riyasat of the Islamic Community in Bosnia and Herzegovina claims the difference between mosque (*džamija*) and masjid (*mesdžid*), explaining that the word masjid is used by the Islamic Community in Bosnia only for a religious place that does not have a minaret. This explanation, that has neither scientific nor architectural or linguistic justification has been used by many researchers and it has nested as a sort of conventional categorization. That is why the Islamic Community in Bosnia and Herzegovina gives separate figures for destroyed mosques and masjids. The figure given in this essay comprises all Muslim places for prayer, and is based on the statistics of the Islamic Community in Bosnia and Herzegovina. See "Najavljen početak manifestacije „Dani džamija i džemata"." Islamska zajednica u BiH (website), 19 April 2018, accessed 12 December 2018, http://www.islamskazajednica.ba/vijesti/aktuelno/26583-najavljen-pocetak-manifestacije-dani-dzamija-i-dzemata.

While some of the ideas presented here arose out of personal experiences gained through my work at the Commission to Preserve National Monuments of Bosnia and Herzegovina from 2001 to 2016, they do not necessarily reflect the views of the Commission. The research was conducted in the places where mosques had been destroyed, and where I participated in their reconstruction process. My interlocutors were the persons that I encountered during the site works.

III. Dissonance

Superkilen (2012)

Architects: **BIG-Bjarke Ingels Group, Superflex, Topotek 1**
Location: **Copenhagen, Denmark**

Recipient of the Aga Khan Award for Architecture in 2016

A public space promoting integration across lines of ethnicity, religion, and culture. A meeting place for residents of Denmark's most ethnically diverse neighborhood and an attraction for the rest of the city, this project was approached as a giant exhibition of global urban best practice. In the spring of 2006 the street outside the architects' Copenhagen office erupted in vandalism and violence. Having just gone through the design of a Danish mosque in downtown Copenhagen, BIG chose to focus on those initiatives and activities in urban spaces that work as promoters for integration across ethnicity, religion, culture, and languages. Taking their point of departure as Superkilen's location in the heart of outer Nørrebro district, the architects decided they would approach the project as an exercise in extreme public participation. Rather than a public outreach process geared towards the lowest common denominator or a politically correct post rationalization of preconceived ideas navigated around any potential public resistance, BIG proposed public participation as the driving force of the design. An extensive public consultation process garnered suggestions for objects representing the over sixty nationalities present locally to be placed in the area. The 750-metre-long scheme comprises three main zones: a red square for sports; a green park as a grassy children's playground; and a black market as a food market and picnic area.

— AKAA jury citation

In the fall of 2018, anthropologist Tina Gudrun Jensen and photographer Jesper Lambaek met with a number of Copenhagen residents to document their perspectives on Superkilen park. Jensen selected the interviewees based on their professional expertise, first-hand user experience, or personal relationship to the project. The following piece introduces excerpts from these conversations, along with photographs taken during these encounters.

METTE,
architect and resident of Nørrebro, Copenhagen

When choosing a place to live, I always consider infrastructure and flow. Superkilen spans from outer *Østerbro* through Nørrebro towards Frederiksberg, which is great. The peculiarity is that I can accidentally bump into my son, who lives up in nearby Nordvest, when riding my bike through Superkilen on a Tuesday morning. Then, the town seems smaller with all these intersections. And so, I can take a walk, go out of Kilen toward Frederiksberg, and pick up my friends along the way or whatever, going back and forth.

I know the project idea behind the Superkilen, and for me this is a kind of no man's land, which extends from outer *Østerbro* up to expensive Frederiksberg, which lies on the shore like a huge artificial snake changing colors from black to red to green. It was a great idea to bring the neighborhoods together like that and create the common shared place here. It is a no man's land because different cultures cross here, and it has a lot of free space within. And there is no doubt about the importance of such a place. Of course, it is also worth keeping in mind that it's no easy thing: creating and maintaining a place like this requires deliberate public planning and an enormous amount of money. And it's not just a matter of old coatings and exposures that have to be removed along the way; it's also a matter of the local community's involvement. All these things hanging around, all these strange artifacts and playground frames—they all contribute to the involvement of people who say, "It would be cool to have a playground like I used to have in Yemen," or something like that. There are about a hundred similar artifacts around, some of which they've probably assembled themselves, together with other people.

So for me, the story is really just about the daily joy of seeing democracy that succeeds, about a country succeeding in producing synergistic forces, so to say. Living here, I'm reminded every day that it's good when a society prioritizes this kind of thing; it gives hope: hope for cohesion, hope that we're a community.

MOHAMMAD,
born in Copenhagen and imam at the Imam Ali mosque in Nørrebro

Now, when I work as an imam here in Nørrebro, I not only walk past Superkilen, but we actually frequently sit together here, having some conversations with the mosque community members, and, if we're going for a walk, we usually end up either in the red square or in the black market area. For instance, we could be studying here in the mosque together, or listening to a lecture, or going out together, and then we would either buy some food and sit down at Superkilen, or buy an ice cream, or we would go for a walk and then sit there, and afterwards we would go home. I also know that a lot of people from the mosque take their children to the playground in the black market area, to this slide.

This very place, Superkilen, is a great example of diversity, it represents the different citizens in Nørrebro. It has a different atmosphere; it is a distinct part of Copenhagen that stands out a little. And I think this diversity is the draw. It also provides opportunities for socializing: after all, it's an open space, so there are benches, there are places to sit, and so on. The space itself welcomes you to socialize with other people. Now, I have traveled around many Middle Eastern countries, and I can tell you that these benches that swing, I think they are from Iraq, if I am not mistaken. They bring back memories when you walk by, because you've seen them in many other parts of the world, you know. And then you come to Copenhagen and you think, hey, that was the bench that we saw somewhere in Baghdad, for example. And that's so nice. I think it also arouses a certain kind of feeling that makes people feel welcomed, as they see something that makes them feel represented. I know it's just a bench, and you think well, that's part of something that represents me, but it's also a symbol, a part of a huge diversity, which I actually think is very beautiful and inspiring.

Besides being a really, really good place, the fact is that it reflects Nørrebro itself as a whole; its inherent diversity. And this diversity is most distinctive here, in Superkilen. Here you really get the feeling of, "Okay, that's Nørrebro, and that's what this place is known for." And that's what Superkilen actually underlines for us. It is a sculpture of Nørrebro as a whole, so to say.

JULIE,
studies anthropology at the University of Copenhagen and lives next to Superkilen

In my daily life, Superkilen is a sort of major artery, as I ride my bike through it every day, one way or another. I watch what is going on while biking; there are always people there and something is always going on. I visit red square probably the most frequently, because it is a kind of meeting place for me and my friends. We almost always say, let's meet in the red square, and then we meet at that elevated spot in the middle, and we sit there, and we talk about life and smoke cigarettes and drink beer and watch skaters and people swinging and whatever else is going on. There's always life there, and it's just such a homey place to be, somehow. And, of course, since I live right next to it, it is to a greater extent my own local environment. I guess this also has something to do with the space being beautiful—there is something about the red color and it feels kind of cool to hang out there. Plus, the combination of people there. I like that there are skaters and families with children, and all kinds of ethnicities being together; so the whole place feels very Nørrebro-like. For me, it's like the essence of living in Nørrebro, hanging out on the red square, and I really feel like I'm a Nørrebrogner (laughing a little).

I have a friend Laura, who had been in the United States for a year, and then she came home, and we agreed to meet in the red square. It was just so dramatic—I had been waiting for her on that elevated spot, and then she came and I met her, and we were crying standing and hugging for several minutes in the middle of the square in the midst of the crowd. We eventually sat down on that spot, and drank some beer, and told each other what had happened during that year we hadn't seen each other, and just sat for hours and felt reunited as friends after having been apart for a long time. So, that red square was just the rendezvous place. And that was a wonderful experience indeed, seeing my friend again. Things like that make it even more my own place where I belong, where I have so much affection and so many personal experiences.

UZMA,
social activist whose work deals with coexistence and citizenship in Nørrebro. Lives close to Superkilen.

I work a lot with place-based identity, with some residents who live close to Superkilen, up the Super-kilen, where the young people identified themselves particularly by the way they live; after all, Nørre-bro is divided into zones based on gang areas. When we really get under the radar, many young people will not go to different neighborhoods, because they are associated with the place they live. So if children and young people go from one end of Nørrebro to the other, from inner Nørrebro to outer Nørrebro, they risk getting bullied or beaten up because they are associated with certain groups belonging to certain parts of Nørrebro. That's why, in order to do something serious, and, at the same time, to expand my thinking, I ran a project called "I'm Nørrebro." I couldn't get the young people to say, "I'm Danish" or "I'm Denmark," but there was no problem with "I'm Nørrebro." For that reason, I used Superkilen as a starting point to make an audio walk, which was GPS-controlled, where the app's GPS points were positioned in Superkilen. They started with playing chess down by the black market, because there are tables made with a chess board, or in the red square, where we recorded a conver-sation about Muay Thai boxing, because there is a boxing ring there. One of the players had come from out of the area. You can walk through Superkilen and hear the different stories. For example, a mother who has chosen to live differently, that is, to build a family, but not in the way she was brought up. Or you meet the local police officer further down, and he tells you about the local roots with such great love. So, in order to promote this local knowledge, we actually involved Superkilen in that way. I too have a great deal of my own good experiences with Superkilen.

So, in that sense, this place, the physical place, merges with the awareness of belonging, and to me, it's a lot about making those worlds meet: it's not just a place for going out, but also a place for opening up. It is not about physically meeting this mother who has chosen a different life style, another form of family, or that cop, it's rather about finding where our realities exist in parallel, and having this awareness that we are all quite different, that this place is very diverse, but we live here together, and we own it, and share it, too. We don't necessarily have to sit in the same living room drinking coffee together to be sympathetic to each other; we can use our imagination and our empathy or sympathy to put ourselves in each other's shoes, and this is what I do in my work all the time.

RIKKE,
urban sociologist specialized in the spatiality of Superkilen.

I live next to Superkilen, close to the black market. I haven't really used Superkilen for many years, but it has always seemed quite exciting to me. And at some point, when I started my studies in urban sociology, I began to realize more and more how unique this urban space actually is. To some extent, it is an urban space where some objects were explicitly taken from different cultures and integrated into an urban space, based on an idea that this will result in some form of integration of the people living here. At the same time, they all have their own specific effects, as they represent all the countries that the residents of Nørrebro come from; I thought it was fascinating from the beginning and so I took a closer look. My thesis in urban sociology was focused on human interaction in the black market section. I've been out doing a lot of fieldwork there. I think I was out doing seventy-two field observations and ten interviews with twenty-five different people over the summer of 2017, which just happened to be the wettest summer ever (laughs a little). And you might at first think that because it was raining all the time, there wouldn't be many people using the space. They wouldn't be there when it was raining cats and dogs, but as soon as it cleared up there were actually a lot of people out there.

What I found out in doing my thesis is that the layout of the black market, both spatially (that is, how its elements interact in the space), plus the integration of objects and the fact that these objects come from the different countries, has a positive impact on the people who come there. I remember talking to three young girls in hijabs who thought it was so cool that there were all these objects. When I asked them why they had chosen this particular place, they were like, "Well, we had just bought a hot dog, and then we thought that this Danish hot dog and multicultural Nørrebro and this place just seemed like an awesome combo." And I actually thought it was rather nice that they managed to so succinctly express what the place was about, and that they somehow felt such a connection with, maybe not so directly, the other people who come to the place; it's not because they sit and talk to them, but in being there they feel part of something bigger. I thought that was really interesting and awesome, yeah.

When I did my fieldwork, I was amazed at how many people there were who do not live near the square, but still actually decided, perhaps not to visit it directly, but to walk through it or walk by and then just stop, buy a cup of coffee, at least, and linger a little while. And then there's the whole other thing with the parents and kids at Superkilen. Today, I am also working on play, and that's something I've observed when I was writing my thesis, that is, how important playgrounds are for people to meet. There must be some sort of triangulation if people are to meet directly, that is to say, have a direct interaction. They simply need something to meet about, and that may be different things, like two dogs meeting on the street, or people sitting side by side on the bus, or "Can I borrow your newspaper?" But the most direct interactions I observed at Superkilen was kids playing with each other—that is, how two kids in the playground would start playing together, and then the parents would start talking to each other. That's where the longest interactions take place and where there are the most interactions. I thought it was pretty crazy how playgrounds could work like that.

SOHEIL,
architect specialized in multicultural design. Born in Iran, lives and works in Copenhagen

When I came to Denmark and first visited Superkilen, I saw the writing in my language on one of the benches, saying: "If you want to have a good city you have to take care of it." A really positive attraction for people, especially me, is this bench, and also the bench at the end of Superkilen, designed with ceramics with that pattern that somehow reminds me of home. I came to this country as an immigrant and find it comforting to see some of elements, some reference points, of my home country. One element is a fountain in the middle of Superkilen. It's not so similar, but still it reminds me of my country. The ceramic material and geometry they used for the fountain is my point of reference—the fountain, it's water, is basically the element of origin of Islamic architecture, which I recognize in some of the furniture and their features when passing through Superkilen. I feel some sympathy and understanding and respect from designers toward my identity, which I appreciate. I connect to these pieces. If you go to Superkilen you can see lots of foreigners who come to Denmark; they are sitting there, all surrounding these objects. Or maybe they don't think about it, and they unconsciously gravitate to these spots.

Most Islamic countries have some similarities in design: they share elements, but of course these elements inspire architects in different ways. Still, they all use the geometry of the fountain or water or writing, and because of that, I can identify myself with some of the Superkilen objects. These elements represent a kind of meeting place for people from a design perspective. And this originates in the Mosque. Basically, in all Muslim countries they have this similar place, where people wash their hands and go to pray. In modern architectural form, the space is open, with an open design, and the water cools the space in the hot season. So this kind of basic cultural connection to the element of water is what reminds the people of home, in a way, when they are sitting here in faraway Copenhagen. Particularly because they might feel that this is lacking in Denmark, where design-wise "less is more." The Scandinavian design is minimalistic, which is amazing in its own way, but many people living here come from countries where they appreciate a different element of design. And this stuff reminds them of the country they came from, no matter how long they have been in a country like Denmark. Me, personally, I feel that I'm Iranian. I'm married to a Dane, but still I feel Iranian and I am proud of that; and I'm proud to be married to a Dane as well. But I see a lot of people here who have come from war, and many of them can't go back to their country, so some element of home can help them to feel while they are really missing their country that perhaps "this country is okay." I think that spaces like Superkilen can unconsciously help people integrate, in effect, because when they encounter design that respects them in such a way, they can feel that there is sympathy and appreciation for them here. And maybe they can also contribute to the system. There is also good potential here for tourists and also for Danes to see design and architecture from other countries.

Rhetoric of Segregation, Everyday Forms of Coexistence: Diverging Visions of Diversity and Coexistence in Denmark

Tina Gudrun Jensen

The last four decades of immigration to Denmark has resulted in public debates on ethnic and cultural diversity as a challenge to the country's social cohesion and welfare. These debates problematize the presence and coexistence of migrants and migrant culture in urban spaces, such as squares and mosques. The contrast between how diversity and coexistence is played out in public debate and everyday life points to the inherent complexities, contradictions, and frictions of coexistence. These complexities derive from a xenophobic turn triggered by the moral panic surrounding immigration in public debates, on the one hand, and a conviviality of everyday life, on the other. Coexistence is thus simultaneously mediated by forms of everyday racism and by co-presence involving sentiments of togetherness.[1] This contrast also manifests in, on the one hand, multiculturalism as a political concern that focuses on negative aspects of diversity, and, on the other, the "everyday multiculturalism" constituted by practices of routine and unreflective forms of encounters and interactions.[2]

Different contexts may envision urban diversity and coexistence in various ways, as a scenario for either assimilation, integration, separation, or mixity.[3] For example, national and local authorities may envision diversity and coexistence in contrasting ways.[4] Still, they rarely capture the cultural complexities of everyday life: the multiple daily forms of urban relation-making often refute national rhetoric regarding migrants' segregation. Issues of diversity and coexistence are dealt with in contrasting ways in the political arena and in local everyday life.[5] Different representations of space thus include perceived, conceived, and lived spaces[6] that reflect different societal macro and micro levels and perspectives. Visions of urban diversity and coexistence thus involve different levels and scales, such as public debate, national and local policies, and the lived experiences of local everyday life.

Drawing on studies of Danish local and national policies on migration and urban planning and ethnographic fieldwork in a social housing complex in Copenhagen,[7] this essay explores how diversity and coexistence are envisioned and practiced in both general public debate, national and local political life, and in lived spaces of everyday life. I argue that the different representations of space constitute contrasting perceptions and practices of diversity and coexistence. While public debates and national policies on migration and social housing perceive diversity as problematic to social cohesion and coexistence, everyday life in social housing complexes constitute lived spaces of inter-ethnic coexistence.

Danish public debate on migration and diversity

During the last four centuries, Denmark, a small Scandinavian country of about 5.7 million inhabitants, has developed into an increasingly closed nationalistic and culturally homogenous society with restrictive immigration policies.[8] The development of the Danish welfare state focusing on common public sector schemes has contributed to widespread perceptions of Danish civil culture as based on equality as an "imagined sameness" that tends to suppress differences.[9] Ethnic diversity—particularly in the form of migrants—is often seen as a challenge to welfare state and national cultural identity in Danish public debate. For example, Danish politicians broadly seem to agree that, despite the presence of migrants, Denmark is not a multicultural society. Yet today, migrants constitute about twelve percent of the population in Denmark, and a majority come from non-Western countries such as Pakistan, Turkey, Iran, Iraq, Lebanon, and Somalia. Migrants have primarily settled in the urbanized parts of Denmark, and many live in public social housing projects, residences based on modernistic architecture constructed in the 1960s and 1970s. Their settlement in social housing complexes is a matter of constant political concern.

With the increasing number of migrants and descendants settling permanently in the country during the 1990s, "integration" became a highly problematized issue in public debate, and consequently a declared objective in Danish policy aimed at "absorbing" migrants into Danish society.[10] Hence, the concept of integration de facto means assimilation to Danish cultural norms and values, meaning that certain cultural norms and values ("the Danish") are seen to be acceptable and desirable, while others ("the non-Danish") are not. Consequently, integration tends to be a paradoxical concept that in theory has positive inclusive connotations, but in practice has exclusionist effects as the notion of integration relies on heavy cultural models that dichotomize relationships between an "us" ("the Danes") and a "them" ("the migrants").[11] One prevalent expression for the relationship between "us" and "them" is the distinction between "Danes" and "Muslims," in which the category of Muslim include all migrants and has become a signifier for people who are not considered Danish, and thus "othered" in Danish society.

Today, Denmark is one of the highest-ranking countries in terms of racial and religious discrimination (see e.g., http://www.mipex.eu/anti-discrimination). The European Commission against Racism and Intolerance has pointed several times to a general climate of intolerance and discrimination against ethnic minorities—and in particular Muslim minorities—in Denmark.[12] Danes' attitudes toward Islam are interrelated with attitudes to immigration as a threat to national peculiarity, which is related to xenophobia; Islam has become a point of condensation for the aversion to strangers.[13] Vandalism and hate crimes committed by nationalistic extremist groups against Muslim buildings such as mosques and graveyards are recurrent phenomena that mark the perception of Muslim spaces as unwanted.

As the next section describes, national policies on migration and urban planning further emphasize diversity as an obstacle to national and social cohesion.

"Holes on the Danish map"

Planning pluralism in Denmark (as well as other contexts) is related to issues of whether "foreign" culture should be reflected in Danish architecture. While "exotic" culture has historically been implemented in Danish architectural work and built environment (e.g., the renowned amusement park of Tivoli), during the last decades of increased immigration, the design of public spaces has become increasingly problematic. The construction of mosques, as visible and audible symbols of "Muslimness," for example, is a highly contested issue in Denmark and other European countries.[14] In Denmark, which insists on a division between religion and state, mosques are perceived as spaces of otherness whose presence is challenging national identity and social cohesion. The presence of Muslim symbols arouse a debate on how to restriction such symbols. Despite Islam being the second biggest religion in Denmark, there are only a few mosques built for the purpose. The majority of mosques consist of prayer houses hidden away in storage rooms and apartments in neighborhoods inhabited by migrants.[15] Many of these mosques represent alternative public spaces, and are targets of profound controversies. Generally, mosques are seen as unwanted spaces of otherness, and as containers of dangerous segregated parallel lives and radicalization.

Social housing projects in Denmark, where a majority of migrants live, are also the subject of an intense political concern. The most commonly used term to describe challenges in public social housing estates is "ghettoization," a term that signals problems of segregation and isolation in social housing.[16] National politicians have defined public housing projects as "ghettos," or as "holes on the Danish map," conceptualizing social housing as unwanted spaces of otherness, places that are not part of a Danish public space. In 2004, the liberal right-wing government launched its first strategy against ghettoization, directed at public vulnerable residential areas together with a "ghetto list" which makes an annual count of ghettos in Denmark based on criteria such as income, (un)employment, educational performance, nationality, and crime rate. During the 2000s, the government intensified its focus on ghettoization and "bad integration," defining social housing as areas where "Danish values are not rooted."[17] This development went hand in hand with increasing references to Danish values and norms used in the debate problematizing migrants' culture as an obstacle to integration. In 2018, the government issued its third comprehensive strategy against ghettoization, characterizing "ghettos" as "parallel societies," and thereby as "un-Danish" places. This has resulted in radical plans to demolish parts of social housing areas and increase punishment of crimes committed in these areas (Fig. 1). The rhetoric on "ghettos" as holes thus reflects the national assimilation politics where migrants are supposed to assimilate or disappear. Consequently, national policy associates diversity with disorder, conceiving diversity as an obstacle to national and social cohesion. Furthermore, national policy does not cultivate visions about mutual belonging and coexistence.

"The intercultural city"

In Denmark, local authorities such as municipalities are to some extent politically autonomous, and local politics may differ significantly from national politics. For example, the municipality of Copenhagen is primarily represented by social democratic politicians, whereas national politics since 2001 has been dominated by the liberal right. Local political visions, with their focus on urban diversity, social integration, and coexistence, differ from the national rhetoric, which associates public spaces used or frequented by migrants with exclusion and segregation. While municipalities produce shifting visions of diversity, the 2010 integration policy of the municipality of Copenhagen in particular envisioned diversity as an asset in urban planning. The Copenhagen municipality explicitly envisioned the city as a site for fruitful coexistence and interaction between citizens with different ethnic backgrounds. The municipal integration policy emphasized "inclusion" and "citizenship," and defined integration as

Figure 1. A block in a social housing project in Copenhagen

"a dynamic and reciprocal process, where citizens with different backgrounds meet and create future communities."[18] This integration policy particularly focused on Copenhagen as "an intercultural city, a site of diversity, interethnic relations and mixture."[19] However, as Welsch (this volume) argues, the concept of interculturality, despite its good intentions, tends to imply homogenous culture. This is reflected in urban regeneration strategies for the municipality of Copenhagen that generally aim to implement "social mixing" between different groups. Such efforts tend to be premised on essentialist notions of culture that may contribute to their crystallization rather than an encounter on common ground.[20]

Based on principles of "extreme participation," Superkilen, which is located in the super-diverse neighborhood of Nørrebro in Copenhagen, may have a potential to represent a "cross-over-place" that facilitates encounters between entities that otherwise are perceived differing from one another.[21] The story of Superkilen may be seen in light of the city's progressive plans for mosque building. The long-planned mosque in central Copenhagen by architect Bjarke Ingels was ultimately cancelled because of lack of funding. Subsequently, Superkilen constitutes a less controversial public space as it does not represent a religious minority, but a more accessible common public space, which satisfies egalitarian visions that characterize Danish civil culture. As Mack (this volume) states, despite the representation of Superkilen as a public space that celebrates inclusion and invites appropriation, diversity still remains a challenge. Fundamental questions remain about whether it is possible to design urban social life; in that sense, Superkilen represents an emplacement rather than an embodiment of social encounters.

Different public spaces have different geographies of contact, and some may invite to more social contact than others.[22] While Superkilen represents an articulated space of visible coexistence that may invite interaction, other urban spaces such as social housing areas—the "ghettos"—represent invisible yet vibrant forms of intercultural coexistence. The next section describes the practice of everyday forms of coexistence that occur at the level of lived spaces.

"What we do have in common is that we live here"

What are termed as "ghettos" in public debates in Denmark are in reality neighborhoods occupied by many different nationalities, including ethnic Danes. However, the public debate on ghettos often ignores the ethnic mix and intercultural coexistence represented there; Ali and Anders thus live side by side and engage in everyday forms of social relations as neighbors. Green Park (a pseudonym) is one among many social housing projects that represents a site of forms of coexistence, ignored in national public debates. Constructed in 1966 as a new modern residential area situated on the southern outskirts of Copenhagen, Green Park is arranged in ten grey-white blocks of three storeys each, comprising 470 apartments with balconies. About a thousand people reside in Green Park and about fifty-two percent of them are ethnic majority Danes, and forty-eight percent represent migrants from primarily non-Western countries. Besides, diversities in terms of gender, age, family type, and social economical status also exist.

Green Park has been subject to the national urban regeneration strategies to counteract "negative development" such as ghettoization, and has a master plan that was implemented by the municipality of Copenhagen. This plan reflects a concern with immigration, integration, ghettoization, and visions of segregated units and groups that do not interact, emphasizing "problems with integration" and a "lack of dialogue between different [ethnic and social] groups," as well as defining Green Park as a place with "tendencies towards ghettoization." The master plan thus reflects the overall municipal mixing policies that tend to assume a lack of inter-ethnic coexistence in social housing projects. The residents in Green Park are aware that their neighborhood is often described as a "ghetto." In many ways, both ethnic majority and minority residents' narratives about Green Park reflect the public debates on immigration and ghettoization, and tend to reproduce the dominant stereotypes about migrants and identity structures based on an "us" versus "them" relationship of distance and opposition. When speaking about social relations in Green Park, the different categories of residents often express that "Danes and migrants have no relations to one another." Such expressions reflect the influence of public rhetoric that tends to crystallize cultures and build boundaries among ethnic groups. Still, all categories of residents in Green Park were aware of their use of stereotypes and prejudices about one another, and they expressed a need for transcending these issues. Besides, everyday interactions with neighbors did result in encounters on common ground.

Yet despite the "us" versus "them" relationship, ethnic majority and minority residents did relate to one another as neighbors, citizens, friends, and family, and thereby practiced everyday forms of coexistence. The most common social relationship was being neighbors, engaging in relations based on accidental everyday contact, and as co-citizens who are sharing place, and practicing civility based on pragmatic interaction. Neighborhood relations in Green Park are mainly rooted in ways that the physical surroundings instigate interaction: outdoor places such as the small paths that crisscrossed Green Park, common spaces such as the laundry and fitness rooms, windows, balconies, and stairways. Bumping into others at such places constitute informal contact situations. Contact is a form of habituated behavior emerging from unexpected situations, and neighboring is thus constituted in occasional and by-chance activities in the neighborhood.[23] Green Park's outdoor areas provide opportunities for sitting and standing such as benches and walls, constituting buffer zones between the private home and the public spaces. The different categories of residents create possibilities for contact in public spaces by meeting in a "third space" that enables them to be themselves while mingling with strangers. In that way, the public spaces in Green Park constitute spaces of coexistence. The materiality and small-scale architecture of Green Park, with its smooth transitions between private and public spaces that invite interaction among different categories of residents thus entail a capacity to work and function as an open social area.[24]

Daily interactions in Green Park involved gestures of recognition, presumably leading to feelings of connection amongst the many different people who share the place. Prevalent forms of interaction constitute weak ties[25] based on contact situations such as acknowledgement, greetings, and helping others. Much of the neighborly interaction reflect "everyday multiculturalism" in the form of practices of routine and unreflective intercultural encounters.[26] Forms of neigborhood contact are characterized by the flow of everyday life constituted in shared places and practices.[27] Such forms of contact are primarily characterized by "sociation," that is, concrete ways of togetherness in everyday life. Everyday practices thus express the ability to cooperate,[28] for example in ways of approaching one another, coordinating gestures and movements in shared spaces (Fig. 2).

The forms of invisible coexistence in Green Park illustrate that in practices of everyday life, diversity is hardly attributed any meaning.[29] The visible presence of migrants was generally experienced as a normal part of social life, constituting "commonplace diversity."[30] This lack of interest in diversity may reflect a habit of seeing the strange as familiar[31] based on living on common ground with people whose main characteristic is their mutual diversities. For example, fifty-year-old Yvonne, who lived in Green Park for ten years, emphasizes the experience of being on common ground as overshadowing issues of diversity:

> I think it's totally unimportant what nationality my neighbor has, but I also presume that,
> well, we have our lives here .... Well, we are perfectly able to be friends even though we don't
> have the same nationality and language and political conviction or religious or sexuality,
> and so forth. In fact, I couldn't care less about that. But what we do have in common is that
> we live here, and that we want to have a nice place to live. It's our home, this place.

Yvonne accentuates sharing a space and belonging to a particular place. As were many other residents, she was, however, attentive to the current subjects in the debate on Danish immigration and

Figure 2. Everyday life in the Green Park, Copenhagen

integration politics. Yet, she and other residents emphasized aspects of integration that were different from the national discourse on assimilation by conceptualizing integration as a reciprocal local process revolving around ways of belonging. Green Park constitutes a "space of commons": common land and a feeling of common belonging. Such local practices of coexistence are contrasted to national policies on ghettos as "holes" and spaces that do not belong to Denmark.

Conclusion

The different representations of public spaces exemplified in this essay show the contrast between how issues of immigration, diversity, and intercultural coexistence are represented in the political arena and how they are dealt with in everyday life.[32] National rhetoric exemplifies the ways that the public sphere and public space coalesce in arenas of social and political contestation around diversity as a form of disorder that needs to be controlled through a politics of assimilation. Both mosques and social housing projects that are mainly represented by non-Western migrants are subject to intense contestation as spaces of otherness whose presence is challenging national identity and social cohesion. They are often seen as unwanted spaces of otherness and as containers of threatening forms of segregation that do not belong to Danish public space. While local political authorities such as the municipality of Copenhagen produce a rhetoric of diversity and coexistence in public spaces, which is implemented through architecture, their impact on social life can be questioned.

The representations of lived spaces constituted by everyday life in social housing projects such as Green Park offer contrasting perspectives to the national rhetoric by primarily representing practiced forms of coexistence. Green Park represents invisible forms of coexistence that contrast national representations of cleavages between "us" and "them" and of life in the "ghetto" as isolated and segregated. Everyday multiculturalism permeates life in Green Park in the form of unreflected embodied encounters facilitated by small-scale architecture that enable smooth transitions between private and public spaces. The forms of invisible coexistence in Green Park illustrate that in everyday life practices, neighbors hardly attribute diversity any meaning, as sharing a neighborhood characterized by super-diversity means that multiplicity has become a defining norm.

1   Ash Amin, *Land of Strangers* (Cambridge, UK: Cambridge University Press, 2012).

2   Pnina Werbner, "Everyday Multiculturalism: Theorising the Difference between 'Intersectionality' and 'Multiple Identities,'" Ethnicities 13(4) (2013): 401–19; A. Wise and S. Velayutham, eds., *Everyday Multiculturalism* (Basingstoke: Palgrave Macmillan, 2009).

3   Ralph Grillo, "Backlash against Diversity? Identity and Cultural Politics in European Cities," *Working Paper* 14 (Oxford: Centre on Migration, Policy and Society/COMPAS, 2005).

4   Anouck Germain, "The Sustainability of Multicultural Cities: A Neighbourhood Affair?" *Belgeo* 4 (2002): 377–86.

5   Richard Jenkins, *Being Danish: Paradoxes of Identity in Everyday Life* (Copenhagen: Museum Tusculanum, 2011).

6   Henri Lefebvre, *The Production of Space*, D. Nicholson-Smith, trans. (Oxford: Blackwell, 1974/1991).

7   Tina Gudrun Jensen, Sameksistens. *Hverdagsliv og naboskab i et multietnisk boligområde* (Copenhagen: Roskilde Universitetsforlag, 2016).

8   Karen Fog Olwig and Karsten Paerregaard, "Strangers in the Nation," in Olwig, Karen Fog Olwig and Karsten Paerregaard, eds., *The Question of Integration: Immigration, Exclusion and the Danish Welfare State.* (Cambridge Scholars Publishing, 2011), 1–28.

9   Marianne Gullestad, "The Scandinavian Version of Egalitarian Individualism," *Ethnologia Scandinavica* 21 (1991): 3–18; Steffen Jöhncke,"Integrating Denmark: The Welfare State as a National(ist) Accomplishment," in Olwig and Paerregaard, eds., 30–53.

10 Steffen Jöhncke,"Integrating Denmark: The Welfare State as a National(ist) Accomplishment," in Olwig and Paerregaard, eds.

11 Inger Sjørslev, "The Paradox of Integration: Excluding while Claiming to Integrate," in Olwig and Paerregaard, eds., 77–93.

12 ECRI, Rapport om Danmark (Strassbourg, 1999); ECRI, anden rapport om Danmark (Strasbourg, 2001).

13 Mette Tobiasen, "Danskernes verden var den samme efter 11 september: terror, islam og global solidaritet," in *Jørgen Goul Andersen and Ole Borre*, eds., *Politisk forandring: Værdipolitik og nye skillelinjer ved folketingsvalget 2001* (Aarhus: Systime Academic, 2003), 347–62.

14 Jocelyne Cesari, "Mosque Conflicts in European Cities: Introduction," *Journal of Ethnic and Migration Studies* 31 (6) (2005): 1015–24.

15 Lene Kühle, *Moskeer i Danmark: islam og muslimske bedesteder* (Forlaget Univers, 2006).

16 John Pløger, "Planlægning i en kompleks og plural verden – og for den meningsfulde by," in *Hans Skifter Andersen and Hans Thor Andersen*, eds., *Den mangfoldige by* (Hørsholm: Statens Byggeforskningsinstitut, 2004), 169–85.

17 Regeringen, *Ghettoen tilbage til samfundet. Et opgør med parallelsamfund i Danmark* (København: Regeringen, 2012), 5; my translation.

18 Københavns Kommune. *Bland dig i byen. Medborgerskab og inklusion. Integrationspolitikken 2011-14.* (Copenhagen: Københavns Kommune, 2010).

19 Ibid.

20 Kristina Grünenberg and Mikaela Freiesleben (2016) "Right Kind of Mixing? Promoting Cohesion in a Copenhagen Neighbourhood," *Nordic Journal of Migration Research* 6(1) (2106).

21 Stavros Stavrides, *Common Space: The City as Commons* (London: Zed Books, 2016).

22 Amin, *Land of Strangers.*

23 Eric Laurier, et al., "Neighbouring as an Occasioned Activity: 'Finding a Lost Cat.'" *Space and Culture*, 5(4) (2002): 346–67.

24 Sandra Wallman, et al., *The Capability of Places: Methods for Modelling Community Response to Intrusion and Change* (London: Pluto Press, 2011).

25 Mark Granovetter, "The Strength of Weak Ties," *American Journal of Sociology* 78(6) (1973): 1360–80.

26 Pnina Werbner, "Everyday Multiculturalism: Theorising the Difference between 'Intersectionality' and 'Multiple Identities,'" Ethnicities 13(4) (2013): 401–19; A. Wise and S. Velayutham, eds., *Everyday Multiculturalism* (Basingstoke: Palgrave Macmillan, 2009).

27 Sarah Pink, *Situating Everyday Life: Practices and Places* (London: Sage, 2012).

28 Richard Sennett, *Together: The Rituals, Pleasure & Politics of Cooperation* (London: Penguin Books, 2012).

29 Pink, *Situating Everyday Life: Practices and Places.*

30 Susanne Wessendorf, *Commonplace Diversity: Social Relations in a Super-diverse Context* (London: Palgrave Macmillan, 2014).

31 Amin, *Land of Strangers.*

32 Richard Jenkins, *Being Danish: Paradoxes of Identity in Everyday Life* (København: Museum Tusculanum, 2011).

A "Border Concept": Scandinavian Public Space in the Twenty-First Century
Jennifer Mack

The Öresund Bridge opened on 1 July 2000, linking Sweden and Denmark and signaling yet another step in the realization of the growing, borderless Schengen Area of the European Union. Historically, Swedes and Danes were once bitter enemies, fighting numerous bloody wars against one another, especially from the fifteenth to the early nineteenth century. Yet the twentieth century evolved this relationship to one based on a commonly understood Scandinavian identity, a condition that intensified as the two countries became members of a diverse European Union. Denmark and Sweden became members of the Nordic Passport Union in 1952, which allowed travel without passport checks from 1958 onward. The Öresund Bridge solidified this collaborative venture, allowing residents from one side to work on the other, and vice versa, and buttressing a regional identity across the Öresund Strait.

This borderless Öresund became the site of heated political debates in the 2010s, however, when Swedish anti-immigration politicians suddenly portrayed the bridge as the facilitator of a "mass migration" of asylum seekers, largely Syrians fleeing their country's civil war. A new policy of guaranteed Swedish permanent residency for Syrian nationals offered in 2013 led to a sharp rise in those traveling from Denmark northward, as anti-immigration parties and media coverage described a "wave" of asylum seekers flooding the national territory. Migrants were increasingly dehumanized, and the residency policy was quickly changed as Swedish politicians from across the spectrum espoused an increasingly hard line. Border controls between Sweden and Denmark were reinstituted in January 2016.

Keeping people from settling and categorizing the territories that they use in everyday life as "temporary" is a method long used to instantiate social and legal hierarchies in spaces like the Öresund region. Here, asylum seekers have recently been denied the right to move across the border while also being denied the right to stay. The right to remain, the right to permanence, and the right to public space are reserved for those who are not forced to carry or imagine a return ticket. In this case, the right to cross this Danish-Swedish border—previously signaling cosmopolitanism's triumph—became central to the definition of belonging. When the new border checks were introduced, Swedish and Danish passport-holding commuters could still flash a passport and travel at will, while others were held in place or forced to attempt illicit means of travel.

Paradoxically, states like Sweden and Denmark also typically prefer to keep migrants living inside their borders spatially stationary. Both for colonial powers and for modern states, mobile bodies like migrants become, following anthropologist Mary Douglas's phrasing, "matter out of place."[1] Keeping migrants inert and under surveillance in the space of the camp (or perhaps even, from a radical reading, within stigmatized urban and suburban neighborhoods) is a more comfortable position for anxious nation-states.

Stasis within a space like a camp or even a suburban apartment guarantees the migrant's absence from political membership, her or his liminality. In spaces like the modernist suburbs of many European countries, people are fixed in space while also being excluded from social rights of membership. These are penal spaces where, following Loïc Wacquant, migrants become "urban outcasts" who muddle through everyday life without agency.[2]

Yet this condition of externality also allows a new productivity in spaces, where migrants participate in remaking spaces both physically and socially. Giorgio Agamben describes the refugee as "nothing less than a border concept that radically calls into question the principles of the nation-state and, at the same time, helps clear the field for a no-longer-delayable renewal of categories."[3] In this essay, I expand Agamben's notion to explore the migrant, including those who hold permanent residency or even citizenship, as a "border concept."

In this, I follow Chantal Mouffe's notion of "agonistic pluralism," which she outlines in order to argue that a viable democracy requires not consensus or deliberation, pace Jürgen Habermas and John Rawls, respectively.[4] Instead, she writes:

> I agree with those who affirm that a pluralist democracy demands a certain amount of consensus and that it requires allegiance to the values, which constitute its "ethico-political principles." But since those ethico-political principles can only exist through many different and conflicting interpretations, such a consensus is bound to be a "conflictual consensus."[5]

In Mouffe's view, the frictions of pluralism are at the very heart of democratic political systems, when holders of differing opinions should be regarded as "adversaries" not "enemies" and thus treat one another as "legitimate opponents."[6] With this logic in mind, I argue that migrants not only uncouple nation and state but also renew the category "public space" in urban settings when designers ask them to engage in radical new forms of participation in the creation of new urban spaces.

Etienne Balibar writes that "citizenship understood in its strict sense [is seen] as the full exercise of political rights and in its broad sense as cultural initiative or effective presence in the public space (the capacity to be 'listened to' there)."[7] Urban spatial practices (including building) emerge as a result of "cultures of exile" and are potentially productive when they, like the migrant, unhinge traditional claims about membership and territory. This view disrupts the notion that legal citizenship is the goal of migration and, in turn, the idea that public spaces are exclusive to one public: the public defined as citizens only. Many public spaces are not open (if not legally, then socially) to people who are stuck or invisible.

Here, I investigate three projects to create new Scandinavian public spaces that radically reinterpret a key paradigm in contemporary urban design—"participation"—to imagine new and more inclusive ways to conceive of public space. In each case, the designers have explored ways to give both voice and visibility to people who are otherwise excluded from public space, treating them, following Mouffe, not as "enemies" of the existing spaces and paradigms but as catalysts for the "vibrant clash" of opinions that she claims is necessary. At the same time, with designers as the interpreters and authors of the projects, these three designs also illustrate that even radical new forms of participation in design may be seen as forms of emancipation but should not be equated with democracy itself.

The three projects include a private space made public in an asylum seekers' residence in a high-rise building in northern Sweden, a redesigned late modernist public square in a "segregated" Malmö suburb, and, in brief, a public park predicated on collaging diverse urbanisms in Copenhagen. These projects demonstrate how both a migrant's personhood and a territory's status may be reconstituted as the boundaries between guest and host, designer and user, and familiar and foreign are blurred. All three implicitly invoke the migrant as a "border concept," a figure who can counteract the hegemonic power of the nation-state, of other local residents disquieted by the injection of mobility into their midst, and, in particular, of exclusionary public spaces based on outdated models of belonging.

Guests and hosts in Boden's newest "living room"

Anthropologist Liisa Malkki describes the "social imagination of refugeeness,"[8] writing that "social significance of the refugee category can reemerge [...] when people [...] appropriate the category as a vital, positive dimension of their collective identity in exile."[9] Nation-states and international aid groups alike mostly fail to recognize the agency of migrants, and they typically avoid addressing the need for communal spaces in refugee camps or housing areas where political or social actions and gatherings might occur. Instead, to refuse the social categories that confine migrants and to regard liminality, following Malkki, as both vital and positive, migrants claim rights to a new spatial history as they absorb, deflect, and rearticulate the meaning and content of "public space."

In Decolonizing Architecture Art Residency (DAAR) member Sandi Hilal's "Living Room" performance piece in the northern Swedish city of Boden, new kinds of physical spaces understand the potential for migrants as social agents in an urban society that frequently does not recognize them as full or permanent members. Boden's location near the Finnish border and in closer proximity to Russia than most of Sweden has historically been determinant for the town's identity (Fig. 1). A military outpost during the Cold War, Boden lost its hegemony as a regional hinge space because of shifts in geopolitics. For this place—where cognizance of borders is part of the local ontology—the arrival of migrants

Figure 1. The Living Room/المضافة in the yellow house, Boden, 2018

does not fit the existing paradigm. Boden's borders are those between vulnerable Sweden and proximate and powerful nation states, not the borders crossed by individuals fleeing violence and crisis.

Rather than victims or passive recipients of the aid and the existing built environment, however, Hilal's "Living Room" suggests a new path to political agency. Migrants who are seeking asylum, she writes, must often perform the role of "perfect guests" and are confined to both physical stasis and social invisibility.[10] Hilal asks, "What does it mean to be someone who has no access to the public?"[11] Seeing the position of the migrant as one of "eternal guest," her work considers how to reposition the migrant in the role of "host," a role with considerably greater agency. With echoes of Agamben's "border concept," her DAAR partner Alessandro Petti has written that we must start "understanding exile as a political practice of the present capable of challenging the status quo."[12] DAAR's work, he writes, seeks to "reframe the position of the refugee from one of weakness to one of strength."[13]

A Syrian couple, Yasmeen and Ibrahim, arrived in Boden two years earlier and, unlike most other migrants in the town, planned to remain there. They had, of their own volition, opened their living room in a refugee housing block to guests, offering conversation, food, and drinks to those who wished to join them, even at a moment's notice. In this, they reclaimed the role of the host and reclaimed the Arab world tradition of the living room, *Al-Madafeh,* as the room of hospitality, where coffee, fruit, and nuts should always be on offer, and no guest should be questioned about her plans for the first three days of her visit. Yasmeen and Ibrahim and other migrants frequently felt unwelcome in Swedish public spaces, meaning that "hospitality became only a public domain in the sense of state domain," as Hilal remarked in a lecture.[14] Instead, in their living room, they again have "the right to host."[15]

In the *Al-Madafeh,* Yasmeen and Ibrahim reject both the idea of their powerlessness and of their limitation to the role of guest, according to Hilal's interpretation. They inspired the "Living Room" project, which opens another private space as a public one for a group whose access to traditional Swedish public spaces in Boden is limited. To create the "Living Room," Hilal converted an apartment in the refugee housing block into a new public space for those residing in the building. Here, being in between, being outside the public, and being a border concept create new kinds of social interactions. An unhinging of personhood and nation within a high-rise housing block creates a new Scandinavian public space that, following Agamben, renews categories: of public and private, guest and host, migrant and resident.

Disordering the public spaces of Malmö: Biblioteksplatsen and Tandläkarplatsen

Political theorist Michael Walzer labels territory a "non-exportable good,"[16] and migrants often find that they cannot claim territory even after years of living on it. This fact is clearly visible in the many modernist suburbs around European cities where migrants form a majority of the location population, and this has even been extended to their children, who are labeled "second-" or "third-generation" migrants. Despite the dominance of migrants and their descendants demographically, they are not conceived as members of the public for which the public spaces of the European past were made. This often leaves current residents, implicitly, without the right to remake and design spaces for the future.

This is clearly the case in the context of the late modernist Swedish housing initiative known as the Million Program, which constructed over one million dwelling units across Sweden between 1965 and 1974 at a time when Sweden's population was under eight million people. The Million Program was intended as the ultimate demonstration of Swedish prowess in the art of nation- and homebuilding. Here, the welfare state would triumph over the past, where squalor and overcrowding had predominated, and where the category "Swedish citizen" was thought to be ethnically bounded and legally static.

Today, however, many Million Program neighborhoods have been stigmatized as sites of social problems that are frequently implied to be causally related to their large proportion of migrants. Rosengård, on the eastern edge of Malmö, has long been one of the major offenders, receiving particularly negative attention for its crime and unemployment. This has also made it the focus of numerous renovation efforts over many years, including work by Jan Gehl's office in 2006, which determined that eighty-four percent of the space in Rosengård is public space.[17] It is these public spaces that are often the sites of the very acts that stigmatize the neighborhood, and many are either disused or monopolized by certain social groups who exclude others.

Since 2016, a new renovation effort for Rosengård has been given the name Amiralsstaden (Admiral's City), collaging several projects related to the development of Station Rosengård, which will allow rail connections from Rosengård to central Malmö and to Hyllie in Denmark. This is an explicit attempt to connect parts of the city that have been underserved by public transit. In 2018, Malmö municipal council leader Katrin Stjernfeldt Jammeh of the Social Democratic Party penned an article in the Swedish newspaper *Expressen,* explaining the project's rationale as primarily economic: "Linking housing construction and urban development to station and collective transit nodes is a strategic effort to attract investment, develop, renovate, create jobs, and connect the city in a smart and attractive way. This is about counteracting segregation and making sure that the entire city is taking part in the development ...."[18] The Amiralsstaden development project has also meant renewed municipal attention to the public spaces of Rosengård. In today's media, these spaces are often presented as sites of crime and danger.

Into this mix has come the landscape architectural firm Disorder Collective, comprising Johanna Bratel and Karin Andersson; they have established a critical practice that focuses on norm-critical, participatory projects. One effort has focused on Biblioteksplatsen (Library Square), outside the Rosengård Library, which was critiqued for its exclusionary use by men. Disorder Collective initially approached the owners of the space, a private developer called Trianon, with a proposal to make Biblioteksplatsen more inclusive and explicitly framed their work as a temporary "test" to make it more palatable. The owners expressed concerns that any improvements would be subject to disuse and/or destruction. Yet the short-term plan paradoxically paved the way for what became a permanent intervention.[19]

Disorder Collective explicitly sought a new methodology for their work, arguing that "to take space in the public space is a political act."[20] In their work in Rosengård, they have drawn on participatory planning models by inviting local residents to "vision workshops" held on site. For them, the public inclusion was not the typical one comprising local leaders or even merely adults. Instead, Disorder

Collective explicitly emphasized a process of participation with local children living in Rosengård, all between the ages of five and fifteen. When Biblioteksplatsen was remade and inaugurated in December 2017, it included new benches and murals that emerged directly from these workshops with children (Fig. 2).

Despite their effective participatory practice in Amiralsstaden, Andersson and Bratel nonetheless describe a certain frustration with the reception of their efforts, especially around the definition of which publics are allowed to participate in participatory planning processes. In an article entitled, "We are not playing with children; we are developing Sweden's democracy," Andersson wrote:

> We are often told that we play with children .... I become confounded—but unfortunately no longer surprised—that people I meet in our branch have this point of view. That our strategic and long-term work is reduced to play and regarded as unserious just because we work with people who have very little power in society, on places that are not seen as being "attractive" and on projects with a relatively small budget.[21]

The projects by Disorder Collective illustrate how, following Mary Steedly, the nation "find[s] expression in the complementary idioms of home and homelessness."[22] Here, in Rosengård—a housing area intended to showcase modern Swedish citizenship in the mid-twentieth century—children who are primarily migrants or their descendants become integral to the processes by which disused public spaces are designed for new uses. The forms of participation used by Disorder Collective depart from those used by Sandi Hilal but nonetheless follow Mouffe's prescriptions for "conflictual consensus." In so doing, these children, together with Disorder Collective, remake both the spaces and the content of the Swedish public. This collaboration both redefines children as key members of the twenty-first-century Swedish public and makes their access to public space integral. The new Biblioteksplatsen renews the category of the public for whom public space exists and is critically important.

Superkilen, an invitation to appropriation

Participation in the recreation of public spaces has, in fact, become a major theme for designers working to inject new energy into stigmatized urban and suburban neighborhoods in Scandinavia. Perhaps the most famous contemporary example of such an approach lies in the Copenhagen neighborhood of Nørrebro, in the urban park of Superkilen. This three-part park—with red, black, and green sections—has been labeled by CNN as "the world's most surreal public space."[23] Superkilen (Super Wedge) was intended to splice together a neighborhood previously wedged apart, since Nørrebro had become associated with social problems often, as in Rosengård, ascribed to its large migrant population. This had been exacerbated as non-residents pass through the neighborhood on bicycles but rarely stop.

The designers of the project, Superflex, Topotek1, and BIG (Bjarke Ingels Group), invited local residents to contribute ideas for objects to include in the park, both online and through meetings. The area is home to residents from sixty different countries, and the project was intended as "a giant exhibition of urban best practice."[24] With 108 objects chosen, the collage of urban furniture, signage, and

Figure 2. Grand opening of the temporary installation, summer 2016. The girls who took part in the workshops during the summer build a pattern of stickers on the wall at Biblioteksplatsen.

décor includes Armenian picnic tables, a Japanese octopus-shaped play structure, palm trees from China, and a neon sign advertising a Moscow hotel (Fig. 3). Superflex describes this mixture as "a sort of surrealist collection of global urban diversity that in fact reflects the true nature of the local neighborhood—rather than perpetuating a petrified image of homogenous Denmark."[25]

Based on what the designers term "extreme participation," this collection brings together objects that have not only never appeared in Denmark before, but that also have never met one another in urban space. In this, the residents and designers have provided fertile ground for considering how inclusion should occur in forms of participation that accept people positioned, following Mouffe, as "adversaries," as "legitimate opponents," to earlier models of Scandinavian public space, and with what forms. Superflex and partners argue, through the project, for that the emergence of new public space can occur by the sheer act of curation; here, a collection of existing objects renews the categories of what belongs together. And the significant international media and professional design attention given to Superkilen suggest that the park has had an influence on the direction of inclusive public design for the future.

Figure 3. The Black Market in Superkilen, Copenhagen, 2016. The neon sign comes from
Dr. Sena's Dental Clinic in Doha, Qatar.

Even so, the architectural and urban historian Mariana Mogilevich argues that this uncanny collection is "an urbanistic spoof …. These disparate objects do not blend into a happy whole but rather exist in cultural and aesthetic tension, demanding to be interpreted and appropriated."[26] In this way, the innovation that Superkilen represents is perhaps not in its extreme participatory model, or in the unusual results of the project. Instead, the dissonances of its adjacencies and its very literal approach to diversity provide a challenge both to earlier Scandinavian public spaces and to the visitor. Here, the forms of participation used to create this public space question existing hegemonies by collaging new urban forms with a goal not to arrive at a consensus but to coexist in their dissonance with one another, neither enemies nor partners in deliberation, but adversaries keeping the democratic process alive.

Public space as moebius strip

In a 1953 essay, African-American author James Baldwin describes himself as "The Stranger in the Village" while living in Switzerland.[27] As he walks through the streets, villagers stare and touch his hair and skin without permission. In their eyes, he feels permanently alien, foreign; the villagers see him "as a suspect latecomer, bearing no credentials, to everything they have—however unconsciously—inherited."[28] While they are citizens, as a "latecomer," he remains outside, without the right to privacy, without personhood in public space, and without a claim to history or heritage.

As "latecomers," migrants are thought to inhabit a space outside history and are not the intended users of lived urban space. Statelessness is translated into discrimination in the form of segregated neighborhoods, permanent mobility, or the lack of rights to claim spaces and their futures. The assumption is that design should result in consensus, a consensus that is often predicated on earlier models of urban design. These public spaces are spaces like the imaged Öresund Bridge, where cosmopolitans would enjoy quotidian travel across the twenty-first-century public space. Touted as "public" infrastructure, the same space excludes others for whom crossing is often a matter of life and death. The bridge selects its publics parsimoniously and demonstrates the need for new models of public space that accept differing positions and opinions at the same time.

From the "Living Room" to Bibliotekstorget to Superkilen, the three projects explored here demonstrate three different ways of creating inclusion in public space through collaboration and participation that does not seek agreement but understands frictions between positions as necessary and desirable. All three explicitly include migrants in the making of new Scandinavian public spaces: as social innovators who redefine the private as public, as minors whose ideas are taken seriously by adults, and as collectors who contribute to a curated exhibition of "best practices." As asylum seekers are disparaged as "criminals," and xenophobic and fascist groups are emboldened to bar their entry to the public sphere, these projects understand the creation of architecture and landscape architecture as critical practices that facilitate or inhibit encounters in everyday spaces. They regard the migrant as a permanent and active part of the Scandinavian public sphere in the twenty-first century.

Agamben argues for a space between people and the nation that "would not coincide with any homogeneous national territory, nor with their topographical sum, but would act on these territories, making holes in them and dividing them topologically, like in a Leiden jar or in a Moebius strip, where exterior and interior are indeterminate."[29] Seeing the migrant as a "border concept" means that we can seek new models of public space in Scandinavia, where publics remake not only the space themselves but the very definition of who has rights: the right to host, the right of a child to be a member of the public, and the right to have one's dearest symbols, whatever their origin, included in the public realm around you. Through participation, a "conflictual consensus" produces new spaces that include frictions and incongruities as desired elements of the designs. They make the future by rejecting the need for agreement about the form and content of Scandinavian public space. In Italo Calvino's *Invisible Cities*, the city of Ersilia is a place where connections between people are constantly remade.[30] Strings tied from one house to another symbolize social ties more enduring than the city itself, which is constantly abandoned and rebuilt. It contains "spider webs of intricate relationships seeking a form."[31] In such places, the material representation of human bonds simultaneously reflects their contingency, and their durability.

1   Mary Douglas, *Purity and Danger: An Analysis of Concepts of Pollution and Taboo* (New York: Routledge, 1966).

2   Loïc Wacquant, *Urban Outcasts: A Comparative Sociology of Advanced Marginality* (Cambridge, MA: Polity, 2008).

3   Giorgio Agamben, "We Refugees," trans. Michael Rocke, *Giorgio Agamben Symposium* 49(2) (Summer 1995), 117.

4   Chantal Mouffe, "Deliberative Democracy or Agonistic Pluralism," *Reihe Politikwissenschaft/Political Science Series* 72 (2000): 14.

5   Mouffe, "Deliberative Democracy or Agonistic Pluralism," 16.

6   Ibid., 15.

7   Etienne Balibar, *Masses, Classes, Ideas: Studies on Politics and Philosophy Before and After Marx*, trans. James Swenson (New York: Routledge, 1994), 724.

8   Liisa Malkki, "Speechless Emissaries: Refugees, Humanitarianism, and Dehistoricization," *Cultural Anthropology* 11(3) (August 1996): 380.

9   Malkii, "Speechless Emissaries," 377.

10 Sandi Hilal, "Al-Madafeh: The Hospitality Room," KU Leuven, accessed 12 April 2019, http://www.mahsmausp.be/events/2017-fall/76.

11 Hilal during keynote lecture by DAAR, "Decolonizing Architecture and Campus in Camps," Making Effect Symposium, ArkDes, 15 September 2017.

12 http://www.decolonizing.ps/site/architecture-of-exile-iv-b/.

13 Ibid.

14 https://www.youtube.com/watch?v=XQKIss0gB-s.

15 https://arkdes.se/en/hosting-is-power-and-by-having-power-you-become-visible/.

16 Michael Walzer, *Spheres of Justice: A Defense of Pluralism and Equality* (New York: Basic Books, 1983): 48.

17 "Malmö: Rosengård, One Size Doesn't Fit All," Gehl, accessed 12 April 2019, https://gehlpeople.com/cases/malmo-rosengard/.

18 Katrin Stjernfeldt Jammeh, "Rosengårds nya station lyfter Malmö," *Expressen*, 22 January 2018.

19 No damage has thus far occurred to the new additions to the site.

20 Karin Andersson and Johanna Bratel, "Debattinlägg: Vi vill inspirera till ett kreativt anvandade av Lunds gator," *Sydsvenskan*, 30 October 2014. https://www.sydsvenskan.se/2014-10-30/vi-vill-inspirera-till-ett-kreativt-anvandande-av-lunds-gator.

21 Karin Andersson, "Vi leker inte med barn – vi utvecklar Sveriges demokrati," Sveriges Arkitekter, 5 October 2017, accessed 12 April 2019, https://www.arkitekt.se/vi-leker-inte-med-barn-vi-utvecklar-sveriges-demokrati/.

22 Mary Margaret Steedly, "Modernity and the Memory Artist: The Work of Imagination in Highland Sumatra, 1947–1995," *Journal for Comparative Study of Society and History* 42, no. 4 (2000): 811–46.

23 Lars Hinnerskov Eriksen, "Superkilen: Welcome to Europe's strangest public park," CNN, 6 October 2014, accessed 12 April 2019, https://edition.cnn.com/travel/article/copenhagen-surreal-park/index.html.

24 Superflex, "Superkilen," accessed 12 April 2019, http://superflex.net/tools/superkilen.

25 Ibid.

26 Mariana Mogilevich, "Ambulatory Therapy: Psychologies of Pedestrianization in New York and Copenhagen," *Candide* 9 (2017): 108–110.

27 James Baldwin, "Stranger in the Village," *Harpers*, October 1953.

28 Ibid., 83.

29 Agamben 118, emphasis in original.

30 Italo Calvino, *Invisible Cities*, trans. William Weaver (New York: Harcourt Brace & Co., 1974).

31 Ibid., 76.

Conflictual Constellations: On Superkilen
Barbara Steiner

After its completion, Superkilen was quickly celebrated as the dawn of a new type of urban public space and featured in numerous architecture, design, art, fashion, and life-style magazines. However, there have also been critical voices accompanying the genesis of Superkilen, claiming that it would just create a representation of difference, promote "place marketing" instead of "place making," and play into a capitalist world's hands. Designed by the architecture group BIG, the landscape architecture firm Topotek1, and the artist group Superflex, Superkilen is a 750-meter urban park wedged within one of the most ethnically diverse and socially challenged neighborhoods in Copenhagen. It is composed of globally sourced objects from sixty different parts of the world, chosen in collaboration with the people inhabiting the areas surrounding it. The selection ranges from exercise gears from muscle beach in Los Angeles to sewage drains from Israel, palm trees from China, and neon signs from Qatar and Russia, among others.

Superkilen is located in Nørrebro, an urban district in Copenhagen's northwest and is part of a greater urban development project for the area. From the beginning, it was accompanied by heightened suspicion from nearby residents. This partly had to do with observations of developments in other European cities, and partly with changes in Copenhagen's urban fabric itself. Special distrust was shown to the Realdania, a private foundation with a philanthropic agenda, which has been involved in many other refurbishment and public space projects in Denmark.[1] The foundation has mainly been criticized for its enormous power in shaping public life. In particular, grass-root movements, which had protested against previous demolitions and real estate speculation, had reservations when Superkilen was announced as a "participatory, integrative project," one that fully ignored past projects.[2] In 1973, for example, citizens of Nørrebro had already built a playground and public space in an empty lot. The project was kept alive until 1980, accompanied by constant struggles with city authorities. Later, the Initiative Group, a group of self-organized residents, aimed at establishing a community space in the old privately owned freight halls of Danish Railway (Danske Statsbaner). During those years, Nørrebro was considered to be a rough, even dangerous place. The open street-gang violence was even highlighted in a travel warning from the British Foreign & Commonwealth Office in 2009.[3]

"This project was all about integration," says Bjarke Ingels from BIG about Superkilen.[4] According to Martin Rein-Cano from Topotek1, the project brief said simply: "Deal with the issue of migration in this neighborhood. Can you somehow make this situation better?" He remarked that the original subject—"migration"—"was not the project team's idea," but the group had an interest in "taking it very serious, almost literal."[5] The heightened suspicion that Superkilen would become a gentrification project that aimed to pacify the area and make it attractive to new, wealthier residents and investors, seemed at first glance justified and supported by the call, driven by ambitions of the City Council of Copenhagen, which wanted to develop "the potential of Nørrebro."[6] In this regard, Nørrebro stands in line with urban renewal zones in many other places all over the world. For some years now, architects, landscape architects, and artists have been invited together to design public and semi-public spaces in order to give the place an identity that is internationally marketable and provide local identification.

Moreover, municipal authorities tend to outsource the task of finding solutions for the integration or inclusion of individuals and social groups within the majority society. This all takes place against the backdrop of an enormous economic perforation of the public space, resulting in new alliances of municipal authorities, private philanthropic foundations, and corporate businesses.

Since the 1960s, artists have had an interest in introducing participation into public arts projects responding to the social fragmentation of societies, and later to the economic perforations of cities and their branding and marketing policies.[7] However, what has begun quite promising has later ended up in a strategy of "radical chic, one that is en vogue with politicians who want to make sure that, rather than producing critical content, the tool itself becomes what is supposed to be read as criticality,"[8] says Markus Miessen in *The Nightmare of Participation*. The architect looks at participation as a kind of sedative that removes criticism of decision makers because it is the people who "participate" and therefore "decide." Participation is celebrated as a horizontal form of decision making, but is, according to Miessen, "only a currency for those who offer it."[9] The legitimate need for participation can thus be relatively easily manipulated to justify political decisions or, rather, non-decisions. Against the background described here, the call for participation cannot be considered as an emancipatory tool for all intents and purposes, nevertheless it remains an important issue. Needed is an increasing awareness of when and how to use the tool. As a consequence, in many works of contemporary artists, the intricacies that emerged alongside participation have become an intrinsic part of public art projects. Superkilen is one such example.

This situation briefly summarized above informs the point of departure for BIG, Topotek1, and Superflex. First, the project team's concept for Superkilen responds to recent developments where activities in the public space are overloaded with (conflicting) expectations. The group is aware of the problems associated with participation and participatory processes. Martin Rein-Cano from Topotek1 puts it like this: "They are kind of trendy, but for ambitious design they are quite an impediment. One tries to involve people in things that they do not have a clue about. Usually the outcome is just chaotic, leading only to mediocre results."[10] Bjarke Ingels from BIG considers public participation "almost like a disease. It sometimes turns into a retroactive justification, and you need an army of people to get qualified for projects. One has to have artists on board, public participation specialists, communication managers, and so on. And quite often one ends up with a lot of workshops, with a lot of post-its in different colors; and certainly all ideas are great."[11] BIG, Topotek1, and Superflex embraced the difficulties of participation and participatory processes as a point of departure for Superkilen.

At first glance the project's concept is strikingly simple: 108 objects and eleven trees from all over the world populate a wedge-shaped urban space.[12] The wedge is structured along three spatial zones following the topographic map, which already suggested three parts. These parts evolved into the "Red Square," the "Black Market," and the "Green Park." The objects, which usually furnish cities—ranging from litter bins, benches, manholes, bicycle racks, play and sport items, street lighting to ads (light boxes), bus shelters, a fountain, and even to sculptures—were to be selected by the people from Nørrebro with very different cultural backgrounds.

The realization of this concept, however, showed a more complex approach: colors and objects are carefully related. The objects and trees are embedded in three zones, red, black, and green, which serve as a sort of backdrop for the objects collected from different places. In the red zone, for example, various shades of the red surface accord with red maple trees, whereas the prevalent colors of the black part are black and greyish, a concept even the cedars and palm trees follow. Yet the colors do not only play an important role in terms of aesthetic considerations: they shape and define space, connecting the objects with one another and with the neighborhood. Moreover, the colors define the identity of the three areas pointing to different uses and functions: the "Red Square" was conceived as an activities zone with partying and music events; the "Black Market" as an "urban living room," serving as a space for lingering, a catwalk, and a trendy meeting point; and the "Green Park" would be as "green as possible" and suggest leisure activities, such as biking, playing ball, and barbecuing by addressing mainly children and families.[13]

Although everyday objects, they were supposed to have certain qualities: each "amazing, unique and special," such as the fountain from Morocco, which refers to a tradition of artisanal water features. Nanna Gyldholm Møller from BIG stated that the project group wanted to have "the best practice items from all over the world." She recalls the group's first visit to the area, when its members noticed that the litterbins and the telephone boxes were blown up and that almost everything was destroyed. "City Council had only the cheapest telephone boxes installed. Not everything was good quality; so we decided to give the people better things."[14] Besides the quality of the design, the objects were intended to create emotional relationships between different people.

Superkilen started with a call on the internet, as well as announcements in newspapers, handouts, and posters in libraries, inviting people to come up with proposals for their future park. The first proposals, however, were mainly for functional items: "we want a slide, we want benches, we want a lot of light because of insecurity in the neighborhood, we want more green, and we want to have a playground for the kids."[15] After numerous sessions with residents from Nørrebro, a catalogue of objects was made from which people could choose, which stimulated, in return, further proposals.[16] Ultimately, the final selection of objects was done by a jury.[17] The problems associated with this procedure point to a basic set of challenges in all participatory projects: How to stimulate participation without forcing people and without being patronizing; how to open up to thoughts people might have not considered themselves; how to promote an exchange of different expertise (aesthetical, technical, local) at eye level? And finally, what if people do not want to participate for whatever reason, if they do not want to play the game for which others set up the rules?

On closer inspection, the project depicts various modes of citizen involvement; or, to put it differently, Superkilen is deliberately based on, and plays through, various modes of participation and non-participation, from "ineffectual," "indirect," to "democratic," and "extreme participation." "Ineffectual participation" refers to a lack of feedback despite numerous public calls, and "indirect participation" means that objects were proposed and people just agreed or disagreed. Formal, schematic participation is most commonly used in contemporary democracies. It follows strict rules in regards to public announcements, time schedule, meeting venues, public hearings, and election procedures, but runs the danger of only addressing people who are willing to engage in such long and rather bureaucratic processes. Mostly this excludes women, young and elderly people, and migrants. In response to this, Superflex set up its subproject Participation Extreme, in which they literally pushed citizen involvement to the extreme: in five exemplary cases, they asked people who usually do not show up to the announced meetings—mostly elderly people, kids, and migrants—what kind of object they would like to have for Superkilen if they could choose anything they wanted. With these choices, Jakob Fenger, Bjørnstjerne Christiansen, and Rasmus Nielsen traveled to Bangkok, Palestine, the United States, Spain, and Jamaica to research and find a handful of the longed-for items. The work Superflex invested in their project, comprising five trips altogether, took one year. If one imagines the same procedure for every object at Superkilen (with its more than 100 objects) the realization of the park would have required approximately forty years. Furthermore, the human and financial resources for doing such projects are usually very limited, and the regulatory frameworks of public art projects such as Superkilen do not allow for certain expenses. In light of this, it is no surprise that the funding for the subproject came from the Danish Art Council. With its subproject, Superflex created a what-if scenario that invited speculation: What if this had happened with everything on display? What if they had followed this form of extreme participation?[18]

Essentially, Superkilen is a curated project based on citizen involvement, which deals with various forms of participation. The project team set up the frame, directed the project, but gave space to interests, views, and desires not necessarily fully congruent with its own. It never retained absolute control of the results, but it also never gave up control. Yet, authorship was also challenged within the project group: although working closely together from the beginning, working methods and manners of speaking to the public differed slightly between the architects, landscape architects, and artists. Working together, incorporating chance, and letting other proposals in basically meant that authorship was permeable and, above all, that the team was receptive.

Beyond turning participation into a leading issue, it is worth taking a closer look at the objects themselves. Some were bought from catalogues, others reconstructed from photographs or built anew onsite. Some were redrawn or modified according to technical, economic, or legal requirements and eventually produced by Danish firms. Some were done in collaboration, such as the giant Japanese Octopus, which was built onsite by Japanese and Danish workers. Particularly in regards to the collaborations and the productions commissioned in Denmark, misunderstanding, mutual approximation, and translation became obvious and important issues, which the project team has pointed out repeatedly. Martin Rein-Cano from Topotek1, being a migrant to Germany himself (he was born in Argentina) bridged the migrating objects that populate Superkilen with people's migration. With this, he raised debates about integration, cultural appropriation and annexation—sensitive and heavily debated issues also connected to projects like Superkilen. The questions of how to deal with cultural appropriation and exploitation critically, how to take a stance beyond a purely consumerist, swallowing attitude, accompany the project still today. In this regard, it might be helpful to recall montage techniques, which were developed by avant-garde artists and filmmakers.[19] Based on contradictory constellations of what are in principle familiar elements, frictions that stimulate new readings and evaluations are produced. Even though Superkilen is full of deliberate and legible frictions, it differs from avant-garde projects in that it flirts with the commercial sphere in equal measure. Certainly, this does not necessarily mean in return that it is abandoned to the world of consumerism. Let us have a look at the frictions first: they can be found in the material of the objects themselves, in the constellation of objects, and in the relationships between objects and their surroundings. And it is exactly the use of frictions that makes cultural incorporation and annexation at least very difficult, if not impossible—in the objects themselves, in the constellation of objects, and in the relationships between objects and their surroundings. Some objects were cheaply produced originally, such as the neon sign with the half-moon and the tooth. Looking at this and other objects, one may notice little strange details caused by the changes—blocked swings, solid, shatterproof glass, graffiti-protection surfaces—which stimulate reflection about security standards, regimentation, protection, economy, and nonchalance. Some objects, such as the bull, look kind of monstrous, others simply awkward, such as the barbecue grill from Canada, an object whose functional use is quite unclear at first sight.

Apart from the objects' immediate appearance, symbols, motifs, patterns, and signs slip into the Danish context, which may be considered alien, provocative, or simply folkloric, depending on the position of the viewer. Furthermore, there are deliberate conflictual constellations, such as soil from Palestine and a manhole cover from Israel next to one another. Summarizing, one could say that the objects remain alien to one another, in a way, and do not match fully with their surroundings. Yet, even if the objects "do not sit comfortably in the same space," as one critic put it, they inhabit nevertheless a common space.[20] Superkilen offers visual coherence but disrupts this coherence in many places. It is "deliberately ambivalent" and challenges standards of "looking good."[21] Essentially, the visitor/reader/viewer is addressed twice: firstly in terms of their consumerist desires and secondly in terms of their willingness to partake in discourse. Actually, Superkilen provides and interconnects these two alternatives in order to manifestly complicate both a purely consumerist as well as an analytical or discursive understanding of its object relations. The park, its objects, and their relation to the surroundings are not completely seductive; there is also something uncomfortable about the whole composition.

Superkilen shows exactly the troubles architects, planners, designers, and artists must deal with nowadays. To work with participation, diversity, hybridity, migration, inclusion requires an awareness of the range and tension inherent to those terms and, most notably, their application. The proclamation of, let's say, participation, does not say anything about how much people are really involved in decision making regarding their environment. It could simply turn into a hollow gesture. Besides, not every form of participation (here I am thinking above all of standardized procedures) is suitable in specific situations, simply because it does not reach certain people. Sometimes more time is needed for participation projects, which would make them very time-consuming and expensive. This is the reason why half-hearted solutions are often found. With Superkilen, the project team responded to the given situation in Nørrebro, to shifts in the conception of public space, and to the enormous expectations connected to public undertakings. Particularly in connection with participation, it stirs up a hornet nest. By playing with various modes of participation and non-participation, and by pushing participation to the extreme, it opens debates about various forms of participation. Furthermore, Superkilen deliberately complicates a consumerist as well as an analytical or discursive understanding of public art projects and sets them in relation to one another. Rivaling ideas about parks, its function and uses, about nature and artificiality, security, safety, and laissez-faire, are literally exposed and stimulate debate. In short: Superkilen allows various positions, values, and identifications without leveling or embracing them in an all-reconciling gesture. It offers a visual expression for an inherently heterogeneous, yet shared, space.

1 https://realdania.dk, accessed 23 September 2018.

2 Brett Bloom, *Participatory Park Extreme!* See chapter "Battles Over City Space in Nørrebro," http://www.academia.edu/3344295/Superkilen_Participatory_Park_Extreme, accessed 23 September 2018.

3 http://archive.li/sFu1d, 3 March 2009, accessed 23 September 2018.

4 Bjarke Ingels, "A Kick in the Nuts of Good Taste (Conflict and Consensus)," in *Superkilen*, ed. Barbara Steiner (Stockholm: Arvinus + Orfeus, 2103), 70.

5 Martin Rein-Cano, ibid.

6 Tine Saaby, "More urban life for all, more people to walk more, and more people to stay longer" (Urban Development)," in *Superkilen*, 75.

7 Claudia Büttner, "On Changes in the Conception of Public Space, Art in the Public Space, and Public Art," in *The Monograph Project*, ed. Barbara Steiner (Berlin: Jovis Verlag, 2018), 98 f.

8 Markus Miessen, *The Nightmare of Participation* (Berlin: Sternberg Press, 2010), 44.

9 Ibid.

10 Martin Rein-Cano, "If you could do anything you want, what would you do? (Participation)," in *Superkilen*, 49.

11 Ingels, ibid.

12 The name "Superkilen" is derived from the park's outline. Kilen means wedge in Danish.

13 The information is taken from: *Superkilen, 3 Zoner, 3 Farver – Et globalt kvarter*, Projektforslag/Hovedprojekt 2009/10, Archive Superflex.

14 Nanna Gyldholm Møller, "Imagine a Moroccan Fountain! (Selection and Realisation)," Interview in *Superkilen*, 58.

15 Jakob Fenger, "Imagine a Moroccan Fountain! (Selection and Realisation)," in *Superkilen*, 56.

16 Bjarke Ingels: "We had to trigger the imagination of people like: 'Imagine a Moroccan fountain!' People were invited to propose something, however, it was not meant to be politically correct. The objects were not chosen, because they are from Morocco: they were chosen, because they were amazing, unique and special. And there was a careful selection process." Ibid., 57.

17 The jury consisted of BIG Topotek 1, Superflex, and Kilebestyr-elsen (local governance board). The realization took place between August 2010 and June 2012.

18 "Participation Extreme," in *Superkilen*, 145–60. Superflex's first idea was to choose all the objects for Superkilen in this way.

19 The method of estrangement was developed by Victor Shlovsky in 1917. See Aage Hansen-Löve, *Der Russische Formalismus. Methodologische Rekonstruktion seiner Entwicklung aus dem Prinzip der Verfremdung* (Wien: Verlag der Österreichischen Akademie der Wissenschaften, 1978), 19f.

20 Brett Bloom, *Participatory Park Extreme!* See chapter "Scripting Democracy and Difference," n.p.

21 Martin Rein-Cano, "A Kick in the Nuts of Good Taste (Conflict and Consensus)," in *Superkilen*, 73.

This text is based on an essay written for the book *Superkilen* (Arvinus + Orfeus, 2103). It has been extended and modified.

IV. Convergence

Islamic Cemetery Altach (2011)

Architect: **Bernardo Bader**
Art installation in the mosque interior: **Azra Akšamija**
Location: **Altach, Austria**

Recipient of the Aga Khan Award for Architecture in 2013

The Cemetery serves Vorarlberg, the industrialized westernmost state of Austria, where over thirteen percent of the population is Muslim. It finds inspiration in the primordial garden, and is delineated by roseate concrete walls in an alpine setting, and consists of five staggered, rectangular grave-site enclosures, and a structure housing assembly and prayer rooms. The principal materials used were exposed reinforced concrete for the walls and oak wood for the ornamentation of the entrance facade and the interior of the prayer space. The visitor is greeted by and must pass through the congregation space with its wooden lattice work in geometric Islamic patterns. The space includes ablution rooms and assembly rooms in a subdued palette that give onto a courtyard. The prayer room on the far side of the courtyard reprises the lattice-work theme with Kufic calligraphy in metal mesh on the qibla wall.

— AKAA jury citation

In the fall of 2018, architectural historian Robert Fabach and photographer Nikolaus Walter met with different stakeholders of the Islamic Cemetery Altach to discuss their personal viewpoints on the cemetery and the effect this project had on coexistence in the region. Fabach selected the interviewees based on their involvement in the development and construction of the project, as well as their relevant experiences of migration and life in Vorarlberg. The following piece introduces passages and photographs recorded during these conversations, along with Fabach's personal observations on the architecture of the cemetery.

A wonderful place of eternity
— Ralf Schubert, Tourist Guide

A gift of time and continuity

Before the River Rhine enters the Lake of Constance, leaving behind steep and snowy alps, it passes through a wide valley along the border of Switzerland and Austria. Its open fields and reedy marshlands are laced with a string of busy settlements and industry bearing witness to peculiar historical traces, like the Turkish roots of the traditional embroidery in Vorarlberg. Red-brick historic chimneys and

factory halls mark the very edge of the city of Hohenems, but beyond, the landscape doesn't really turn into wilderness. The scenery is dominated by steep walls of rock coming close to the open road, but also features a huge farm house, a gravel pit, and the strange flying roof of a pit-stop looms in the distance. Driving along this expanse, lines of reddish walls appear, slowly revealing the form of a massive reddish cube. Beyond the walls are people, sunk in prayer, silent and alone. They somehow become a picturesque detail, carefully embedded in front of awesome rocks and meadows.

The cemetery. Only walls and nature, nothing shiny. Stepping in doesn't make a difference. The wide openings of the building emphasize the garden, the praying people, the towering backdrop. One's hand instinctively glides over the rough, wood-like texture of the concrete walls. Autumnal leaves on the floor unite with fine hairline cracks to form sketches of mindfulness.

It's not only individual life and death that is encountered when talking to people at the Islamic Cemetery in Altach. Most of them are descendants of men and women that came to the region from Turkey, Bosnia, or Chechnya as migrant workers, arriving during the economic boom of the 1960s. Most of these stories begin in distant worlds, distant years, distant lands. They are marked by new beginnings from scratch and major cultural discontinuities. Social ascent and acceptance took generations, if it ever happened, and so it is comforting to find a place that seems like it had always been here. It is not only a gift of space, but also a gift of time and history.

TUNCAY,
local resident of Turkish origin

We gladly come to this place, every fortnight. We make our prayers and remember. When the cemetery opened, we were very pleased that we finally achieved it, but with the death of my father last year it became crucial for us, especially for my wife, whose brother passed away unexpectedly this summer. It is important for her to come here and feel that he is present.

Asked if he was aware of the beauty of the site, Tuncay nodded silently. We stood there for a while. The quietness of the cemetery and also the design of the landscape are comforting, as are the birches, the waving grass, the sunlight falling in, especially during spring and summer. Tuncay described the calmness and a certain strength the cemetery grants him and his wife.

My father, he continued hesitantly, was blessed with a peaceful death. He was resting on the sofa and just fell asleep. He was 89. A fulfilled and fascinating life; he lived up to a dream. He, raised in the city of Istanbul, landed here in 1964 as one of the first. The reason he went abroad was a divorce—a scandal in those days. He was actually doing well. He was a master shoemaker and he had wanted to come here for two years or so—as was the idea of many Turks—to gain a little distance, earn some money and then return home again. He didn't quite manage that. He stayed. In 1968 he got to know my mom. I was born in 1970 and since then we have actually been here in Vorarlberg.

He never continued his craft, but worked in factories, like my mom, until his retirement. Three years ago I said to him, when he was 87 and in really bad shape: "Dad, we have to be realistic. What should I do if something happens? Do you want to go to grandma and grandpa, so to your parents grave in Istanbul?" And he replied, "No, we have an Islamic cemetery and if something happens, I want to be buried there. Because, the whole family now is here. In our former homeland, in Turkey, we don't have so many relatives anymore. Who will find me there? Nobody. I want to be buried here so that my descendants don't forget their roots and they should know that grandpa is here and you can always come and visit me." That was his wish.

The claim that the cemetery is not accepted, Tuncay insisted, is not true at all. It takes time. We are in a transitional phase. It will be increasingly important and it will be an important point of reference for many, but it simply takes time. Having this cemetery, this beautiful cemetery, is very important for us, because it connects us with our ancestors and we also have the chance on special occasions, like Ramadan, to say: "Let's go, let's quickly visit Daddy."

At family funerals, Tuncay meets many friends and relatives, from abroad, from Germany, from Switzerland, who have come to Altach for the first time. They often tell Tuncay that he and his family are really lucky to have such a great, modern and beautiful cemetery in Vorarlberg. Especially the architecture pleases many of Tuncay's family members. Many people like the simplicity and the quietness of the cemetery: *Everyone tells me they are so happy to have this cemetery here.*

Encountering letters

Visitors are welcomed by a huge lattice of wooden beams alongside the cemetery building, which resumes the scale of the landscape and allows a view inside. Everything seems open here. The repetitions of its patterns are ornaments, are prayer, are geometry. The actual entrance steps back from all this. A plate of brass in a niche receives the entrants. It's just as narrow as the wooden boards in between the single-pour reddish concrete—all veins, all rough—materializing as a kind of petrified reflection. Therein, inserted flush, is a dark, dense mass of brass featuring two sequences of words cut out: One German, *Islamischer Friedhof Altach* and one Arabic, *al Maqbarat al'islamiat fi Medinat Altach*. "The Islamic Cemetery in the City of Altach," translates my Arab companion with a faint smile: "Oh, how mindful! The German phrase—set in firm capitals and neutral typography—was not simply trans-ferred. No, they preserved also the politeness of the Arabic language and the skillful swing of its handwriting."

Roland Stecher, who took care of the graphic design, explains that he kept the Arabic lettering un-touched, out of respect... and due to his lack of ability to understand a word of it. For the German he chose a sober, extremely balanced typeface. "The Corpid, he adds, was originally designed in 1997 by Lucas de Groot as a typeface for a Dutch ministry. Hence the solidness. The German letters with bold strokes stand next to each other quite self-contained, as buildings do. The German lettering on the left runs to the right, and on the right side, the Arabic runs to the left, so they are encountering each other.

المقبرة الإسلامية في مدينة ألتاخ

GOTTFRIED,
Mayor of Altach

I have a certain relationship to Jordan due to a chronic skin disease. For two decades, I have been in Jordan almost every year for four weeks at a time. Maybe I know the country better than my homeland, because I use these stays not only to care for my skin, but also to travel a lot when I am there. So I have a bit of access to Muslim countries and people. You also see that our relation to migrant populations is different than in a country that is basically Muslim, with only a ten percent Christian share of the population. You know, the whole biblical story is practically located at the Dead Sea, where you meet Christian history everywhere. But they can deal with it very well over there. The religious peace is very obvious. There are mosques, like the King Hussein Mosque, standing side by side an orthodox church. Only on Fridays and Sundays do you realize that the shopkeepers are Palestinians and Christians, when either the Muslim or the Christian shops are closed. They all get along surprisingly well.

The mayor of Altach, Gottfried Brändle, has been doing his job for over twenty-five years. He has worked in close cooperation with the neighboring communities Götzis, Mäder, and Hohenems for some time now. At a time when integration became an issue in Vorarlberg, the *Gemeindeverband* (Association of Municipalities) was in search of a possible location for an Islamic cemetery. During one of their joint *jour fixe* they unanimously agreed on the current location.

The opportunity to make a practical contribution to the ongoing process of integration was ultimately the trigger for us. Friendly words are not enough; you should also do something. At that time, September 2004, state elections, and half a year later municipal elections, were scheduled and we agreed with all political parties that we would consistently exclude this topic from the election campaigns. That held. This already signaled a certain maturity in the process and we indeed reached a joint decision afterward, within half a year, to build a cemetery.

The working group responsible for the project soon found out that a cemetery means different things to different people, that a cemetery is something very personal and private. The need for a cemetery, the place where you put your loved ones to rest, was never questioned. But people in the village questioned whether a mosque would follow—like Christian cemeteries surrounding village churches. Another issue raised was whether the distant location of the cemetery would be interpreted as an act of discrimination. Both could be clearly denied by the Muslim communities as a misconception: "In Islam, mosque and cemetery are distinctly separated," they explained to us. "The dead are in no way a matter of worship. On the contrary, that suits us, because we are used to cemeteries on the edge. So, no mosque and not in the center."

In 2006, the assignment was handed over to the Islamic communities. Nothing happened for years. The local administration approached them again and learned that they lacked experience to organize a building process like this. Then Mayor Brändle offered, together with the community association,

that the municipality of Altach would professionally run the cemetery parallel to its existing local cemetery. The Muslim communities gratefully accepted and Altach also took over management of the entire construction process. A communally run cemetery was created, financially supported by all the ninety-six Vorarlberg communities. This was unique.

Overall, I think we were really lucky with the designer. They were both, artist and architect, very attentive and at the same time very warm personalities who also brought in their ideas and expression. Originally I would have expected a more classical form, as we know it from the mosque and other Islamic buildings that have Turkish influence, especially in our country. It surprised me that something like this was possible. I personally was enthusiastic from the beginning. It expressed a certain neutrality. A classic form of architecture, firstly modern, but very neutral and therefore able to connect everything. After all, there are no religious elements. The wooden screen, for example, is not religious. It's architecture with an Arabian touch, but it's not a religious symbol. We do not actually have any religious symbols, anywhere, at the cemetery. We had been expecting that there would be religious symbols and ornaments, but the representatives of the Muslim communities said: "No decoration. Graves are not decorated. They are simple."

But this started to change over the years, Gottfried Brändle pointed out. *Now some of the graves are beautifully decorated at the Islamic Cemetery. At some point the relatives even came and asked: "Please, can't you install a water outlet somewhere?" And I said to myself: "Aha. Water, flowers. Maybe they see how flowers are kept on a grave. In the heat of typical Arab countries, that's not possible. I am convinced they will not behave differently in terms of grave decoration than we do." We also learned that the people started to visit the graves more often, contrary to what they were told beforehand. The mixing of cultures was happening.*

In the second year after the opening of the cemetery, Mayor Brändle received a call from a collaborator: *"We have to do something. There is decoration on one of the graves, which is not appropriate. I cleared it all up for you and put it in the office." Then he talked to Ali Can, who does the organization and administration for us. He was already quite concerned and said that nobody was allowed to do that, which is true; graves are the property of the relatives. Now, he told me, there were candles with cross symbols on them—the ones you can get from us at the local cemeteries. Then came the lanterns and angels, and that shouldn't be. With these candles, we knew (Ali had already told me) that they were brought here by a neighbor of one of the deceased, unaware that there was a cross symbol on them. That was the trigger. Then he called the caretaker of the cemetery and told him: "We have to be careful now. If something like that happens, do you think we should remove it or may we leave it?" He understood immediately. "Thank you for telling me that—we should leave those decoration, no question." So also here we notice that we simply have to let these borders be crossed. And that is beautiful.*

Modern ornaments

My conversation with the mayor took place inside the open courtyard and afterwards, when he was receiving a group of visitors, I just stayed and took the opportunity to contemplate on the huge wooden lattice, on its crossing lines and the ornamental shadows they were casting. Bernardo Bader, the architect, described the decision for this element as an architectural and aesthetical consideration, but also emphasized the spiritual depth of these geometrical patterns. The simplicity of three overlaid patterns of squares manifests in uncoated oak beams of 6 x 20 centimeters, engineered by a computerized cutter. I contemplated the oneness of these patterns created by multiplicity.

My reflections were suddenly interrupted by the opening of the heavy oak door and a crowd of young students pouring in, chatting, wondering, taking pictures. The mayor and I gave our farewells and I dedicated the time until my next encounter to a retreat into the prayer room.

Gamze,
local resident of Turkish origin, third generation

I was impressed by the change of acoustics. The woolen carpet and the wooden cladding on the wall seemed to embrace the visitor. The *mihrab,* the ritual niche indicating the direction of Mecca, was a window with a kind of wooden curtain providing an abstract writing of the name of Allah and His prophet and, at the same time, a wonderful view toward the landscape. The door was open, so I could hear the voices and steps of my next conversation partners as they slowly approached the prayer room. Gamze was a young woman of Turkish origins, who grew up as a third-generation Austrian in Vorarlberg. She wrote a seminar paper about her experience as a third-generation Turkish-origin Vorarlbergian at her high school and was for this reason also invited to the ceremony of the Aga Khan Award.

It was my grandfather who came to Vorarlberg, Gamze told me. *But we have no relatives in the cemetery yet. For us, it is important to know that we can also be buried here. Not everyone has the financial means to bury a relative in Turkey. Especially in the case of young deaths, parents would like their children to be buried here.*

The realization of this cemetery took over nine years. When we first read about it in the newspaper, we were immediately interested. At last we are doing something for Muslims. It meant for us to be noticed and also the official support from the country meant for us that our community had value. It is the case with many mosques that they are often much too small and crowded into corners. If someone then asks for the address, one has to explain the way to a backyard in an awkward way. With this cemetery, it is a different story altogether. Simply giving the name is enough.

I asked her about her first impressions of the place.

It was a bit unusual when we first passed by. It took some getting used to because it stands out so distinctly from its natural setting. Little by little, its appearance has become more commonplace for me, but it remains something special.

And did the place strike her as fitting into Vorarlberg culture, I wondered.

Not really. But the way it's done, and how you adapt when you're here, I think that's very nice. This place is a bit different as a cemetery, but it integrates itself into the Vorarlberg landscape by using contemporary architecture. From the outside, it's Vorarlberg architecture, it looks like Vorarlberg, with concrete and everything. There's the reflex "Ah, a Vorarlberg architect made that for me," and when I'm inside I think of something completely different; I become melancholic, as if I were in another world.

In 2008, we built our house, a duplex house with its own garden, our own house in Rankweil Brederis. I grew up with two identities. I see this as a bonus point, being able to enlighten Austrians a bit and balance reality with what they are shown in the media. I tell them what I see and experience.

I've had an identity problem before. In Turkey they see me as a foreigner and here they used to see me as a Turk, but that's no longer the case... I was very concerned at the time because I hadn't passed the German Matura on my first attempt, which made me very sad. Then I tried to master the German language. I wanted to study at all costs, but I couldn't do that until now, now that I've completed my apprenticeship and can resume this path.

Do you also read specifically on the subject of identity? I asked her.

Today I don't dwell so intensely on the topic of integration. From time to time, but not often. I want to live here. I grew up here. I couldn't live in Turkey anymore—family, children, but perhaps also work and professional life there would be difficult.

Pear wood under a cover of glass

The architectural model on the fourth floor of the Vorarlberg Museum has a mild and gentle complexion. It is made of slightly reddish pear wood. Fine-textured and consistent with the intentions of the architect, it provides a good idea of the real material. Abstract, but still true to scale. A glass cover shields it from the hands of curious visitors turning it into something precious or ancient, something abstract, out of time. It was only two years after the cemetery's opening that the curators of the museum decided to integrate the model of the Islamic Cemetery in Altach into the exhibition *Making of Vorarlberg*. "I presume that by far more people have seen the model than the real cemetery, so it became somehow an important part of the exhibition idea," explains Fatih Özelik, member of the team of the museum but also part of its story: he too was raised by parents who migrated to Vorarlberg in the 1960s. He was very surprised when he heard the model would be exhibited in the museum, but views it positively as it introduces visitors to the wide spectrum of influences that formed the Vorarlberg of nowadays.

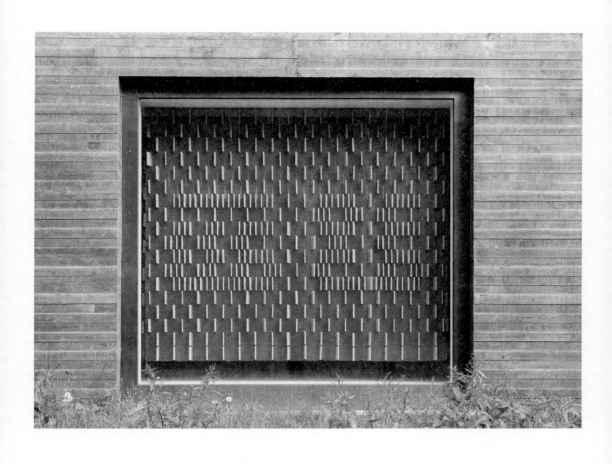

BERNARDO,
architect of the Islamic Cemetery Altach

I never actually had office partners. But I like to reflect about my projects with outsiders. One of them is my wife, of course. I show her almost everything; not every drawing, but every project. There is therefore a strong "amateurish" component. That was also a very important part of the process with the cemetery. In the working group, it was all about soliciting, pitching, and expanding ideas. What do people say? What moves them? Otherwise the project would never have come about like this. That was a very important approach. Listen first, then insert something, and see how it develops. Of course you must never lose the thread; that's crucial. But these open discussions are important.

I was curious to see if I could actually fulfil all of these expectations in a meaningful way, touching people, touching them sustainably—not that they simply say "yes, it is beautiful," but that they also say, "I like to go there." It's not necessarily the prizes I'm after, but quite simply the visitor feedback. And there was a lot of personal feedback at the cemetery, where you felt that it worked well and also touched people—that they go there often and it had become a "nice place" for them. There is, of course, a bit of irritation too, because it is not as tidy a cemetery as usually expected and it's now also being slowly encroached upon by nature; wild plants are growing into it, but that's exactly what I find very exciting about it.

This place also provides a good opportunity for the country in general to discuss sites like these— their design and significance. I do some guided tours at the cemetery from time to time and the same questions appears again and again. Why is the prayer room so reduced, so barren? But people then feel its mood and find it quite fascinating. They are mostly architectural laypersons, not many Muslims. Muslims are rather familiar with this type of reduction, because most Islamic cemeteries are not excessively decorated.

I have my own way, my own approach as an architect, to the site of a project. Of course, I have to act and react as an architect at this point. What is given landscape-wise, the light, the analysis of the place, the classical architectural themes, and of course, the influence of the working group. It's a soft process of letting ideas rise, letting a project grow. Some might have analyzed ten mosques, read the Koran three times, and so on. I didn't do that. I went twice to Istanbul, once with an excursion team. You feel very soon what the project could be; it's not so complicated. Sure, it's a different context, but the gist is the same everywhere. So you approach the project in terms of craftsmanship and in an architect's way. You have a plot of land, you have to structure it. There is the building and there is the cemetery. You figure out about the topics and tasks in a structured way and try to find what works, again and again.

Finally, you need a clear concept. In Altach, this was the orientation toward Mecca. It was important to me that an element also shows the transience and the annual rhythm, which is why the filtering lattice

is right next to the entrance, as an interface between outside and inside, which is different in spring than in winter—an incredibly beautiful effect that you don't really have to explain to anyone. Of course, this effect can be designed only to a certain extent. The fact that the sun falls so flatly in autumn that the shadow of the pattern appears on the back wall surprised me. A clear focus also helps when considering other inputs and additions. Is it now enough, or does something need to be added? And then you have to decide very clearly. No, it is good now, we must leave this element out, otherwise we weaken that other element. Focus supports discipline, and I learned that again very clearly from this project.

I wondered if there had been any impressions for Bernardo that had gained importance as the project went forward.

The site, primarily. That was the inspiration, first and foremost. Very strong. On one side there is the country road, but fortunately the view toward Mecca is incredibly beautiful. We did not build anything huge, just this light shell set back from the road. You can concentrate there. It's very strong, this scenic approach, but at the same time it is very delicate, almost fragile, open, completely open. Wall. Simply a wall. Begin with an element low, then bring it a little higher, then let go and let it end in a building.

The opening ceremony was quite emotional for me, I have to say. There were some people who I didn't even know and they said: "Thank you for doing this for us," or "It is very beautiful." And this "very beautiful" has become a platitude where you think "Oh, he's just saying that now," but they couldn't describe it any other way. They couldn't somehow verify it architecturally. They just said, "Super. Thank you for making it that way. Thanks to the group and everyone, too." You also noticed this appreciation in Mayor Brändle's internal presentation of the project. You could feel without many words spoken an incredible thank you.

"This has become a wonderful building," and so on. Yes, it's nice, I don't want to belittle these speeches. But that is what's so special about such projects. In fact, that's exactly why I studied architecture, because of this motivation. With the great teachers one used to have, with a Josef Lackner, for example, they worked out of a deep conviction. A little world-improving, and that's something I already find totally absurd in today's architectural discussion. You see the projects around on ArchDaily; they look the same all over the world. But this attempt to do something better, somewhere, is a nice motivation. You don't do jobs like these to earn money, and you don't do them to be congratulated on the many publications that follow. That's all nice, but it's about more.

Material

The choice of materials always follows a logic that corresponds to something functional or useful. The door handles and lock are made of brass contrasting to the oak wood of the doors. The brass faucet and basin stand out from the wall. The choice of materials is never trivial, but creates an artistic balance of carefully crafted materials. Their number is deliberately reduced to a minimum. One kind of wood, one kind of metal, one kind of solid stone. The principle of reduction sharpens the senses and makes their order visible. It emphasizes the form, the changes of light, and the traces of people. But the material itself is also transcended: it's not only a handle on a door, but it conveys something about the hands using and touching it. It silently becomes meaningful and timeless, superseding fashions and caprices of today's accelerated and commercial daily life.

It was surprising to me what architectural language can do. I worked in the textile industry for a long time and have always been close to design, but how much architecture can actually move people has become visible here at the Islamic Cemetery in an excellent way.
— Gottfried Brändle

Cultivating Convergence:
The Islamic Cemetery
Altach, Austria
Azra Akšamija

Figure 1. The Islamic Cemetery Altach, Austria (2011). Located along the federal road L190 between the municipalities of Hohenems and Götzis, the facility can accommodate approximately seven hundred graves; on its grounds there is also a structure for the ritual washing of the dead, as well as a small prayer space.

Homeland is the place where we would like to find the final resting.
— Dr. Fuat Sanaç, 3 June 2012

With these words, Fuat Sanaç, president of the Islamic Religious Community in Austria, addressed several hundred people at the inauguration of the newly built Islamic cemetery Altach, Vorarlberg.[1] Describing what this project means for Muslim immigrants in Austria, Sanaç's opening remarks point to the shifting conceptions of homeland for Muslim diasporic communities in their adopted country, and more notably, the remarks show that architecture can facilitate that shift.

For many, the cemetery's openness and design, which is grounded in Islamic and local building traditions, bear witness to a constructive dialogue between cultures (Fig. 1).[2] This essay probes the architectural parameters that shape such a dialogue, examining how Islamic funerary architecture can contribute to cultivating pluralism in Europe. Islamic cemeteries represent an opportunity to widen the scope of representation for Islam in the West beyond the mosque. This opportunity necessitates new approaches to creating Islamic architecture in non-Islamic environments that would be sensitive to local context and Muslim immigrants who have found a new homeland.[3] While most of the new Islamic cemeteries in Western Europe are focused on fulfilling the functional requirements of Islamic burial, the Altach cemetery, I argue, reveals a new route by creating a bridge between cultures and fostering intercultural exchange.

The cemetery was designed by the architect Bernardo Bader from the Bregenz Forest region of Vorarlberg, and the interior prayer space was conceived by myself, a Sarajevo-born Austrian Muslim artist and architectural historian.[4] The cemetery was completed in late 2011, nine years after the initial idea was born. The large amount of interest in the project has persisted even a year after the inauguration—the mayor of Altach, Gottfried Brändle, has given more than sixty guided tours.

It is even more astonishing that, throughout the entire implementation process, there have been no protests or media campaigns against the construction of this cemetery. This is very unusual, given that the visibility of Islam in the context of the immigration and integration politics in Austria represents a sensitive issue and that conflicts in response to construction of new mosques and Islamic cemeteries in Western Europe are very probable.[5] The Islamic Cemetery Altach was not only spared from conflicts, but it also found major international recognition in both Islamic and non-Islamic contexts, receiving the highly prestigious Aga Khan Award for Architecture in 2013, the Austrian Client Award 2013 and the International Piranesi Award in 2012.[6]

The reasons for the success of this project are manifold and, as I intend to explain in this essay, have to do with the ways in which the project has been communicated to the public and the ways in which it functions as a form of intercultural communication.

Root-taking in a new homeland

State law has recognized the Islamic religious community in Austria for over a hundred years, but only recently have burials according to the Islamic rite become possible. An Islamic burial rite helps the mourning community in overcoming its loss by placing emphasis on the spiritual journey of the deceased to afterlife, rather than mourning the physical loss of the beloved person. Inhumation burials are the only form of burial in Islam, which, according to the Islamic belief, allows for a resurrection.[7] The deceased is prepared for the burial though a ritual washing conducted by a specialized personnel, and then wrapped in simple white cotton sheets. To facilitate quick decay, the grave is constructed in such a way that the soil can touch the corpse. No coffins are used—the corpse is placed directly on wooden planks placed in the grave hole. This is very different from burials in Europe and the United States, where the use of coffins is at times obligatory. In fact, burials without a coffin are prohibited in Austria by law, which means that Muslims in all Austrian cemeteries are buried in coffins. Finally, the family and friends of the deceased accompany the deceased person's "journey" to the hereafter with collective prayers. The corpses and graves are oriented toward Mecca. Being buried within a community of Muslims is also important; this practice of being buried within one's own religious community is common to other cultures, as evident, for example, from the developments in the European funerary architecture. Since the end of the nineteenth century, communal cemeteries in European cities with religiously mixed population have witnessed proliferation of cemeteries with distinct grave fields for their Catholic, Protestant, and Jewish communities.[8]

The Islamic Cemetery Altach is the first of its kind constructed in the western Austrian province of Vorarlberg.[9] It is only the second Islamic cemetery ever constructed in all of Austria; the first was built in Vienna in 2008. The two cemeteries differ in their administrative status: the Islamic cemetery in Vienna is a confessional cemetery run by the Islamic Religious Community of Austria, whereas the Islamic Cemetery Altach is a municipal cemetery managed by the city of Altach for the different communities of Vorarlberg. Before these cemeteries, Austrian municipal cemeteries were not built to accommodate Islamic funerals, making it necessary to transport the dead (after a long, expensive, and bureaucratically complex process) to their countries of origin.

The Altach cemetery serves the 51,000 Muslims who live in the ninety-six communities of Vorarlberg (thirteen percent of the local population).[10] The Muslim community in Vorarlberg is predominantly comprised of Turkish immigrants who came to Vorarlberg in the 1960s as "migrant workers"; Bosnian Muslims who sought refuge in Austria during the Yugoslav wars in the 1990s; and immigrants from Chechnya and North African countries who came to the region in the last two decades.[11] The assumption held in 1960s Austria that these migrant workers would one day return to their countries of origin has long been proven wrong. Austria has now become home to many Muslim immigrants; their third- and fourth-generation descendants have become part of the culturally heterogeneous Austrian population. The immigrants' decision to bury their dead in Austria, rather than in the country of their origin, points at the process of "root-taking" in the adopted country.

The Altach cemetery is part of the ongoing processes of Europe's social and cultural diversification, which is manifested in the increasing number of Islamic cemeteries. The oldest Islamic cemeteries in Germany and the United Kingdom date back to the nineteenth century, and some cemeteries in Western Europe have facilitated special burial grounds for Muslims.[12] The building of separate Islamic cemeteries, however, represents a novel phenomenon in Western European funerary architecture. Most of them opened in the past ten years, such as the one that opened in London in 2002; in Zurich in 2004; in Brøndby, near Copenhagen, in 2006; and in Paris in 2012. These new developments in European funerary architecture provide an opportunity for representation and mediation of Islam in the West. Most of these new Islamic cemeteries, however, have been built to fulfill primarily functional necessities, missing the opportunity to shape Europe's diversity from an architectural standpoint.[13]

In order to understand how the Altach cemetery takes a lead in addressing the changing notion of a Muslim homeland, we can consider related debates over identity and representation in other realms of Islamic religious architecture. Over the course of the past century, the mosque has been the primary architectural repository of identity and authenticity for those Muslims displaced from their countries of origin.[14] The sociocultural transformation processes in a postcolonial and globalized society and the related fear of loss of identity are architecturally reflected in the attempts to preserve identities by insisting on Islamic signifiers such as domes and minarets. Consider, for example, the mosque in Vienna, Austria (1979) or the more recent Essalam al-Maktoum Mosque in Rotterdam, Netherlands (2006); both are inspired by their monumental Ottoman and Mamluk predecessors.[15]

This traditionalist (and predominant) approach to designing contemporary Islamic architecture has been criticized for its reliance on historic forms that project an image of Islamic cultures as static and "stuck" in time.[16] The insistence on domes and minarets as the defining elements of the mosque contradicts its fluid architectural definition and historical richness of forms and types.[17] The traditionalist designs have also been interpreted as an expression of "homeland nostalgia," lacking an architectural relationship to the local context.[18] These designs are often perceived as "alien" to their surroundings and are interpreted as an indication of the immigrant community's lack of integration in the dominant society.[19] What connects all these criticisms, regardless of the validity of the claims, is the concern for the references chosen to represent contemporary Muslims in the West. Central to this concern is architectures that can express both the identity of their users and engage the specific cultural context in which they are located.

More and more, architects are taking on this challenging task and investigating different methods to address Muslim immigrants' quest for more visibility under a less negative spotlight. Examples such as the newly built Islamic Center in Penzberg, Germany (2005) and the design for the mosque and Islamic Center in Aarhus, Denmark (2007) signal both an Islamic and European identity through a marriage of Islamic ornaments with modernist forms. However, when they are more generic or too abstract, designs such as these often fail to facilitate a sense of identification for their Muslim users.

None of the issues discussed above have affected the funerary architecture in Europe so far, except for the Islamic Cemetery Altach. The cemetery is pioneering in the way it addresses both functional and representational needs, thereby fostering coexistence, culturally sensitive design, and an inclusive building process that reveals the dialogic dimension of architecture. This last dimension fosters cultural convergence and fosters mutual understanding.

Architecture as community-making process

The Altach cemetery has made community through the process of building and public mediation. Before the Altach cemetery was built, there was no other possibility for Muslims of Vorarlberg to be buried there according to their traditions. Vorarlberg's cemeteries are managed by municipalities and none of them possessed a burial ground that could have been used for Muslims. The growing number of the deceased Muslims in Vorarlberg necessitated the need for Islamic burial grounds. Hence, a new solution had to be found. One option was to create separate burial grounds within different municipality cemeteries, which would then be open to burials of Muslims from different Islamic sects. The other option, which was then also finalized, was to create a single Islamic cemetery for all Muslims of Vorarlberg. The solution eventually settled on was unique: a separate Islamic cemetery managed by a single municipality, as a cooperation of all municipalities in Voralrberg, and that can be used by Muslims of different confessional affiliations.

This unique solution evolved an inclusive and participatory process bringing together all Muslims of Voralberg who live in ninety-three of ninety-six municipalities of Vorarlberg, the municipal and regional governments, institutions of the Catholic Church and minority-culture organizations such as okay.zusammen leben, an informational and advising center on immigration and integration issues in Vorarlberg.[20] The cemetery project was carried out through an intense mediation carried out by Eva Grabherr, an academic expert in history and Jewish studies and founding director of okay.zusammen leben, Attila Dincer, the spokesperson for the Islamic Community in Vorarlberg, and Mayor Brändle, who is an enthusiastic advocate for the cemetery.

In 2004, different Muslim communities and associations of immigrants in Vorarlberg founded Initiative Islamic Cemetery, hoping to create a common burial ground in their adopted homeland. The subsequent process was guided and mediated by Eva Grabherr who, in her role as the director of the okay.zusammen leben, commissioned an expert report to demonstrate the need for an Islamic cemetery in Vorarlberg. This report was created by Elisabeth Dörler, the envoy to the Islamic community for the Vorarlberg Catholic Church, in 2004.[21]

That same year, the Islamic community of Bregenz, the Islamic Religious Community of Austria, and Initiative Islamic Cemetery filed an application with the Vorarlberg state government for the construction of the cemetery. The Association of Local Authorities in Vorarlberg issued a recommendation document for the cemetery in 2005. The next step was to find an adequate site—not an easy task given the politically sensitive debate about the presence of Islam in Austria. The municipality of Altach voluntarily approached the project initiators to offer them a plot, which the Association of Local Authorities in Vorarlberg purchased in 2006.

Figure 2: The small prayer space within the Islamic Cemetery Altach, Austria (2011).
The qibla wall-curtain and the prayer rugs were designed by artist Azra Akšamija.

Subsequently, an invitation-only architectural idea competition was launched, and the winning project was designed by Bernardo Bader.[22] Between 2007 and 2010, Bader's office carried out the planning phase and preparatory work on the site.[23] A group of imams from Vorarlberg and a "Working Group Construction" (*Arbeitsgruppe Bau*) composed of representatives and experts from the local Islamic communities selected by communities themselves and invited by Eva Grabherr assisted in the development of the project and advised planners about the particular ritual requirements for an Islamic cemetery.[24] I was commissioned to create the interior design of the masjid.[25] My concept for a space that bridges different cultures though the qibla wall and the prayer rugs was implemented in close collaboration with Bader.

Throughout the planning and construction process of the cemetery, there was only very little public critique.[26] The few points of critique that were publically discussed in response to diverse informational events and media reports regarded the following three issues: 1. The fact that a separate Islamic cemetery was to be built was seen by some as a sign that Muslims want to separate themselves from their Christian neighbors, while others understood this as a diametrically opposite tendency; 2. The remote location of the cemetery was understood as something that would underscore social exclusion of Muslims from the dominant society; and 3. The reasons for the need of a large plot of land was seen as unjustified (regardless of the required inhumation burials).[27]

A major constraint on the development of the design was the lack of organizational structures in the local Islamic communities and associations, which made the decision-making process difficult. Executive bodies first needed to be formed and their representatives chosen. The fact that Islamic groups and associations living across ninety-six communities in the region wanted to jointly realize this project added to the communication and organization challenges. The project would have taken far less time had the establishment of these organizational networks and communication channels not been necessary.

The process of mediation and building the cemetery put a spotlight on the organizational structures of the local Muslim groups because the activities of planning, administration, and construction required the presence of representative decision-making bodies. On a social level, this project brought together very diverse Islamic groups for a common purpose. The will to share the burial ground necessitated networking and collaboration between people with ideologically diverging positions (i.e., orthodox Sunnis and the Alevis), demonstrating that a building process can stimulate community-making and encourage conciliation.

Converging in design

From the design perspective, the Islamic Cemetery Altach demonstrates how architecture can inspire a process of finding common ground between different cultures without having them become the same. The subtle simplicity of the cemetery's architecture and its integration with the surrounding nature provide a calm and dignified place for spiritual contemplation and mourning. Bader and his consultants worked with the idea of "the cemetery as a primordial garden"— a recurring theme across different religious traditions. To create a garden means to demarcate a plot of land from its surroundings for cultivation. This idea was architecturally translated into a lattice-like system of light-red exposed concrete walls of varying heights, embedded in the marshy terrain and enclosing distinct burial areas. The "finger-shaped" grave fields allow for the ritually correct orientation toward Mecca, as well as for phased occupancy.

The delicate mesh of red concrete walls patterned by formwork surrounds the burial fields and the structural facilities. The cemetery's main entrance is perpendicular to a long outer wall; the visitor is welcomed by an ornamental opening in a wall that bears a wooden lattice featuring Islamic geometric patterns in an octagonal motif. Crossing the threshold, the visitor enters a partially roofed space large enough to accommodate a congregation and a crowd of mourners. This space opens onto the courtyard and is characterized by a lively play of light and shadow. The position of the openings guides the visitor's gaze toward the burial garden and the foothills of the Freschengebirge (Freschen Mountains) that can be seen in the background.

My design of the masjid's interior was intended to symbolically and visually connect the different cultures in Vorarlberg though formal and material references to local and Islamic traditions. The qibla wall was executed in the form of three stainless steel mesh curtains covered with an array of wooden shingles (Fig. 2). These curtains are positioned parallel to the wall and the mihrab window at different distances, an arrangement that emulates a prayer niche with the muqarnas. Since the shingle curtains also function as blinds, they break the light, making it more dramatic and underscoring not only the architectural significance of light in mosques, but also highlighting the analogy between light and spirit, light (An-Nūr) being one of the ninety-nine names of God.

The qibla wall was designed to be seen differently by different observers, depending on their position in the space and their angle of vision. Upon entering, the qibla wall appears to be a wooden shingle wall, which resonates with Vorarlberg's local architectural tradition. To a moving observer, the pattern of the shingle curtains appears animated. Arranged in the direction of Mecca, the shingles are parallel to the visitor's direction of prayer. Because the shingles are positioned orthogonally to the window, the visitor has a clear view of the park surrounding the cemetery outside, which symbolically reiterates the notion of mihrab as a gateway to the afterlife (Fig. 3).

Six prayer rugs with long, alternating beige and brown colored stripes indicate prayer rows. Their pattern reiterates the rhythm of the shingles from the qibla wall. The color gradient of the carpets increases the perception of spatial depth, brightening in the direction of Mecca and continuing the theme of directionality of prayer and purity of the prayer space.

The prayer carpets (kilims) were hand-woven in a specialized workshop, the "Association for the Preservation of the Bosnian Kilim," based in Sarajevo, Bosnia and Herzegovina.[28] The choice of the workshop was significant not only because it addressed the cultural origins of the Bosnian Muslim communities in Vorarlberg, but also served as a contribution to preserving the craft in Bosnia and Herzegovina, where war in the 1990s inflicted massive destruction on cultural heritage. The workshop employs women who were victims of the war, and working in the craft serves as a form of trauma recovery for them. The Islamic Cemetery Altach also recognized the importance of such humanitarian efforts.

The principal materials used in constructing the cemetery's buildings include exposed reinforced concrete for the walls and oak wood for the ornamentation of the entrance facade and the interior of the prayer space. Special attention was paid to the appearance of the exposed concrete, the design of which evolved from advances in structural and material technology involving coloring and the design of formwork patterns. To achieve the desired color tone, ten wall samples were tinted by mixing black and red pigments in different ratios. The final tone was chosen based on the wall's appearance at the site. The aim was to create a contrast between the colors of the surrounding cliffs, the fields, and the architecture. The texture of the exposed concrete walls was created though a particular arrangement of formwork planks of varying thicknesses and widths. The surfaces of the exterior walls reflect the texture of the rough-sawn boards used for the formwork (in three different thicknesses), while the inner surfaces remained smooth and plain. This created a subtle distinction between the interior and exterior walls.

The use of wood was important in evoking the local building traditions of Vorarlberg, a region known for its woodcraft. For the wooden lattice ornament in the entrance, wall oak was crafted using traditional carpentry and mechanical techniques. The individual wooden boards were first milled with CNC machines and then linked without glue or screws using conventional carpentry techniques. Wood played an important role in the design of the prayer space interior, which is entirely clad in white-stained wood. For the qibla wall, fir wood shingles with a natural finish were used.[29] Invisible bolt connections pierce tightly through the mesh of the stainless-steel curtains at two points and provide a rigid and stable positioning of the shingles perpendicular to the mesh. This was important to achieve the animated appearance of the overall pattern while simultaneously maintaining the textile look of the curtains.

Conclusion

The Islamic Cemetery Altach is a product of a fruitful dialogue between Muslim immigrants and the dominant society in Austria, underscoring the importance of Islamic religious architecture for more expansive integration politics in Europe. In light of the project's religious requirements, the political sensitivities of the program, and the lack of organizational links between local Islamic communities and associations, the building of the cemetery necessitated intense collaboration among many diverse groups. The remarkable achievement of this project is that the participatory process contributed to the forming of continuing organizational structures for Muslims in Vorarlberg.

With the construction of the first Islamic cemetery in Vorarlberg, local Muslim immigrants and the local community signaled that Austria is welcoming to Islam and that architecture can be a bridge between cultures. The project symbolically acknowledges the coexistence of different religions and ethnicities in Austria. For Muslim immigrants in Vorarlberg, the cemetery is a symbol that Austria has

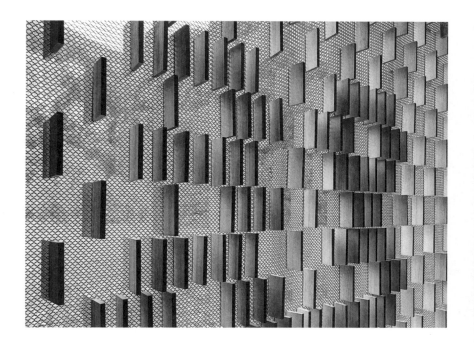

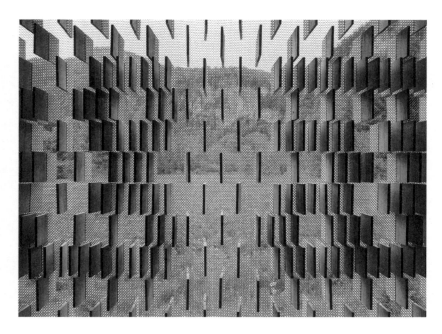

Figure 3: Detail of the qibla wall-curtain. At eye level, an array of gold-coated shingles is arranged more densely to spell out the words "Allah" and "Muhammad" in Kufic script.

become their new homeland, in which the remains of their ancestors can lie buried according to Islamic rituals. For many of them, as Fuat Sanaç put it, the cemetery symbolizes the fact that a homeland is no longer where one came from, but where one chooses to bury one's dead.[30]

This meaningful dimension of the project is most poignant in regard to the connections that were forged between Muslims and non-Muslims, as evident from the very large local interest in this project. The cemetery's pedagogical potential continues to nourish a sense of pride and ownership within Islamic communities. The architectural significance of the project has come to the fore. By moving beyond the "dome vs. cube" and the "traditionalist vs. modernist" design dichotomies that dominate the architectural discourse concerning the choice of symbolic markers of Islamic identity, the cemetery in Altach renders visible a new culturally sensitive aesthetic that is simultaneously local, Islamic, and European.[31]

1 Sanaç stated: "Heimat ist dort, wo man gerne die letzte Ruhe finden möchte." Brigitte Hellrigl, "Ein Stück Heimat Für Muslime," *Vorarlberg Online*, 4 June 2012, http://www.vol.at/ein-stueck-heimat-fuer-muslime/3270716. My translation.

2 With "many," I am referring to the local community members and the local media reports.

3 It should be noted that not all Muslims in Europe are immigrants; there are converts and also people who were born in Western European countries as Muslims. In this essay, I am referring mainly to first- and second generation immigrant communities.

4 Bader originates from the Bregenz Forest (Bregenzer Wald) region and his office is based in Dornbirn, Austria. For more information about the architect Bernardo Bader and his work see: http://www.bernardobader.com

5 Stefano Allievi and Ethnobarometer, eds., *Mosques in Europe: Why a Solution Has Become a Problem—NEF Initiative on Religion and Democracy in Europe* (London: Alliance Publishing Trust, 2010).

6 The project was also nominated for other renowned international awards, such as the DETAIL Prize in 2012 and the 2013 European Union Prize for Contemporary Architecture Mies van der Rohe Award.

7 Elisabeth Dörler, "Eine Begräbnisstätte für Muslime und MuslimInnen in Vorarlberg," okay.zusammen leben. Projektstelle für Zuwanderung und Integration, 2 October 2004, www.okay-line.at/file/656/empfehlungspapierislamischerfriedhof.pdf.

8 Last year, Austria celebrated the 100th jubilee of its "Islamic law," issued in 1912 following the Austro-Hungarian annexation of Bosnia and Herzegovina. This law recognized Sunni (Hanafi) Muslims as a religious community and guaranteed them the same religious rights as those of the Empire's other recognized religions.

9 For the chronology of the project realization, see "Eine Begräbnisstätte für MuslimInnen in Vorarlberg," *Okay-line Für Zuwanderung Und Integration in Vorarlberg*, accessed 10 December 2012. http://www.okay-line.at/deutsch/okay.zusammen-leben/doku-prozessbegleitung/.

10 The number of Muslims living in Vorarlberg in 2019 was 50,797 persons. Eva Grabherr, "Die aktuelle Demografie der muslimischen Bevölkerung Vorarlbergs," in Eva Grabherr, ed., *Vorarlbergs Moscheegemeinden: Die Organisationen und ihre Entwicklung*, commissioned by okay.zusammen leben, Projektstelle für Zuwanderung und Integration (September 2019), 13. downloadable at https://www.okay-line.at/Wissen/religioesevielfalt-in-vorarlberg/vorarlbergs moscheegemeinden.html, accessed 18 January 2020.

11 Dörler.

12 Germany's oldest Islamic cemetery is the Turkish Cemetery of Berlin-Şehitlık dating to 1863. In the United Kingdom, there are a number of historic Islamic burial sites, such as the Brookwood cemetery near Woking in Surrey.

13 I am using the problematic phrase "Islam in the West" for the sake of word limits, but I would like to point out that neither of the two can be understood as homogenous entities. In my understanding of these terms, both Islam as religion and the West as a geographical region standing primarily for Western European countries and the United States, Canada, and Australia, are ideologically, culturally, historically, and politically heterogeneous.

14 For developments of mosque architecture over the course of the twentieth century, as they evolved in response to the nationalist movements in the Islamic world and the identity formation of the Islamic diasporic communities in the West, see: Renata Holod, Hasan-Uddin Khan, and Kimberly Mims, *The Mosque and the*

Modern World: Architects, Patrons and Designs Since the 1950s (Thames and Hudson, 1997); Omar Khalidi, "Import, Adapt, Innovate: Mosque Design in the United States," *Saudi Aramco World* 52(6) (December 2001): 24–33; Nebahat Avcioglu, "Identity-as-Form: The Mosque in the West," *Cultural Analysis* 6 (2007): 91–112.

15 While the broadcasting of the *athan* is often not permitted, the function of minarets remains primarily symbolic. They act as architectural anchors for identity of immigrant communities.

16 Khalidi, "Import, Adapt, Innovate: Mosque Design in the United States."

17 Azra Akšamija, "Generative Design Principles for the Contemporary Mosque," in *The Mosque. Political, Architectural and Social Transformations*, Ergün Erkoçu and Cihan Bugdaci, eds. (Rotterdam: NAi Publishers, 2009), 129–39.

18 Christian Welzbacher, *Euro Islam Architecture: New Mosques in the West* (Amsterdam: SUN, 2008).

19 We could, of course, argue that domes and minarets can indeed be understood as contemporary forms, and that having them is both a matter of personal taste and freedom of religious expression. We should also keep in mind that architectural arguments often conceal xenophobic politics and Islamophobic populism. As a whole, however, the ongoing debates over mosque appearances demonstrate the vital role of architecture in mediating the challenges of European society to come to terms with its own cultural diversification and social integration. For more information on mosque conflicts, see Stefano Allievi and Ethnobarometer, eds., *Mosques in Europe: Why a Solution Has Become a Problem—NEF Initiative on Religion and Democracy in Europe* (London: Alliance Publishing Trust, 2010).

20 okay.zusammen leben describes itself as "an information and advice centre for immigration and integration issues in the Austrian province Vorarlberg. The Aktion Mitarbeit society is responsible for the centre. It was founded in the autumn of 2001. The majority of the funding is provided by the Vorarlberg State Government." For more information, see "okay-line für Zuwanderung und Integration in Vorarlberg," accessed 10 December 2012, http://www.okay-line.at/deutsch/okay.zusammen-leben/english-portrait/.

21 Dörler.

22 The competition brief specified the parameters concerning the burial grounds and their supporting structures, including a space for the ritual washing, a mortuary facility for a maximum of two deceased, ablution facilities for the mourners (four to eight persons), sanitary facilities, a small masjid (for individual prayer for five to ten people), a weather-protected area for about fifty people for the congregational prayer (not an enclosed space), a well, off-road, and parking. The competition aimed for a design that would address the following issues: programming at the site (access, facilities, parking lots, grave sites, and footpaths), fencing, choice of materials, and planting.

23 Unsuitable soil properties posed a major concern at the very start of the project. The existing clay soil at the site was too soft for the construction and inappropriate for burials. Consequently, this soil had to be removed and replaced with soil containing more sand and gravel, which was then allowed to settle for a year before construction work on the site could begin.

24 The constant members of the "Working Group Construction" who accompanied the entire planning and construction process of the cemetery included: Attila Dincer, Eva Grabherr, Baki Kaya, Jusuf Mesic, and Nuri Sarıgül.

25 The commission of Azra Akšamija for the interior design of the prayer space was part of the "percent for the arts" program to foster contemporary arts within public constructions.

26 "Islamischer Friedhof Altach," Information brochure by the Municipality of Altach, accessed 10 December 2012, http://altach.at/buergerservice/bestattung/islamischer-friedhof-altach.

27 Ibid.

28 Founded by the artist and rug specialist Amila Smajović, this workshop is committed to fostering research and to preserving and reproducing traditional Bosnian kilims, which are a historical product of diverse Islamic and local weaving traditions.

29 Following unsatisfactory tests with traditional planed shingles, it was decided to use machine-cut shingles, which allowed for better precision and legibility of the curtain-wall pattern and its calligraphy.

30 Hellrigl.

31 Parts of this chapter, such as this sentence, were written by myself and were used for the description of the project for the Aga Khan Award submission.

This text has been slightly revised and edited from the previously published article: Azra Akšamija, "Cultivating Convergence: The Islamic Cemetery Altach," *International Journal for Islamic Architecture* 3(1) (March 2014): 131–45.

The Islamic Cemetery as an Expression of the Process of Muslim Belonging in Vorarlberg

Simon Burtscher-Mathis

On the way through the middle of the Rhine valley region in Vorarlberg, there is a bus stop named "Islamischer Friedhof" (Islamic Cemetery) between Götzis and Hohenems. Directly next to it is a building of striking simplicity and impression, whose function would be unrecognizable were it not for the information on the bus stop. Visitors coming from outside the region probably ask themselves why an Islamic cemetery is situated here in the middle of the Rhine valley, near the historic Jewish cemetery. If interest is awakened and visitors enter the cemetery, they find a few lightly occupied fields of graves and, generally, only a few visitors; questions might then arise as to why and for whom this particular cemetery was built.

The answers are found in the history of immigration to Vorarlberg. Muslims currently comprise around thirteen percent (51,000 of 394,000) of the population of Vorarlberg and live in ninety-three of the ninety-six municipalities in Vorarlberg. There, immigration is hence not a purely urban, but also a rural phenomenon, and one that is occurring in all communities. And, nevertheless, there are no individual burial sites for Muslims in the municipalities' local Christian cemeteries, but instead one large Islamic cemetery for all the Muslims of Vorarlberg.

With the cemetery, which is located in the zone between Hohenems, Altach, and Götzis, a "landmark" for this region was also created. Just as people have spoken for centuries about the area around the Jewish cemetery in the Schwefel district of Hohenems, the Islamic Cemetery is also part of the landscape and has thus also become a reference point. At the same time, the population can also drive past without taking any notice, since the cemetery is situated in an area that is largely unused by the public. It is an intermediate space frequented mainly by cars and otherwise used primarily for agriculture and for walks by local residents. In other words, the cemetery is visible, but does not need to be noticed, necessarily.

With that basic backdrop, this text deals with the positioning and sense of belonging of Muslims in Vorarlberg. To this end, it starts by taking a look at the history of Muslim immigration to Vorarlberg, and explains the reasons for it as well as specific characteristics. The process by which Muslims have become established in Vorarlberg will then be addressed from the perspective of the "established outsider" model of the sociologist Norbert Elias[1] on the basis of research and data about the second generation in Vorarlberg[2] and the TIES Study (The Integration of European Second Generations)[3] for Vorarlberg. Further, the relationship between Muslims and established local residents will be examined based on the example of immigrants of Turkish origin.

Immigration history and the profile of Muslims in Vorarlberg

Muslim immigration from Turkey occurred as part of economic developments after the Second World War.[4] As in other nations in Europe (e.g., Germany), the majority of the immigrant population of Vorarlberg arrived as a result of the labor migration of the 1960s to 1970s and the subsequent reunification of families in the state. Strong growth in the textile and metal industry led to a large demand for an uneducated, low-skilled workforce, which was met for the most part by the migration of guest workers from Turkey and the former Yugoslavia. Since the Turkish workers were Muslims, Islam also came to Vorarlberg along with them. Until today, the largest group of Muslims by far (ca. 80%) in Vorarlberg comes from Turkey.

In 1964 and 1966, agreements for recruiting labor migrants were concluded between Austria and Turkey and/or Yugoslavia. In 1973, 22% of payroll employees in Vorarlberg were guest workers. With the decline in industry and the transformation of the economy, the demand for unskilled labor decreased, so that no new bilateral contracts were concluded in the 1980s or 1990s. Nonetheless, migrant guest workers did not return to their country of origin, as had generally been expected. Instead, further immigration took place as a result of family reunification.

In comparison with the rest of Austria, the rate of naturalization in Vorarlberg was low until the late 1980s, in particular with respect to immigrants of Turkish and ex-Yugoslavian origin. It was first in the 1990s that naturalizations increased strongly in both groups of immigrants. This can be regarded as an indication of Vorarlberg's transition to a state of immigration. Since the 1990s at the latest, the rotation model (guest worker model) has also been superseded by the remain model in the public discourse on integration. With this transition to a state of immigration, integrating the second generation into the educational system in Vorarlberg as well as into other socially relevant areas increasingly gained in importance given this demographic and economic transformation.

Since the changeover from population censuses to registry censuses, reliable information about religious affiliation in Austria is no longer available. The last reliable figures on religious affiliation in Vorarlberg thus come from the final population census in 2001. The religious affiliations[5] of the population of Vorarlberg are currently (2018) estimated at 61% Catholics, with Muslims comprising 13% (of 394,000 residents = 51,000 individuals). With the decreasing percentage of Catholics, the percentage of individuals with no religious affiliation has also been growing in recent years (2018: 18%).

In the course of the preparations to construct a Muslim burial ground, Elisabeth Dörler provided the last comprehensive description of the Muslim population of Vorarlberg based on the population census of 2001.[6] At that point in time, 75 to 80% were Sunnis (Hanefitic school of Islam), with 90% coming from Turkey and 10% from Bosnia. Twenty to 25% were Alevi from Turkey. In addition, there were a few Muslims from other schools of Islam and Islamic countries such as Egypt, Algeria, Morocco, or Tunisia. Based on the latest estimations in 2018, 45% of the Muslims in Vorarlberg were born in Austria, 34% in Turkey, 7% in the former Yugoslavia, and 14% in other countries.

The civil war in Chechnya also resulted in a new wave of Muslims leaving that country. Currently, 1,768 Muslims from Chechnya live in Vorarlberg.[7] With the forced migration of the past four years, additional Muslims from Afghanistan (1,637), Pakistan (137), Iraq (572), and Syria (2,561)[8] have immigrated to Vorarlberg. As of today, immigrants from Turkey still comprise the largest share of Muslims in Vorarlberg, with Bosnian Muslims as the second-largest group. The autochthonous majority population thus continues to equate Muslims in Vorarlberg with the Turkish population. Thus, if one wants to comprehend the relationship of Muslims to the autochthonous majority, it is particularly important to focus on the relative stability and mobility of the Turkish-origin population vis-à-vis the majority. What serves as an orientation framework in such a comparison is Norbert Elias's established outsider model,[9] according to which, for at least two to three generations, new groups of immigrants find themselves in an outsider position that is inferior in power compared to population groups that have been established for a longer period of time. The central question is how the process of integration and becoming established of the second generation of Turkish origin can be described within the context of their outsider status in relation to established local residents.[10] To this end, the author consulted data on the integration status of the second generation in Europe from the comparative, international TIES Study[11] (The Integration of European Second Generations), for which data on the first and second generation of Turkish origin in Vorarlberg were collected.

Socialization, educational attainments, and language competence of the first generation of Turkish origin

The first generation of Turkish origin arrived in Vorarlberg in the course of the migration of labor from rural regions, which were poorly developed in terms of industry and hence struggled with high unemployment. Seventy percent of the fathers and 67% of the mothers of the second generation of Turkish origin grew up in rural villages and came from structurally weak, preindustrial regions, which were characterized by premodern social structures and correspondingly limited educational and work opportunities.[12]

As expected, the majority of the parents of the second generation of Turkish origin reached the highest level of schooling in their country of origin: 86% (224) of the fathers reached their highest level of educational attainment in a Turkish school and only 6% (16) in Austria.[13] The situation for mothers is similar: 73% (190) obtained their highest level of schooling in Turkey and only 6% (15) in Austria. Thus, various educational backgrounds are connected with this. A comparison of groups of immigrants from Turkey and the former Yugoslavia with the autochthonous majority population in the TIES Study Vorarlberg[14] shows that considerably more fathers (78%) and mothers (77%) of the second generation of Turkish origin only attended an elementary or compulsory school. This figure is the lowest in the group without a migration background. Among fathers without a migration background and fathers of the second generation of ex-Yugoslavian origin, nearly half have completed vocational education as their highest level of schooling, while, in the case of fathers of Turkish origin, this only applies to four individuals (1.6%), and thus indicates a lack of qualification opportunities. The percentage of fathers who attended a school with a Matura (matriculation examination) level or obtained a tertiary level of education after Matura is considerably higher in the group without a migration background than in groups with a migration background. In the case of mothers without a migration background, the largest share, and, in the case of mothers of the second generation of ex-Yugoslavian origin, the second-largest share completed vocational training as their highest level of schooling. For mothers of the second generation of Turkish origin, this only applies to one person (0.5%). The percentage of mothers who attended a school with a Matura level or reached a tertiary level of education is some-what higher in the group with an ex-Yugoslavian migration background than in the group without a migration background. In both groups, the percentage is considerably higher than in the group of Turkish origin. The educational level of fathers and mothers of Turkish origin is by far the lowest, and that of autochthonous parents without a migration background the highest.

The international comparison in the TIES Study[15] generally shows that, in all countries, parents of the autochthonous comparison group without a migration background obtained higher levels of edu-cation than the parents of the second generation; the latter are strongly overrepresented in the lowest area (no schooling, solely religious school, elementary school), and quite strongly underrepresented in the upper level (postsecondary and tertiary area). With just a few exceptions (parents of Turkish origin in Linz, fathers in Vienna, Zurich, Basel, Paris, and Stockholm), in all countries, the parents of the second generation have a considerably lower level of education than the parents of the comparison group without a migration background, a fact that should be taken into account in particular when analyzing the educational trajectories and attainments of the second generation.

Study respondents with a Turkish migration background and parents with factually low education levels also subjectively assessed the German language knowledge of their parents as lower than re-spondents of ex-Yugoslavian origin.[16] Correspondingly, a larger share of respondents with an ex-Yugo-slavian migration background stated that their parents are able to read and write German more often than the second generation of Turkish origin. This difference is particularly clear in the case of mothers.

In the international and national comparison to other groups of immigrants, it is thus shown that Muslim immigrants from Turkey in Vorarlberg come from rural, premodern environments, completed short educational trajectories, and correspondingly have few formal educational attainments. For the questions raised in this text and/or in the second generation's process of integration and becoming established, this means that they are only able to assist their children to a limited extent with their educational paths, and that their immigration to Vorarlberg necessitates a process of transformation over several generations within families.

The second generation of Turkish origin and their process of becoming established

The comparative analysis of the educational trajectories of the second generation in the TIES Study Vorarlberg[17] shows that the autochthonous group without a migration background has obtained considerably higher qualifications than the second generation, and that the second generation of ex-Yugoslavian origin as a whole obtained higher qualifications than the second generation of Turkish origin. Both second generation groups have achieved upward mobility above all in the area of vocational training/apprenticeships, but this holds true to a greater extent for the second generation of ex-Yugo-slavian origin. At the same time, the group of the second generation of Turkish origin with its highest educational attainment in the area of compulsory schooling is strongly overrepresented. In the second generation of Turkish origin there are hence considerably more so-called early school leavers, who have at most completed a secondary education, and, simultaneously, fewer so-called high achievers, who obtain a post-secondary degree following their Matura.[18]

The international comparison of groups of migrants first facilitated by the TIES Study[19] shows that the second generation of Turkish origin is consistently one of the most disadvantaged groups, but performs well to varying degrees in different countries. Educational mobility is greater in educational systems with an earlier preschool education that differentiate to a lesser extent and at a later point in time than in educational systems in Austria, which differentiates relatively early. This effect of early differentiation in Austria is intensified by entering preschool care at a later point in time and by the reduced emphasis on preschool education in general. As a result of the large share of learning achievements that have to be realized outside of school in Austria in the form of homework assignments and learning tasks at home, the educational attainments of parents also have an effect: parents with higher educational attainments are able to assist their children better with school-related tasks at home. Parents of the first generation of Turkish origin, in contrast, were only able to support their children to a very limited extent due to their low formal educational attainments and limited language skills.

In summary, it can be determined that the second generation has realized upward educational mobility in comparison to the first generation, but the distance from the autochthonous population group remains. The upward educational mobility of the second generation is also confirmed by a current analysis by August Gächter (2017),[20] even though his study and the data on the labor market integration of the second generation in TIES[21] show that this is still only reflected to a limited extent in higher professional positions. This upward mobility of the second generation, which takes place above all in the area of vocational education, at the same time becomes visible to some extent socio-spatially in the establishing of companies and buying of real estate, as well as in the renovation and erection of new mosque buildings. Muslims have thus become structurally integrated and settled. According to this, the Islamic Cemetery Altach is further proof of this process of becoming established.

Connections with the receiving society and the society of origin

In comparison with autochthonous young people without a migration background, the second generation has had to overcome specific challenges in the formation of its identity. The members of this generation have to unite their relationship to the country of origin of their parents with their relationship to the society in which they have grown up. The vast majority of the respondents in all TIES Study countries have reacted by developing a form of identity that is described and designated as a "multiple identity" and is expressed in the following quote by Tansel Terzioğlu from a talk on the occasion of a book presentation at the Pförtnerhaus in Feldkirch:

> Sitting on a fence in the no man's land between cultures, ... this is how the lament of my and subsequent generations has sounded since my youth. I have always refused to see this as a negative aspect of my life. I don't feel lost or lacking in identity. I have created my own identity. I am a cherry picker who extracts the best of both cultures. The fact that my

potential cultural horizons are much broader than if I were only an Austrian or only a Turk fills me with joy and gratification. This is only possible because I have access to both cultures as a person sitting on a fence. Life sitting on a fence is not a handicap for me, but a privilege.[22]

Correspondingly, he also does not want to be a Vorarlberger or a Turk, but instead hopes that "it will be normal at some point to be an Austrian of Turkish origin, and that people are able to accept this unconditionally."

The results of the TIES Study on solidarity with the country of immigration[23] show that it seems to be easier for the second generation to develop stronger feelings of belonging to the cities and/or, in Vorarlberg, to the federal state, than to the national level. The concrete living environment thus offers more points of contact for developing positive feelings of belonging than the more abstract national level, which is determined much more by ideological aspects. The multi-country depiction of the results connected with these questions in the TIES Study shows, moreover, that respondents in all big cities who reported of having *weak/very weak/no* feelings of belonging for the level of the city and/or region in which they live, or for the national level, are clearly in the minority.

Established or outsider? Relationships to the majority population and experiences of discrimination

The comparative analysis of the network of friendships of the second generation in Vorarlberg[24] shows that the groups of both Turkish and ex-Yugoslavian origin and the group without a migration background are quite isolated from one another during and after school, and that boundaries between networks of friends are based on ethnicity and educational attainments. The results thus illustrate that networks of friendships and their educational attainments are an important indicator in comparing the living environments of the different milieus of these different groups. In particular, the second generation of Turkish origin in Vorarlberg remains within its own group of origin to a relatively great extent and predominantly within the group with low educational attainments. Due to limited ethnic and social mixing, what thus arises is also a specific social milieu that shares the same life experiences and has a common understanding of its living environment and conditions. Such images are not called into question due to the lack of mixing. This also applies conversely to the group without a migration background, especially to the group with higher educational attainments.

In spite of educational upward mobility and solidarity with the country of immigration, the second generation of Turkish origin continues to find itself in an outsider position, something that is shown in particular by the lack of mixing of networks of friends between the groups and also by experiences of exclusion and discrimination. Both the self-reporting and assessments of the group with a migration background refer to more frequent experiences of discrimination and exclusion. Men of the second generation, especially of Turkish origin, also seem to be more strongly affected than women. The results make reference to existing forms of everyday exclusion and discrimination based on ethnic and/or religious affiliation. The outsider position connected with this and how they are viewed from the outside also influence the self-image of the group. This is reinforced by the limited social and ethnic mixing of the groups, as becomes visible in the segregated circles of friends. Many young people of the second generation of Turkish origin have grown up in ethnically and socially homogeneous peer groups. The external images that are ascribed and the self-images related to them are not questioned within the group. The same double images can also be observed in the group without a migration background: in it, self- and external images are also questioned to a very limited extent as a result of the lack of social and ethnic mixing, and thus contribute to perpetuating the boundaries between groups.

In connection with these dynamics, in the results of the TIES Study Germany, Sürig and Wilmes make reference to the fact that the more Germans one has in one's circle of friends, the fewer reports of ill will there are.[25] With regular contact, the experience of discrimination apparently changes, a factor that can be understood in line with the established-outsider dynamic as a process of becoming established.

Conclusion

The Muslims of Turkish origin who immigrated to Vorarlberg are distinguished by their socialization in premodern, rural regions and the limited educational and labor opportunities connected with them, which are reflected in their low formal educational attainments and limited knowledge of German. The analysis of the process of upward mobility of the second generation of Turkish origin in comparison to their parents indicates that Muslims immigrants in Vorarlberg are in the process of becoming established. In comparison to their parents, the second generation has achieved upward mobility through education. They deal with the challenge of feeling that they belong to both the country of immigration and the society of origin with multiple identities: they identify both with Vorarlberg as the state to which they immigrated and with the origin of their parents. In spite of educational upward mobility and a feeling of solidarity with the country of immigration, however, experiences of discrimination and exclusion and the limited mixing of networks of friends simultaneously point to the persistence of the established outsider dynamic. The process of becoming established has therefore not been completed. In this context, the construction of the Islamic cemetery can also be understood as a manifestation of the process of becoming established, which affects both autochthonous residents and Muslims. For autochthonous residents, the construction of the cemetery denotes recognizing Islam and Muslims as part of society. For Muslims, accepting Vorarlberg as their home means being born and dying there. The cemetery offers both groups an opportunity to do so. It is thus a symbol of the possibility of positive coexistence within the context of diversity. Whether this possibility is progressively actualized in day-to-day life depends, of course, on the evolving social and economic relationships between the two groups.

1 Norbert Elias and John L. Scotson, *The Establishment and the Outsiders* (London: Sage Publications, 1994).

2 Simon Burtscher-Mathis, *Zuwandern, aufsteigen, dazugehören: Etablierungsprozesse von Eingewanderten* (Innsbruck, Vienna, and Bolzano: Studienverlag, 2009).

3 https://www.okay-line.at/okay-programme/ties-vorarlberg-studie-zur-integration-der-zweiten-generation/, accessed 18 January 2020.

4 Erika Thurner, *Der "Goldene Westen"? Arbeitszuwanderung nach Vorarlberg seit 1945. Beiträge zu Geschichte und Gesellschaft Vorarlbergs 14* (Bregenz: Vorarlberger Autoren Gesellschaft, 1997).

5 Eva Grabherr, "Die aktuelle Demografie der muslimischen Bevölkerung Vorarlbergs," in Eva Grabherr (ed.), *Vorarlbergs Moscheegemeinden: Die Organisationen und ihre Entwicklung.* Commissioned by okay.zusammen leben, Projektstelle für Zuwanderung und Integration (September 2019), 11–18. downloadable at https://www.okay-line.at/Wissen/religioese-vielfalt-in-vorarlberg/vorarlbergs-moscheegemeinden.html, accessed 18 January 2020.

6 Elisabeth Dörler, "Eine Begräbnisstätte für Muslime und Musliminnen in Vorarlberg," commissioned by okay. zusammen leben, Projektstelle für Zuwanderung und Integration, *okay-Studien*, 2 (October 2004); downloadable at https://www.okay-line.at/file/656/islamischerfriedhofstudie.pdf, accessed January 2020.

7 Source: Population statistics, State of Vorarlberg, reporting date: 30 June 2018.

8 Ibid.

9 See Elias and Scotson, *The Establishment and the Outsiders.*

10 See Burtscher-Mathis, *Zuwandern, aufsteigen, dazugehören.*

11 https://www.okay-line.at/okay-programme/ties-vorarlberg-studie-zur-integration-der-zweiten-generation/, accessed 18 January 2020.

12 Simon Burtscher-Mathis and Nina Formanek, description of the study, survey groups, and socio-structural characteristics of the parent generation, TIES Vorarlberg/paper 1, 2012; working paper in German downloadable at http://www.okay-line.at/okay-programme/ties-vorarlberg-integration-der-zweiten-generation/erkenntnisse-zu-integrationsprozessen-in-vorarlberg.html, accessed 18 January 2020.

13 Ibid. The remaining percentage points can be attributed to the categories "never went to school," "different state," "don't know," "not specified."

14 For further details and charts see Simon Burtscher-Mathis, "Bildungsverläufe und Bildungsabschlüsse im Gruppenvergleich und ihre Bedeutung im internationalen Kontext," TIES Vorarlberg/paper 2, 2012; working paper in German, downloadable at http://www.okay-line.at/okay-programme/ties-vorarlberg-integration-der-zweiten-generation/erkenntnisse-zu-integrationsprozessen-in-vorarlberg.html, accessed 18 January 2020.

15 Laurence Lessard-Phillips and Christopher Ross, "The TIES respondents and their parents background socio-demographic characteristics," in Maurice Crul, Jens Schneider, and Frans Lelie, eds., *The European Second Generation Compared: Does the Integration Context Matter?* (Amsterdam: Amsterdam University Press, 2012), 57–100.

16 Burtscher-Mathis and Formanek.

17 For further details and charts see Simon Burtscher-Mathis, "Bildungsverläufe und Bildungsabschlüsse im Gruppenvergleich und ihre Bedeutung im internationalen Kontext," TIES Vorarlberg/paper 2, 2012; working paper in German, downloadable at http://www.okay-line.at/okay-programme/ties-vorarlberg-integration-der-zweiten-generation/erkenntnisse-zu-integrationsprozessen-in-vorarlberg.html, accessed 18 January 2020.

18 Academies, college after Matura, university/technical college, and doctorate.

19 Maurice Crul, Philipp Schnell, Barbara Herzog-Punzenberger, Maren Wilmes, Marieke Slootman, and Rosa Aparicio Gomez, "School careers of second-generation youth in Europe: Which education systems provide the best chances for success?" in Crul, Schneider, and Lelie, eds., *The European Second Generation Compared* 101–64. Philipp Schnell, *Educational mobility of second generation Turks in cross-national perspective* (Diss., University of Amsterdam, 2012).

20 August Gächter, "Entwicklung der Integration von aus dem Ausland zugezogener Bevölkerung und ihrer Kinder in Vorarlberg," commissioned by okay.zusammen leben, Projektstelle für Zuwanderung und Integration, 2017; downloadable at https://www.okay-line.at/file/656/integration-in-vlbg-gachter.pdf, accessed 18 January 2020.

21 Simon Burtscher-Mathis, "Arbeitsmarktpositionen im Gruppen-vergleich und ihre Bedeutung im internationalen Kontext," TIES Vorarlberg/paper 4, 2013; working paper in German, downloadable at http://www.okay-line.at/okay-programme/ties-vorarlberg-integration-der-zweiten-generation/erkenntnisse-zu-integrationsprozessen-in-vorarlberg.html, accessed 18 January 2020.

22 Burtscher-Mathis, *Zuwandern, aufsteigen, dazugehören*, 238f.

23 Eva Grabherr and Simon Burtscher-Mathis, "Zweiheimisch als Normalität: zu identitären und kulturellen Dimensionen der Integration der 2. Generation in Vorarlberg," TIES Vorarlberg/paper 3, 2012; working paper in German, downloadable at http://www.okay-line.at/okay-programme/ties-vorarlberg-integration-der-zweiten-generation/erkenntnisse-zu-integrationsprozessen-in-vorarlberg.html, accessed 18 January 2020.

24 Simon Burtscher-Mathis, "Soziale Beziehungen, Diskriminie-rungserfahrungen und politische Teilhabe und ihre Bedeutung im internationalen Kontext," TIES Vorarlberg/paper 6, 2018; 2018, downloadable at http://www.okay-line.at/okay-programme/ties-vorarlberg-integration-der-zweiten-generation/erkenntnisse-zu-integrationsprozessen-in-vorarlberg.html, accessed 18 January 2020.

25 Inken Sürig and Maren Wilmes, *Die Integration der zweiten Generation in Deutschland. Ergebnisse der TIES-Studie zur türkischen und jugoslawischen Einwanderung, IMIS-Beiträge,* 39 (2011), 172, edited by the board of the Institute for Migration Research and Intercultural Studies (IMIS) at Osnabrück University.

An Offer of Leadership
Eva Grabherr in conversation with Azra Akšamija

Azra Akšamija: When the architect of the Islamic Cemetery Altach, Bernado Bader, talks about his inspiration and ideas for the project, the human dimension is always central. To him, a cemetery needs to provide an atmospheric space for people who are grieving and who want to commemorate their loved ones. His design accommodates the experience of mourning through the sensory engagement of the space, materials, color, and light. Different from many contemporary buildings initiated by Islamic communities in Europe, who desire to represent their identity through traditional Islamic architectural features, Bernardo's design is elegantly minimal. It exhibits the many qualities that Vorarlberg architecture is celebrated for: contextual integrity, meticulous craftmanship, and material sensibility. That this design was chosen by the community over the more traditional competition proposals is quite unusual. Is this project indicative of some specific local phenomena, or does it point to some broader dynamic of Islam in Europe? How does the Islamic Cemetery Altach contribute to the notion of cultural convergence?

Eva Grabherr: I can offer my perspective on the term convergence as a societal process. Through my work with the center okay.zusammen leben I have the opportunity to see many instances that demonstrate how, currently, in addition to the process that Muslims are becoming increasingly integrated as individuals (e.g., by exhibiting upward mobility), there are also processes at an organizational level. For example, an academic Islamic theology has been emerging in Austria and Germany at state universities for a few years now. All these processes of becoming established at different levels are driven by various dynamics. This fits with the notion of convergence.

The Islamic Cemetery Altach is essentially a project within the framework of this process. I think that specifically this cemetery connects many different layers of society. For me, it's like a crystal stone through which this phenomenon is expressed and becomes more evident. It allows you to recognize the conflicts that are taking place, the irritations, misunderstandings, and misinterpretations that go hand in hand with engaging in something new. This is all part of the societal pluralization process, which is naturally fraught with tension.

In the context of the cemetery, the architecture represents one dimension of convergence, and the other is the social process between its stakeholders that has been taking place. While the entire process of initiating, designing, and building this cemetery was not formally organized, it was fascinating to see how these very diverse stakeholders have been repeatedly interacting and working together. There wasn't an established church community to which one could have said: Do this now! It was as if this project extracted what it needed from the joint responsibility of its stakeholders, who were, of course, converging on an ongoing basis. No particular organizational structure was stipulated. It's as if this project found its own sponsors and stakeholders—stakeholders who had to constantly adapt and open up to one another to address the ongoing issues of the project. Miraculously, this informal process worked and, in the end, everyone recognized that the success of the cemetery resulted from all these stakeholders shaping the project together.

In the introductory chapter of her book *Europäischer Islam: Muslime im Alltag* (European Islam: Muslims in everyday life) the Turkish born French sociologist Nilüfer Göle emphasizes that one cannot grasp the emergence of a phenomenon like European Islam with macro-historical categories like "Islam" or "Europe." For her, there are realities and actions of Muslim and non-Muslim individuals and groups, which encounter, interact, ... and all this contributes to an ongoing formation and creation of European Islam. Göle promotes working on a micro-historical level to describe and understand this phenomenon and the processes associated with it. To me, our Islamic cemetery project was and is a project in that sense. There have been and are ongoing encounters, ongoing contacts, ongoing exchanges—and as a result of such projects and processes, something like a Vorarlbergian Islam comes about.

AA: How do you see your position in this process of Islam becoming established in Vorarlberg in relation to your role in the creation of the Islamic Cemetery Altach? For me, you were the project's lead, but you weren't a project manager. You have had a very elastic leadership quality; people could sense that they were being led. You set the direction and created the conditions and the framework in which the people could get involved and be able to find a way to come together. What type of leadership does such a project need so that people are able to come together?

EG: I actually like the term elastic leadership, it really appeals to me. I would say, yes, one could call it that. But, I would rather say it was an offer of leadership. And it was only when someone reacted to it that my role became leadership.

Essentially, I realized that a cemetery requires an architect. A cemetery also needs a building contractor, its need an organizational structure. Such a cemetery naturally requires the communities. My role was not absolutely necessary, let's say. Thus, my leadership contribution was basically to make sure that people who had not come together in a formal structure could find a way to collaborate. Since no prior organizational structure existed in this project that would take on the leadership role, it was necessary to have a person who could provide a framework for all these people to be able to work together in the absence of formal organization. I would really say that that was my role: not formal leadership in a traditional meaning of the term, but instead, care, making sure that the project, when it needed something, received what it needed—and that the stakeholders and people who could address these needs could do it together.

AA: The Altach cemetery is then a great example for how architecture brings people together and crystalizes organizational forms. What are the conditions, people, or processes that make this possible? What would the difference be if an architect or simply the city were to lead the project? You had a very different role in the creation of the cemetery through your work with okay.zusammen leben. You also have personal access to all these stakeholders. You know the people very well and have also provided them with a platform for working together. That's interesting because it differs so much from a ' standard, participatory building process. Perhaps your role could be given a name of its own: not mediation, but architectural navigation?

EG: I would say that navigation is a very apt description for my activities and practice. We can call it elastic leadership and/or an offer of leadership, if need be. But it's still always merely an offer. It isn't any official or formal leadership. So, what was the decisive aspect? I'd say it was the timing. I think that it would no longer work that way today, or the process would be very different: much more formal, much more explicit, much more organized, because the establishment of Islam has reached a different place. The topic of migration and integration is also on a very different level. Projects like the cemetery today would need explicit stakeholders. But back then, when the cemetery was first initiated, there wasn't really a formal structure for organizing such a project.

I think, this leadership style was a very constructive and productive approach in such a pioneering phase, but certainly not for later phases in processes of becoming established. And this form of leadership is perhaps also something that this federal state allows: the culture in this state allows for things that have already been valued and accepted to be taken on and led by people. Our government structure offers opportunities and is open for individual initiatives. I find the way of working in the state of Vorarlberg supportive. The same goes for the field of architecture. The way architecture is connected to the land and its history, as well as our contemporary architectural movement, is related to the government's openness to initiatives. Somehow, people in Vorarlberg go ahead and get things started.

The fact that the initiation of the cemetery project became productive has something to do with the phase in which the need for a cemetery arose. In a later phase of Muslims becoming established in the region, when everything became more formally organized, and more official, I don't think the cemetery would have been done the same way.

It is as if this project always found its stakeholders. That's how people have experienced it. Just as you became part of it. Although he'd already won prizes, Bernado Bader was not that well known and established as he is today. It was also a sort of risky project for him, but he accepted that risk. He didn't wait to see whether the project had an officially established leadership or not. He relied to the same extent on the fact that this network of stakeholders was responsible for the project. I don't know whether an established architecture firm would have accepted those particular risks. Yet, if you look at the career of the architect Bernardo Bader—you also see that it was one of his first bigger projects.

AA: What role has this project played for okay.zusammen leben and its aims of cultural integration?

EG: The managing board of the association is not made up of people who have a strong connection to religion. I would even say that its internal culture is atheistic. Therefore, there was no great fascination with the topic of an Islamic cemetery. But, despite its very traditional organizational format (at that time consisting only of men), the board never told me what I had to do. That was really fascinating. This project began as an open-ended process in which people didn't know at first whether the result would

be simply one section in a municipal cemetery or in a new cemetery for one confession. The outcome was totally open. That it would become a special cemetery, and that it would receive the amount of attention that it has received with the Aga Khan Award and other international architectural prizes—that surprised the board and certainly contributed to the association's reputation.

But I was also not religiously motivated when I started with the project. Context sensitivity as a way of working, however, is very important to me, independent of the Islamic cemetery project. When I established the center, I didn't want to approach the task like a director of a theater or a museum, working with a fixed program based on international standards of art, culture, or scholarship. Instead, I wanted to be able to work in a way that's sensitive to the regional context. That means tuning in to the energies that are found in this state, and detecting a small flame, where something already exists, and asking: How can one do something there? We do not develop the topic of coexisting in diversity around a conference table of scholars and art curators. We instead travel through the state in search for existing needs and potentials.

From the initial conversations that I had with very diverse migrant organizations and mosque associations, I got the sense that this topic of burial and having their own cemetery represents a central issue in relation to feeling at home. I didn't invent this issue—I've heard that from a wide variety of people who haven't even spoken to each other. It simply struck me when people said that a cemetery gives them a feeling of being at home. And it struck me that this notion came from very different individuals and groups, which were organizationally not even affiliated with each other.

It was also immediately clear to me that there was a sort of small avant-garde in the first generation of immigrants, which was in some parts less tradition-oriented than many of the people they were speaking for. I think that is also evident in the way the cemetery is used today.

That all these different aspects came together resonated with me: a cemetery, feeling at home, the idea that a cemetery is more than just a place for a specific function. Those ideas gave rise to an approach where we didn't a priori say that a cemetery is necessary, but we rather continued listening to different groups, to be able to learn and take something from them: Would this project work or not? In the end, it bore fruit.

Today, people say that the cemetery is a project of the second generation, since many people from the first generation are still buried in their country of origin. But the same people whose parents are buried in their country of origin confirmed to us in interviews that the Altach cemetery is a central, symbolic project for them, because it was possible to build it in Vorarlberg.

I follow the use and reception of the cemetery quite closely, and it makes me happy that the stakeholders who initiated everything at the beginning were not all part of mosque associations. People also came in part from secular associations. It makes me happy to see that today people from the traditional milieus are slowly beginning to make use of the cemetery, not necessarily starting with burials, but to learn about the religious rites. For instance, groups of women contacted the Altach mayor Gottfried Brändle to ask if they can practice performing ablutions. It is really fascinating to see that both male and female Muslims are getting involved in the cemetery.

AA: Do such processes connected with coming to feel at home in turn need an expanded navigation and a navigator after the project has been built? Or does it simply suffice that the building now exists? How and who does it catalyze? Is it the agenda of the building, of people, or of both?

EG: The cemetery is both a form of expression of identity and a catalyst for the process of belonging and feeling at home. It was first and foremost a crystallization medium for bringing people together. Once it catalyzed the existing energies, it provided a form of expression for them, and then subsequently inspired other processes. These are three phases and all different.

This place inspires something. It's a catalyst. It's incredible to observe such processes of coming to feel at home in a new country, with all the associated pain and controversy, namely letting go and changing. And here I find Nilüfer Göle's idea that European Islam is coming about on a micro-social level so fascinating, because I've heard dozens of stories representative of the kinds of debates that the cemetery has provoked within families about feeling at home. For example, in many mosque associations that we visited within our most recent study, we were told about conflicts over the burials taking place within families. The parents would say: "Yes, the Islamic cemetery in Altach is a great project, but will I be buried there? Will you promise me that you will have me buried in my home country?" And the children would say: "Yes, but you know, Mama, Papa, we would really like for you to be buried here in Vorarlberg."

But I would also like to show the other side. In German-speaking countries, we are currently talking about the fact that the emotional dimension of integration—to put things in sociological terms—is a very important topic at the moment. Now that the immigrant groups are experiencing upward mobility through education and the job market, all these questions of homeland and belonging are coming to the surface. And, the host society suspiciously questions whether migrants really want to find a home here or not, with the underlying idea that it must be an either-or decision.

In response, young people say, for instance, in Twitter campaigns: "Please also accept a different feeling of being at home than you had for centuries based on your family's history. It's a feeling of being at home nonetheless. You shouldn't take that from me."

As far as questions of belonging are concerned, we are really having an intense debate in this respect in Vorarlberg. An increasing perception, above all in the second or third generation, goes like this: "What can we actually still do? Every little thing that's a bit different is immediately held against us. In the sense, you don't want to feel that you belong." We are also having micro-debates in Vorarlberg, for instance, when a commentator from the biggest daily regional newspaper brings up the cemetery in a critical comment on Turks in Austria voting for R.T. Erdoğan as Turkish president despite his undemocratic attitudes. When he writes (in an undertone of disappointment) that "they don't even let themselves be buried here yet," he takes the fact that the first generation of Muslims, especially of Turkish origin, hesitates to be buried in Vorarlberg as evidence that Turkish migrants hesitate to belong to and identify with the new country. And the young people then respond: "We are the second, the third generation, and we will surely let ourselves be buried here, but don't be angry with us now because we aren't at an age to die yet." Such debates basically do take place on this level. The cemetery is a very important catalyst in family discussions, but also in such conflict-ridden public debates about belonging. I keep a journal about such debates.

I also take notes about initiatives that took place in or around the cemetery after the construction. For example, there was an initiative by the Muslimische Jugend Österreich, an organization of young Austrian Muslims who are not affiliated with a mosque, and who very intentionally state that the Austrian identity is important to them. They inquired about whether they could do landscape maintenance at the Islamic cemetery as volunteer work and civil engagement during Ramadan.

There's a wonderful project by a young man from a Bosnian family whose father died at an early age and is buried at the Altach cemetery. This young man studied agriculture in Vienna and returned to Vorarlberg to work here as a professor at a school of agriculture. He is now doing a project at the cemetery. Remember those metal frame strips at the cemetery? Poppies are supposed to bloom there. However, that doesn't really work from a horticultural perspective. And hence, this young man has written a landscaping proposal for the cemetery in which he states: "I would like to plant a low-nutrient meadow that would allow all the regional varieties of flowers to grow there." For me, this is also a philosophical concept that I'd like to have realized at the cemetery. It is as if he is saying "I'm really happy that this is exactly the place where my father is buried and has found a home."

AA: The flower meadow is a really beautiful metaphor for all the social processes that have been taking place in, around, and through the cemetery.

EG: The cemetery is patiently awaiting whether people will be buried there or not, and whether this young man who returned to Vorarlberg after his studies in Vienna will plant his wildflower meadow or not. The cemetery is simply there. It is also there for the Muslimische Jugend Österreich, who would like to do something for Ramadan, and to do that representing their identity as Muslim Austrians. The cemetery is also waiting for the news commentator and others to criticize that too few people got buried there. The cemetery exists and awaits—with great patience—what the feeling of being at home will signify on diverse levels of society.

AA: Can we derive a global dimension from these regional issues that might be instructive for other places?

EG: The central topic of the Islamic Cemetery Altach is the process of Islam becoming established in Europe, but catalyzed through architecture and expressed in the different forms of appropriation at different sites. I feel vindicated by Nilüfer Göle in this regard, since she says that it simply doesn't work to write general statements about Islam in Europe. We have to—and it's extremely hard—work on micro-sociological level, because that's the level on which we can really capture what individual Muslims do through their encounters with all the others in society. Writing down what is happening on this level will one day be an important part of the history of Islam becoming established in Europe.

But there is also a global dimension. The values that society holds in regard to the subject of death and the emotions it triggers in people—I think these aspects made it possible for the cemetery to get started in the first place, and they encouraged contacts, encounters, and cooperation. That was also my initial thesis—that death opens up a dimension of empathy in people, since this subject enables an overcoming of individual factions. It prevents the formation of divisions because this subject affects everybody.

And that's why the topic of accommodating Islamic burials was taken up so quickly, in the majority society as well, even though we had very contested minaret debates five years later. While the minaret propelled the formation of factions further, in the case of the cemetery, there was a great readiness for acceptance from all sides. Death in particular triggers something deep in people that touches anthropological dimensions.

AA: We come together in death.

EG: Exactly, or empathy flows. Or there is at least a reluctance to be hostile or adversarial toward others when it comes to death.

V. Epilogue

Islam, Arts, and Pedagogy
Ali S. Asani

As a faculty member who teaches and conducts research on Islam at Harvard, I am often invited to lead study tours for alumni to various parts of the world. Several years ago, during a tour of India, I arranged for a group of alumni to visit a site of great historical and religious significance—the tomb shrine of Khwaja Muin ad-Din Chishti (d. 1236), a renowned Muslim spiritual teacher, in Ajmer, Rajasthan. Over the centuries, millions of people of all faiths and socioeconomic classes have visited the shrine to seek blessings as they regard Khwaja Muin ad-Din to be a holy man and a friend of God (*wali*). So exalted is the status of this mystic that many South Asian Muslims consider seven pilgrimages to his shrine as being equivalent to performing the *hajj,* the Islamic pilgrimage to Mecca.

As we entered the shrine, we were met by Syed Salman Chishti, one of its custodians. He guided us to the tomb to pay our respects by spreading on it a chadar, or elaborately embroidered cloth, and garlands of roses. The crowded room was filled with sweet fragrances of rose petals, jasmine, and incense while someone sprinkled rose water on the pilgrims who were offering prayers and supplications. Reverberating in the background, one could hear rhythmic and enchanting beats of *qawwali,* the genre of devotional music characteristic of such shrines in South Asia. As we reached the tomb, our host instructed us to hold the *chadar* by its edges and raise it above our heads so that we were underneath its canopy. He then began reciting prayers in Arabic and Urdu. Standing next to him, I closed my eyes, focusing on the prayers, the scents, the sounds, and the atmosphere. Suddenly, Syed Salman whispered in my ear, "Look, professor, they are weeping." When I opened my eyes, I could see that my companions were indeed overcome with emotion. After laying the *chadar* on the tomb, we walked out into the dazzling sunlight. Surprisingly, the group was strangely silent; no one said a word about what they had just experienced. The next day, however, a member of our group remarked: "If what we saw was Islam as it is understood by millions of Muslims, how is it that we don't know about it?"

My traveling companion's question was a perceptive one, for it highlights a crucial issue concerning representations of Islam in media and political spaces. Since Islam is a tradition marked by diversity of interpretations and experiences, it is important to ask precisely which Islam and whose Islam is represented in these spaces and why? In this regard, Mohammed Arkoun, an ardent advocate for rethinking Islam, often lamented that public understanding of Islam is sadly inadequate since hardly any attention is given to the way it is practiced and experienced by the majority of the world's Muslims. Simply put, the living Islam of the faithful has been ignored or marginalized in not only media and political spaces but significantly also in the academy. Hence, Arkoun refers to it as "silent" Islam.[1] In other words, an Islam that has been "silenced." Instead, he argues that portrayals of Islam in these spaces are monopolized by contemporary sociopolitical formulations which he proclaims are secular movements "disguised by religious discourse, rites and collective behaviours."[2] Through these "secularized" formulations, Islam is overwhelmingly represented as an ideology of revivalism, identity formation, and political legitimation articulated by competing elites. As an example of this bias, we may cite a recent publication titled *Islam in Pakistan,* which focuses on constructions of the religion by various elites and explicitly excludes from its purview the beliefs and practices of ordinary women and men. In other words, Islam as it is understood by the majority of Muslims in that nation.[3]

We can extend Arkoun's critique of representations of Islam to most accounts of the history of Islam which are almost invariably framed through political and legal idioms. Typically, in much educational literature, the story of Islam is fused with the fortunes of various imperial dynasties, Arab and non-Arab: Umayyad, Abbasid, Ottoman, Safavid, Mughal and so on, perpetuating an orientalist cliché that Islam is an imperialist religion whose fate is synonymous with the fate of these political dynasties. Here again, the voices of ordinary Muslims and how they experience Islam as a faith are missing. In view of Arkoun's definition of "silent" Islam, we may characterize these formulations of Islam and their discourses of power and hegemony as "loud" Islam, as their voices have been greatly amplified in political, social, and cultural spaces, including the academy. As an unfortunate consequence of this amplification, Islam has come to be widely perceived as being a political ideology and not a legitimate religion. In the words of retired US military general and President Trump's former national security advisor, Michael Flynn, Islam is a "political ideology" that "definitely hides behind being a religion."[4] Consequently, for him, "all Muslims who practice traditional Islam are a security risk."[5] Such perceptions, which are responsible for fueling Islamophobia, have become especially prominent in policy circles, not just in the United States but around the world.

In my courses at Harvard, I endeavor to address this widespread misrepresentation resulting from a lopsided reliance on "loud" Islam by highlighting the voices, experiences, and worldviews of "silent" or "silenced" Islam, that is, the diverse ways in which the religion is understood, experienced, and practiced by varied Muslim communities in different parts of the world. My goal is not only to provide students with a balanced, more inclusive and nuanced picture of the tradition, but also to improve literacy about the nature of religion in general.

The arts and Islam

The arts play a key role in shaping and articulating understandings of faith in many Muslim societies. The vast majority of the world's Muslims engage with their faith not as an ideology but as a multisensory experience through which they engage in acts of worship and devotion. Hearing the *adhan,* or call to prayer; reciting and listening to the Quran; chanting the beautiful names of God; contemplating beautifully inscribed calligraphies or geometric designs in a mosque; singing devotional songs or poems in praise of the Prophet Muhammad; listening to stories of the prophets; participating in a *sama,* or a whirling dance, *dhammal*[6] or a *muharram*[7] assembly; venerating visual representations of important religious personalities; taking part in a *taziya*[8] or attending a *mushaira* or a poetry recital; singing *ginans*[9]; or strolling through a garden, are just some examples of the rich sensory repertoire through which Muslims in different regions of the world may experience varied aspects of their faith. For them, knowledge of faith does not come from erudite books on theology, law, and philosophy. Rather, it is inextricably enmeshed in the consumption and production of various arts, principally sound, visual, and literary arts. The poetic arts, in particular, play an influential role in shaping the ethical, theological, and spiritual core of Muslim cultures. By fusing the aesthetic and performative with ethical, theological, philosophical, and spiritual, they convey knowledge about the faith in forms that are emotive, helping audiences relate to and experience it immediate and transformative ways. In this sense, as Nosheen Ali has aptly pointed out, it is appropriate to term this knowledge, "heart-mind knowledge."[10] It is through "heart-mind knowledge," for example, that the worldviews of audiences across the Persianate world have been shaped through aesthetic and intellectual engagement with Jalaluddin Rumi's long epic poem, the *Mathnawi,* often called the Quran in Persian as it is regarded as a poetic commentary on the spiritual or inner dimensions of the Muslim scripture.

The centrality of the arts in Muslim religious life stems from what lies at the very heart of Islam—the Quran. Although we think of the Quran primarily as a written scripture, during Muhammad's lifetime, it functioned as an aural/oral text which he would recite aloud. Hence it came to be called Quran, meaning "Recitation." According to traditional Muslim accounts, people flocked to hear Muhammad's recitations as they had never heard anything more beautiful in the Arabic language. Many would weep openly and uncontrollably.[11] Indeed, some of Muhammad's most bitter enemies broke down in tears after listening to a recitation and became adherents.[12] To paraphrase a Quranic verse, the most beautiful of recitations caused the skin of listeners to shiver and their hearts to melt.[13] The power of the Quran over listeners was such that some people accused Muhammad of being a magician or a sorcerer. Others accused him of being a poet for, in pre-Islamic Arabian society, words recited by poets were conceived to have a powerful spiritual potency as they were inspired by *jinns* or spirits.[14] In response to such accusations, Muhammad declared that he was a prophet receiving revelation from the One Almighty God. The Quran responds to demands that Muhammad prove this claim by challenging skeptics to produce a recitation of equal magnificence.[15] Thus, the beauty of the text comes to be seen by Muslims as proof of its divine origin. Not surprisingly, Muslim narratives attribute the spread of the faith to the literary and aesthetic qualities of the Quran. The association of beauty as a manifestation of the Divine also inspired the famous saying attributed to the Prophet Muhammad, "God is beautiful and loves beauty." Not surprisingly, in contrast to Western views that attribute the success of Muhammad's mission to social, political, ideological, and militaristic factors, Muslim narratives view the literary and aesthetic qualities of the Quran as decisive factors. For example, the Iranian scholar Muhammad Taqi Shariati-Mazinani comments:

> The Arab, already besotted with the beauty of language, suddenly heard an oration like none he had ever heard before .... [H]e thrilled to this oratory and was enraptured, he was amazed and astonished; it transformed, changed and delighted him. The Quran's words fell like rays of light on him; the listener found himself immersed in light; it enveloped his whole being and every particle of his existence, illuminating his heart and mind. The Quran was a light that shone intothe soul through the aperture of the ear; it transformed the soul, and as a result, the world.[16]

After the death of Prophet Muhammad, the orally transmitted recitations were codified into a written scripture in a state-sponsored project that made the text a pretext for the emergent Umayyad state.[17] Its compilation into a text privileged written learned culture over oral culture, eventually leading to the emergence of a class of scholars who claimed their authority to interpret the text and define ortho-doxy.[18] In this way, the written text of the Quran became the basis of "loud" ideological forms of Islam. Yet, for ordinary Muslims, the Quran continued to be an oral/aural text with which they interacted through the medium of sound. It was a text to be recited aloud, listened to, and memorized, publicly performed and privately experienced. Reciting and listening to it provided individuals the means to commune with the Divine aesthetically and intellectually. Over time, Quranic recitation developed into such a highly developed art form that every year thousands of Muslims from around the world gather to participate in national and international Quran recitation competitions with the most outstanding reciters being recognized with cash prizes and high status in society. Today, Muslims encounter the recited Quran in a vast array of contexts beyond spaces of formal worship: in shops and crowded bazaars; recited in the streets by beggars; at the beginning of public events; in taxis, trains, and airplanes; on the radio, television, and internet.[19] In these and in many other ways, the Quran is at the heart of an Islamic soundscape that permeates traditions of spirituality and the art of poetry, music, and dance as vehicles to help individuals transcend the material and the physical and experience the spiritual.

Just as the Quran needed to be melodiously recited so that it moved the heart, it had also to be beautifully written to please the eye. Calligraphy in the Arabic script developed into an important reli-gious art form practiced by Muslims the world over, with distinctive styles emerging in certain regions. As visual texts, Quranic words and phrases began to adorn and lend meaning to all kinds of objects: the domes and walls of mosques; pages of poetry; ceramics; jewelry and other kinds of ornaments created as amulets and talismans. Similar to the way in which the Bible has influenced works of art, literature, music in Western societies, the Quran, too, has served as an important source of metaphors and sym-bols, with concepts and themes inspiring Muslim artists as they engage in creating art. Thus, poems, short stories, novels, folk songs, miniature paintings, calligraphies, architecture, gardens, films, and rap music can provide us with glimpses into Muslim worldviews by representing understandings of Islam that appeal to multiple senses but may often go unrecognized by students of religion.

Teaching Islam through the arts

Given the centrality of the arts in Muslim religious life and their influence in shaping Muslim cultures, it is rather astonishing that they are rarely integrated into introductory courses on Islam in schools, col-leges, and universities. Professor Arkoun's observation that the academy has generally marginalized the study of devotional aspects of Islam and the lived experiences of majority of Muslims is certainly relevant here. Most courses on Islam are predominantly textual, logocentric, and historical in nature, conceiving of Islam within the framework of a European post-enlightenment notion of a religion as a homogeneous, well-defined and systemized ideology with a distinctive set of beliefs and practices. Such a conception cordons off and excludes the experiential multisensory aspects of the faith from consideration as religion.[20] At best, they are regarded as peripheral. "The arts are the icing on the cake," a senior scholar explained to me, while another, who teaches at a distinguished British university, remarked, "If I taught Islam through the arts at my university, it would not be tolerated; I would be laughed out of the room." The overwhelmingly secular environment in the academy, the lacuna in methods and theories to study religion as experience, and the elusive quest for "objectivity" may, in fact, impede the incorporation and appreciation of the multisensory faith experiences in the classroom.

Notwithstanding such biases, for several years now, I have taught an introductory Islam course at Harvard using the arts as pedagogic lenses. In its latest iteration, it is titled *Multisensory Religion: Rethinking Islam through the Arts*. Offered as part of the university's general education curriculum, it fulfills the undergraduate requirement in aesthetics and culture. Hence, it attracts students from a broad variety of disciplinary backgrounds, ranging from STEM to the social sciences and humanities. For many students, the majority of whom are non-Muslim, it is often the only course they will take during their college career that will engage them with the study of religion and/or arts. It, therefore, becomes crucial to provide them the appropriate frameworks and tools to think critically about these subjects. The official course description is footnoted below.[21] The course employs the arts as pedagogic bridges for both teaching and learning about Islam. It has four major goals:

1) To introduce diverse interpretations of Islam, major concepts, practices, and institutions primarily through different artistic expressions and secondarily through the theological or doctrinal contexts, exploring their evolution and interpretations over time in different spaces

2) To foster religious and cultural literacy by exploring the relationship between religion and the arts, together with the ways in which changing historical, political, and cultural contexts influence this relationship and its expressions

3) To explore the role of the arts in Muslim societies as vehicles for social and political reform and critique

4) To promote knowledge and understanding of religion through experiential learning, involving immersive experiences and creative self-expression through art-making, thus providing scope for individual agency and space for self-reflection

In conceiving this course, I was inspired, firstly, by my experiences growing up Muslim with a multisensory engagement with my faith through various arts, especially Quran recitations and devotional poetry. I did not, however, recognize and appreciate the role of the arts in constructing and shaping knowledge about Islam until I came to Harvard and studied under Professor Annemarie Schimmel. An extraordinary scholar who lived and traveled in many Muslim majority countries, she introduced me to the power of the arts as lenses for understanding Islam. She often cited poetry and calligraphy, in particular, as crucial to her own development as a scholar of Islam. The poetic arts provided her profound insights into the various cultures she studied and visited.[22] She emphatically endorsed the perspective of the German philosopher, Johann Herder (d. 1803) who wrote: "From poetry we learn about eras and nations in much greater depth than through the deceitful and miserable ways of political and military war histories."[23]

A second concern of the course is to improve literacy about the nature of religion. For this, I adopt the cultural studies approach as outlined by Diane Moore.[24] It is premised on the notion that constructions of religion are intricately embedded in all dimensions and contexts of human experience—historical, political, economic, social, literary, artistic, etc. As these contexts evolve and change, so do religious ideas and institutions. As a result, religions are not only dynamic but also marked by internal diversity manifested through the existence of many communities of interpretation. Therefore, asking what a religion does or teaches no longer becomes a viable question. No religious tradition is a monolith. Instead, religions can be understood as dynamic cultural constructs constantly being shaped and reshaped by the changing realities of people's lives. In order to highlight and distinguish between competing claims, we should be asking questions such as: Who is interpreting the tradition? In which specific contexts, and drawing upon what authority? Such questions help us to pay attention to the voices of the powerless who are often marginalized or silenced by those who have the power of authority.

A third concern of the course regards the role of the arts in the context of a liberal arts education. For this component of the course, I draw upon the insights and recommendations of Harvard's Task Force for the Arts. It asserts that the arts, which are often relegated to a co-curricular or extra-curricular status in the academy, must be made curricular and robustly integrated into the cognitive life of the university, for "the arts—as they are both experienced and practiced—are irreplaceable instruments of knowledge."[25] Such remarks particularly resonate with my course, based as it is on the fundamental premise that to be literate about Islam, we need to recognize that the arts are not only central to the experience and expression of the religion, but they are also important ways of knowing. They are also a direct immediate way of communicating profound passions and beliefs. Their experiential nature gives rise to meaning. In this regard, the report further recommends that the making of art should be an essential element in the cognitive training of students for it entails engaging in deeper forms of learning that have a lasting impact on them.[26]

Inspired by the Task Force's recommendations, I have incorporated into the course a substantial art-making component which encourages students to express their understanding of concepts they have learnt in the course through creative projects they design, whether individually or in groups. All students are expected to create a portfolio that provides them the opportunity to reflect creatively on the course readings and discussions in class. The portfolio incorporates six creative pieces, each of which illustrates a concept or an idea that resonated most with them. In creating these pieces, students are expected to employ at least four different media or art forms, such as charcoal drawing, watercolor, pen and ink, film, dance, poetry, musical composition, and sculpture. Each entry in the portfolio is accompanied by a short explanation of how the work they created engages with or represents themes and ideas featured in the course content. This commentary must be well-considered and explain thought processes. In addition to the portfolio, students design their own calligram in the Arabic script through which they express an idea or concept related to God using the Arabic word *Allah* in different media. For another project they compose poems in English using the rhyme scheme and the themes typical of the Persian *ghazal* (love lyric), or the *mathnawi* (the romantic epic). If they are so inclined, they can set them to music. Their composition should be accompanied by a short commentary.

One of the art-making highlights for students is the "mosque project" which engages them in envisioning a mosque for a major American city. In producing their vision for an American mosque, the students are encouraged to think about a mosque as being more than a building that functions simply as a place of prayer. As evidenced by numerous attacks and threats on mosques in the United States, the mosque has become a tangible symbol of the Muslim "other." How can it be transformed to become a space of dialogue where one welcomes and engages fellow citizens? In addressing this broad question, students are asked to keep in mind a range of issues: How would they interpret the conventional features of mosque design (*mihrab, minbar, qibla,* decor) within an urban American context? Given the highly charged Islamophobic discourse surrounding Muslims and mosque spaces in the United States, what identity would they choose to express through the facade? What are the advantages and disadvantages of "Orientalizing" it? How do they envisage the mosque engaging with members of the surrounding community? Since mosques are multipurpose buildings serving as community centers, particularly so for diaspora communities, how do they expect to address this function in their design? How will they address questions of inclusion and belonging within the mosque community, especially as they relate to sectarian and cultural divides as well as increasingly important issues of gender equity and sexual orientation?

In undertaking this assignment, students are asked to consult a variety of studies dealing with the historical and functional evolution of the mosque both in Muslim majority and minority cultural contexts, the most important being Azra Akšamija's innovative study, *The Mosque Manifesto,* which responds to the question of what a mosque should look like in the contexts of the Muslim diaspora in the West by outlining ten generative principles.[27]

The mosque design project was an eye-opening exercise for both the students involved as well as for me as their instructor. How students conceptualized mosque spaces and how such spaces would be used to foster community involvement revealed a tremendous amount of imagination, sensitivity, and social conscience on the part of the mosque designers. All believed that environments surrounding mosques should be open to everyone. One project, aptly named The Green Mosque, emphasized that, since mosques have always been seen as places of communal gathering, creating green spaces—including eco-friendly wall-covered vegetation—would not only attract visitors due to the spaces' physical attractiveness, but also enable non-Muslims to understand what is actually at the very heart of Islam, namely that beauty and the care and concern for plants and animals as espoused by the Prophet Muhammad are essential elements of being human. Highlighting the words of Seyyed Hossein Nasr in her presentation, one student aptly stated: "The sacred architecture of mosques is an extension of nature as designed by God within an environment created by Man." Another project emphasized the need to create community gathering spaces in the form of classrooms, bookstores, cafés, and social halls for parties and other celebrations, once again highlighting the importance of making such spaces open for all to enjoy, since Muslims, in addition to the needs of their communities, are also expected to fulfill the needs of society at large. Offering English as second language classes and immigration/citizenship assistance are other examples of the thought-provoking suggestions made by the students which, by the way, is how many mosques in the United States often function. The students intended mosques to open and welcoming to all visitors, not the secretive and mysterious "other." Given the recent rise of sectarianism in certain regions of the world, several projects imagined ways in which mosques could function as spaces of intra-Muslim reconciliation, bringing Sunni and Shia together to create "Su-shi" communities.

From a pedagogic perspective, the most satisfying aspect of the course for many students is that its arts-based approach affords them agency to experience, shape, and express their learning in frameworks of their choosing. This helps them to recognize the potential of the arts as catalysts for social engagement and change. Approaching Islam through the arts provides them with a counter-narrative that presents it as a faith experienced by a marginalized majority whose voices may have been "silenced" in media, political, social, and academic arenas, but are still vibrant and powerful today. In this regard, the arts can play a significant role in humanizing what has been dehumanized.

It is no small statement to say that my students are the inspiration for my belief in the power of the arts to educate, enrich, and foster a greater understanding between the cultures and peoples of this world. I fully acknowledge that through the creative work they have produced in my courses—be it poetry, songs, paintings, or calligraphy—my students have inspired me. I have been stunned by how they have responded to designing mosques replete with all of their logistical, spatial, aesthetic, and historical elements carefully considered while still being socially engaged with the modern urban American landscape. Beautifully designed, with every consideration given to creating environments that were not only eco-friendly but welcoming spiritual enclaves open to everyone, I was deeply moved by the depth of the passion each student put into their work. Their awareness of the needs of others touched me deeply, to the point where I wished such fictional mosques could actually exist. My students have taught me that one need only scratch the surface of imagination and creative expression to uncover a passion just waiting to be set free.

1   Mohammed Arkoun, "Rethinking Islam Today," *Annals of the American Academy of Political and Social Science 588* (2003), 19.

2   Ibid., 38.

3   Muhammad Qasim Zaman, *Islam in Pakistan: A History* (Princeton: Princeton University Press, 2018).

4   https://www.pbs.org/newshour/politics/flynn-critic-muslim-militancy-culture, accessed 29 January 2019.

5   Will McCants, director of the Brookings Project on US relations with the Islamic world, https://qz.com/841197/islam-is-a-malignant-cancer-the-hateful-rhetoric-of-michael-flynn-trumps-new-national-security-adviser/, accessed 29 January 2019.

6   A form of Sufi dance or *sama,* prevalent at several Sufi shrines in Pakistan.

7   An assembly attended by Shia to commemorate the martyrdom of Imam Hussain, the grandson of the Prophet Muhammad.

8   A form of drama, prevalent in Iran, commemorating the martyrdom of Imam Hussain.

9   Devotional hymns of the Nizari Ismaili communities of South Asia.

10 Nosheen Ali, "From Hallaj to Heer: Poetic Knowledge and the Muslim Tradition," *Journal of Narrative Politics* 3(1) (2016), 5.

11 Naveed Kirmani, *God is Beautiful: The Aesthetic Experience of the Quran,* trans. Tony Crawford (Cambridge, UK: Polity Press, 2015), 24–30.

12 Ibid., 15–24.

13 Quran 39:23.

14 Kirmani, 35–37

15 See, for example, Quran 17:88 "If humans and Jinn banded together to produce the like of this quran [recitation] they would never produce its like even though they backed one another." Also Quran 52:34 "Or do they say he has fabricated it? Nay! They believe not! Let them then produce a recitation like unto it if they speak the truth."

16 Kirmani, 25.

17 Mohammed Arkoun, "The Notion of Revelation: From Ahl al-Kitāb to the Societies of the Book," *Die Welt des Islams, New Series,* Bd. 28(1/4) (1988): 74–76.

18 Ibid., 75.

19 Kristina Nelson, "The Sound of the Divine in Daily Life," in D.L. Bowen and E. A. Early, eds., *Everyday Life in the Muslim Middle East* (Indianapolis: Indiana University Press, 2002), 257–61.

20 See Alexandra Grieser, "Aesthetics," in Kocku von Stuckrad and Robert Segal, eds., *Vocabulary for the Study of Religion* (Brill: Leiden, 2015) vol. 1, 14–23.

21 This course explores the influential role that the arts play in shaping the ethical, aesthetic, theological, and spiritual core of Muslim cultures. Contrary to popular stereotypes, the majority of the world's Muslims derive knowledge of their faith from multisensory experiences that involve engagement with the literary arts (scriptures, panegyrics, love lyrics, epic romances, folk songs, and folk tales), as well as sound and visual arts (Quran and poetic recitations, music, dance, drama, architecture, calligraphy, and miniature painting). The course will challenge your assumptions about Islam as well as the relationship between religion and the arts. What does it mean to call some art "religious"? Who decides what counts? On what basis? How can interpreting an individual believer's engagement with the arts as an exercise of religious authority help us see "religion" in a new light? Engaging with these questions will allow us to create a nuanced picture of the rich and multicolored tapestry of the ways in which the arts create religious tradition and innovation, weaving the voices of poets, novelists, short-story writers, folk musicians, and rock stars with those of clerics, theologians, mystics, scholars, and politicians. An important aim of the course will be to explore the relationships between religion and the arts, together with the ways in which historical, political, and cultural contexts influence these expressions. To be inclusive of the cultural diversity of Muslim societies, the course draws on material from regions beyond the Middle East, particularly sub-Saharan Africa and South and Southeast Asia, regions where the majority of the world's Muslims reside. This course assumes no prior knowledge of Islam.

22 In support of her contention of the power of poetry in promoting understanding across deep divides, Schimmel cites, in a speech she made in March 1996 at a ceremony recognizing her efforts to foster better understanding between East and West, the example of a former American student who had been held hostage in Tehran after the Iranian Revolution. The moment he began reciting Persian poetry, his jailers' attitudes changed, and a bridge was built across deep ideological differences. Annemarie Schimmel. "A Good Word is Like a Good Tree," http://www.amaana.org/articles/schimtree.htm, accessed 9 January 2019.

23 As quoted in Annemarie Schimmel, *Occident and Orient: My Life in East and West,* trans. Karin Mittman (Lahore: Iqbal Academy, 2007), 296.

24 See Diane Moore, *Overcoming Religious Illiteracy* (New York: Palgrave Macmillan, 2007).

25 Report on the Task for the Arts, 2008, https://www.harvard.edu/sites/default/files/content/arts_report.pdf, accessed 21 January 2019.

26 "Indeed, in many cases, long after the substance of the courses have dimmed, and the assignments and exams have all faded from memory, what remains most bright and intense in the memories of these students, and what energizes them personally and professionally, are the hours they spent in creative projects." *Report on the Task for the Arts,* 2008, https://www.harvard.edu/sites/default/files/content/arts_report.pdf, accessed 21 January 2019.

27 Azra Akšamija, *The Mosque Manifesto: Propositions for Spaces of Coexistence* (Berlin: Revolver Publishing, 2015).

Appendix

Contributor Biographies

Azra Akšamija is an artist and architectural historian. She is the Founding Director of the MIT Future Heritage Lab (FHL) and an Associate Professor in the MIT Program in Art, Culture and Technology (ACT). Her work explores how social life is affected by cultural bias and by the deterioration and destruction of cultural infrastructures within the context of conflict, migration, and forced displacement. Akšamija is the author of *Mosque Manifesto: Propositions for Spaces of Coexistence* (2015) and *Museum Solidarity Lobby* (2019). Her artistic work has been exhibited in leading international venues, including the Generali Foundation Vienna, Liverpool Biennial, Secession Vienna, the Royal Academy of Arts London, Queens Museum of Art in New York, Design Week Festivals in Milan, Istanbul, and Amman, and the Fondazione Giorgio Cini as a part of the 54th Art Biennale in Venice. Her most recent work was shown at the Sharjah Museum of Islamic Civilization (2019), the Aga Khan Museum in Toronto (2020), and Venice Architecture Biennale (2020). She received the Aga Khan Award for Architecture 2013 for her design of the prayer space in the Islamic Cemetery Altach, the 2019 Art Prize of the City of Graz, and an honorary doctorate from the Monserrat College of Art, 2020.

Mohammad al-Asad is an architect and architectural historian. He is the Founding Director of the Center for the Study of the Built Environment in Amman (CSBE), a private, nonprofit think/do tank established in 1999. He has taught at Princeton University, the Massachusetts Institute of Technology, the University of Jordan, the German Jordanian University, the University of Illinois at Urbana-Champaign, where he was the Alan K. and Leonarda Laing Distinguished Visiting Professor, and at Carleton University in Ottawa. In addition, he has taught Massive Open Online Courses (MOOCs) in both Arabic and English on architecture and urbanism for the Edraak Platform of the Queen Rania Foundation for Education and Development and for the Aga Khan Trust for Culture Education Program. Al-Asad is the author of Contemporary Architecture and Urbanism in the Middle East (2012). He co-edited (with Rahul Mehrotra) *Shaping Cities: Emerging Models of Planning Practice* (2016), and edited *Workplaces: The Transformation of Places of Production: Industrial Buildings in the Islamic World* (2010). In addition, he has appeared in documentary films including *Islamic Art: Mirror of the Invisible World* (2012), and led the production of films including *Arab Women in Architecture* (2014). He was a project reviewer for the Aga Khan Award for Architecture between 1989 and 2007, and has been a member of the Award's Steering Committee for its 2010, 2013, 2016, and 2019 cycles.

Ali S. Asani is Murray A. Albertson Professor of Middle Eastern Studies and Professor of Indo-Muslim and Islamic Religion and Cultures at Harvard University. A specialist of Islam in South Asia, Professor Asani's research focuses on Shia and Sufi devotional traditions in the region. His books include *The Bujh Niranjan: An Ismaili Mystical Poem* (1992); *Ecstasy and Enlightenment: The Ismaili Devotional Literatures of South Asia* (2002), among many others. He is particularly interested in the interaction between religion, literature, and the arts in Muslim societies. His use of the arts in pedagogy is part of his broader effort to combat "religious illiteracy." For more than thirty years, he has dedicated himself to helping others better understand the rich subtext and diverse influences that make religion—in particular, Islam—a complex cultural touchstone. He is the recipient of the Harvard Foundation medal for his outstanding contributions to improving intercultural and race relations. More recently, he received Harvard's Petra T. Shattuck Excellence in Teaching Award.

Velibor Božović grew up in Sarajevo, Bosnia and Herzegovina. When he was in his twenties, the country of his youth became a war zone and Velibor spent the duration of the siege of Sarajevo honing his survival skills. In 1999, he moved to Montréal where he worked as an engineer in the aerospace industry before devoting his time fully to the exploration of images. Subsequently, Božović earned BFA and MFA degrees in Studio Arts at Concordia University where he currently teaches. His projects have been supported by the Canada Council for the Arts and by Conseil des arts et des lettres du Quebec. In 2015, he was awarded the Claudine and Stephen Bronfman Fellowship in Contemporary Art. His work has been exhibited in Canada and internationally.

Amila Buturović is Professor of Humanities and Religious Studies at York University. She holds a BA in Arabic Language and Literature from Sarajevo University, and an MA and PhD in Islamic Studies from McGill University. Her research interests span the intersections of religion and culture, focusing on the Ottoman Balkans and Arabo-Islamic world. She is the author of *Stone Speaker: Medieval Tombstones, Landscape, and Bosnian Identity in the Poetry of Mak Dizdar* (2002), and a co-editor, with Irvin C. Schick, of *Women in the Ottoman Balkans: Gender, Culture and History* (2007), published also in Turkish translation in 2008. Her latest book, *Carved in Stone, Etched in Memory: Death, Tombstones and Commemoration in Bosnian Islam* (2015) examines the spaces and culture of death in Bosnia and Herzegovina, particularly in the context of the Islamization and Ottomanization of the region.

Simon Burtscher-Matis completed his studies in sociology at the Universities of Graz, Austria, Waterloo, Canada, and Innsbruck, Austria. From 2003 to 2016, he was involved in the project okay.zusammen leben, an information and advice center for immigration and integration issues in the Austrian province of Vorarlberg (www.okay-line.at); since 2016, he has worked as an independent sociologist. His work and research explores social change in organizations, municipalities, and regions; processes of integration in the context of diversity; and equality in the education system. He is engaged in the establishment of platforms for social cooperation, responsibility, and solidarity.

Robert Fabach is an architectural historian, publisher, and architect. His studies of architecture at the University for Applied Arts in Vienna were supplemented with cultural field research in the Middle East and on the American West Coast, exploring cultural sources and significance of architecture. Moving to Vorarlberg in 1998, he realized building, consulting, and communication projects at various scales of the formation. Research and editorial work on the building culture of Vorarlberg accompany this practice. In recent years, his focus shifted to teaching at the University of Liechtenstein and to the establishment of the Architectural Archive Vorarlberg, which demonstrates historical evidence of global cultural exchange in the region. The concept of an economy of attention balanced between site and world constitute the basis of Fabach's publications, historical, and architectural work.

Eva Grabherr was the Founding Director of the Jewish Museum of Hohenems, where she served as Director from 1990 to 1996. In 1997, she began research for her PhD at the Department for Hebrew and Jewish Studies of University College London, and in 2001 published her dissertation entitled *Letters to Hohenems: A Microhistorical Study of Jewish Acculturation in the Early Decades of Emancipation*. During this research period, she was involved in various projects in Austria and Germany, including working as a team member at the Center of Democracy-Studies Vienna (2000–2001), teaching at the Institute of European Ethnology/ University of Vienna (2001), participating in the steering committee of the International Summer Academy of Museology (1999–2006), and several museum and project exhibitions. Since 2001, she has been the Founding Director of okay.zusammen leben, an information and advice center for immigration and integra- tion issues in the Austrian province of Vorarlberg. She is also currently a member of the Independent Expert Council for Integration at the Ministry of Europe, Integration and International Affairs in Austria.

Amra Hadžimuhamedović is the Director of the Centre for Cultural Heritage, International Forum Bosnia and holds a PhD in architecture. She has been the leading expert in the process of implementation of Annex 8 of the Dayton Peace Accord for Bosnia and Herzegovina, managing diverse projects of integrating cultural heritage into postwar recovery. She has taught the history of architecture and architectural conservation at the International University of Sarajevo (2010–19), guest-lectured on heritage in war and postwar periods, on the theory and philosophy of conservation across the world, and has published widely, including the books: *Heritage, War and Peace: Human Rights and Destruction of Cultural Memory* (editor); *Bosnia: Destruction of Cultural Heritage* (co-author), and the forthcoming *Reconstruct or Forget: Recovering Heritage in War-traumatized Communities*. She has worked as a consultant for UNESCO, ICCROM, World Bank, ICOMOS International, OSCE, ARC-WH, and Welfare.

Tina Gudrun Jensen is an anthropologist and researcher at the Malmö Institute for Studies of Migration, Diversity and Welfare in Global Political Studies at the University of Malmo, Sweden and is affiliated with the Department of Anthropology at the University of Copenhagen, Denmark. She has done research on migration, diversity, cultural complexity, social integration, and urban spaces. Her work focuses on inter-ethnic relations and everyday multiculturalism in Scandinavia. Her publications include "The Complexity of Neighbourhood Relations in a Multi-Ethnic Social Housing Project in Copenhagen" in *Identities: Global Studies in Culture and Power* (2016) and a monograph on everyday life and social relations in a multi-ethnic neighbourhood in Copenhagen, *Sameksistens: Hverdagsliv og naboskab i et multietnisk boligområde* (Roskilde: Roskilde Universitetsforlag, 2016). She has co-edited the special issue on "Planning for pluralism in Nordic cities" for the *Nordic Journal of Migration Research*.

Jennifer Mack is an Associate Professor at the School of Architecture at KTH in Stockholm. Mack received a PhD in architecture, urbanism, and anthropology from Harvard University in 2012 and also holds an MArch and MCP from MIT and a BA from Wesleyan University. Her work combines history, ethnography, and formal analysis to study social change and the built environment and has recently published the monograph *The Construction of Equality: Syriac Immigration and the Swedish City* (2017), which investigates how one immigrant group has challenged the Swedish welfare state's assumptions that "universal," modernist design standards would create social equality. Mack is currently conducting two multiyear research projects. The first concerns the architectural design and urban planning of new Swedish mosques and churches in the context of shifting national religious orientations, increasing immigration, and the rising influence of neoliberal notions of management. The other concerns modernist ideas of nature in the creation of public and outdoor spaces around housing blocks developed during the Swedish Million Homes Program (when Sweden built one million dwelling units from 1965 to 1974).

Nasser Rabbat is the Director of the Aga Khan Program for Islamic Architecture at MIT. His interests include the history and historiography of Islamic architecture, medieval urbanism, modern Arab history, contempo-rary Arab art, and postcolonial criticism. He has published several books, most recently *The Destruction of Cultural Heritage: From Napoléon to ISIS,* co-edited with Pamela Karimi, http://we-aggregate.org/project/the-destruction-of-cultural-heritage-from-napoleon-to-isis (2016) and *al-Naqd Iltizaman: Nazarat fi-l Tarikh wal 'Ururba wal Thawra* (*Criticism as Commitment: Viewpoints on History, Arabism, and Revolution*) (2015). A volume on the Dead Cities in Syria is slated for publication in 2018. Rabbat regularly contributes to several Arabic newspapers and consults with international design firms on projects in the Islamic World.

Barbara Steiner is a curator, editor, author, lecturer, and the current Director of Kunsthaus Graz (Austria). Until 2017, she was visiting professor for Cultures of the Curatorial at the Academy of Fine Arts Leipzig. Besides monographs of artists including Jorge Pardo, Christine Hill, Superflex, Liam Gillick, Josef Dabernig, and Jun Yang, Steiner brought out a series of theme-related books on conceptions of space, the relationship between private and public, and on art and the economy: *Mögliche Museen* (with Charles Esche, 2007); *Spaces of Negotiation* (with as-if wienberlin, 2010); *The Captured Museum* (2011); *Scenarios about Europe* (2012); *The Europe Book* (2013); *Superkilen* (2014); and *Creative Infidelities* (2016). In her curatorial work, she looks into conditions of cultural production, drawing attention to conflicting concerns and interconnected processes of negotiation.

Helen Walasek is the author of *Bosnia and the Destruction of Cultural Heritage* (Routledge 2015) and is an Honorary Associate Research Fellow in the College of the Humanities, University of Exeter, UK. She was Deputy Director of the London-based campaigning organization Bosnia and Herzegovina Heritage Rescue (BHHR), the only heritage NGO accredited as a humanitarian aid organization by UNHCR during the 1992–1995 Bosnian War. She has been a consulting expert to the Parliamentary Assembly of the Council of Europe, an advisor to the Swedish NGO Cultural Heritage without Borders (CHwB), and an Associate of the Bosnian Institute, London, 1998–2007. In 2016, she was a consultant-contributor for the website Targeting History and Memory (SENSE Center for Transitional Justice, Pula) documenting the prosecutions of crimes against cultural property of the International Criminal Tribunal for the former Yugoslavia (ICTY). Her 2000–01 field trips across Bosnia and Herzegovina (with archaeologist Richard Carlton) made the first independent postwar assessments of damaged and destroyed historic monuments across the country. She has lectured widely on the destruction of cultural heritage and art crime in the context of the Wars of Yugoslav Succession, particularly the Bosnian War.

Wolfgang Welsch is Professor Emeritus in Philosophy of the Friedrich-Schiller University of Jena in Germany. Previously, he taught at the University of Magdeburg, and has held visiting professorships at Stanford University and elsewhere. His work focuses on epistemology and anthropology, cultural philosophy, aesthetics, and transculturalism. Among his publications are *Unsere postmoderne Moderne* (1987); *Ästhetisches Denken* (1990); *Vernunft: Die zeitgenössische Vernunftkritik und das Konzept der transversalen Vernunft* (1995); *Grenzgänge der Ästhetik* (1996).

Image credits

Jacques Bétant / Aga Khan Trust for Culture: pp.12–13

Velibor Božović: pp. 67–70, 72–75, 77–80, 82–83, 85–88, 90–93, 96–98, 103, 283

Amila Buturović: p. 106

Richard Carlton: pp. 116–17

Disorder Collective: p. 179

Cemal Emden / Aga Khan Trust for Culture: pp. 20–21, 195, 196–201, 207, 210, 213, 217–19, 222, 224–27, 229, 239, 286–87

Courtesy of the Gazi Husrev-beg Biblioteka, Sarajevo: p. 114

Amra Hadžimuhamedović: pp. 124, 129, 130

Carol M. Highsmith / Courtesy of Carol M. Highsmith Archive, Library of Congress, Prints and Photographs Division: p. 42

Sandi Hilal: p. 175

Aldo Ippoliti / Aga Khan Trust for Culture: p. 47

Tina Gudrun Jensen: pp. 166, 169

Omar Khalidi / Courtesy of Aga Khan Documentation Center, MIT Libraries: p. 44 (bottom)

Jesper Lambaek: pp.137–40, 142–43, 145–46, 148–49, 151–54, 156–57, 159–61, 180, 285

Marc Lins: pp. 234–35

LPLT / Wikimedia Commons / CC BY-SA 4.0: p. 41

Jennifer Mack: p. 180

Pascal Maréchaux / Aga Khan Trust for Culture: p. 35

Volker Naumann / Staatsgalerie Stuttgart: p. 33

Nasser Rabbat: pp. 54, 59

Courtesy of Aleksander Aco Ravlić: p. 115

Kristian Skeie / Aga Khan Trust for Culture: pp. 16–17

Michael A. Toler / Courtesy of the Aga Khan Documentation Center, MIT Libraries: p. 44 (top)

Nikolaus Walter: pp. 203–5, 208, 214, 220, 256–57

James L. Wescoat: p. 57

Acknowledgements

The creation of this book was made possible with the support of many colleagues, friends, and family members, as well as the generous backing of the Aga Khan Award for Architecture. I would like to thank all the contributors for their excellent essays, interviews, and photographs. I am deeply grateful to my assistant editor, Rixt Woudstra, for her research assistance, brilliant inputs in the conception of this book, and professional dedication to many editorial matters—the completion of this complex project would not have been possible without her. This book was initially conceived in close collaboration with the other three members of the Editorial Board, Bernardo Bader, Farrokh Derakhshani, and Eva Grabherr, to whom I owe my deepest gratitude for their intellectual generosity and organizational support. The book production would not have been possible without the professional project management and excellent teamwork across three institutions: Nadia Siméon (AKAA), Cristina Steingräber (ArchiTangle) and Rixt Woudstra (MIT), as well as the professional support by AKAA staff members Céline Bouchacourt Martenot and Isabelle Griffiths, who helped in administrative matters and in gathering image credits and authorizations, respectively. I am very thankful to the translators Amy Klement (German-English), Esma Zlatar (Bosnian-English), and the company Translated (Danish-English) for helping us overcome the challenges of working and writing across borders. Julia Wagner, grafikanstalt, is responsible for the aesthetic qualities of this book and I thank her for translating our vision for the project into such a beautiful design. *Architecture of Coexistence* greatly benefited from the eloquence and sharp eyes of Lucas Freeman, to whom I would like to thank not only for his professional and timely work on copy editing and proofreading this book, but also for his conceptual insights throughout the development of this project. Special thanks to the publisher, ArchiTangle, for their excellent professional work on the production and distribution of this book. Finally, my work—this project, but everything else as well—would not be possible without the continuous support and love of my family and friends. Privileged to have remarkably devoted parents, two fantastic siblings, a wonderful husband, and a group of friends that I can always count on, I have been surrounded with unconditional love and support throughout my life.

The research and production of this book was made possible with the generous financial support of the Aga Khan Award for Architecture, aimed at continuing the cultural mission that inspired the Islamic Cemetery Altach, which received the Award in 2013. I would like to thank all the stakeholders, creators, and constituencies of this beautiful cemetery, which has demonstrated to all of us that architecture can indeed create a bridge between cultures. My deepest gratitude to His Highness, the Aga Khan, whose vision, generosity, and passion for cultural heritage, architecture, art, and education continues to inspire us to create a world of peaceful coexistence.

Azra Akšamija